SANDRA GUSTAFSON'S

GREAT EATS
LONDON

FIFTH EDITION

CHRONICLE BOOKS
SAN FRANCISCO

Printed in the United States of America

FIFTH EDITION

ISSN: 1074-5041
ISBN: 0-8118-3250-3

Cover design: Ayako Akazawa
Book design: Words & Deeds
Typesetting: Jack Lanning
Series Editor: Jeff Campbell
Author photograph: Marv Summers

Distributed in Canada by
Raincoast Books
9050 Shaughnessy Street
Vancouver, B.C. V6P 6E5

10 9 8 7 6 5 4 3 2 1

Chronicle Books LLC
85 Second Street
San Francisco, California 94105

www.greateatsandsleeps.com
www.chroniclebooks.com

For Tom Large

With many thanks for so eloquently expanding the horizons of the Great Eats and Great Sleeps series.

Contents

To the Reader

London—a nation, not a city.
—Benjamin Disraeli

London's reputation as a first-rate city with second-rate dining has been laid to rest. Great Eaters in London can forget all those horror stories about overcooked mystery meat swimming in gluey gravy, greasy fish and chips, heavy meat pies, soggy puddings, and not a salad or fresh vegetable to be found. Food has become fashionably correct, and as the range and quality of eateries has grown, British cooking has become gourmet. Restaurateurs have become tycoons operating giant, innovative food shrines that feed as many as two thousand people each day, and the media and dining public avidly follow and promote their favorite chefs. According to the British Tourist Association, London has more than twelve thousand restaurants and cafés, with cuisines from more than sixty countries. And that is not counting the fifty-five hundred pubs and bars. Statistics also show that Londoners spend 31 percent of their annual food budget on eating out, paying around £30 per meal.

Today, dining in London can vary as much as your taste allows, and it's possible to travel around the world gastronomically without going beyond the Circle Line of the London tube. In addition to new interpretations of all the English staples, you can sample superb Indian, Southeast Asian, and Italian cuisine. In vogue, too, are minimalist settings and humble foods that challenge creative chefs to make something out of very little. Liver and tripe are enjoying a revival; mackerel and anchovies have replaced partridge, lobster, and prawns. Vegetarian cuisine has grown in popularity, and vegetarians can look forward to hearty meals, as opposed to a diet of cabbage and Marmite on toast. One of the biggest changes in the British food revolution is the emergence of the "gastropub," run by people more attuned to consuming fine food and wine than pints of beer and pub grub.

While London's financially hard times have eased in recent years, savvy Londoners continue to make stinting stylish—no-nonsense quality dining is in, and unchecked extravagance is out. You won't find London's smart diners in high-priced restaurants, eating and drinking recklessly. You will find them eating out, however, especially during lunchtime or after the theater, when they take advantage of the amazing set-price meals offered for a fraction of the price of an à la carte meal.

Longtime readers will notice that, for its fifth edition, *Cheap Eats in London* has a new name, but that in no way changes the spirit in which it is written. The purpose of *Great Eats London* is exactly the same: to lead you to the best values for your dining pound without sacrificing taste or quality in the bargain. To help you do that, I list more than two hundred of the best eateries in London, providing a comprehensive sampling of available cuisines and restaurant types, all the while balancing the considerations of budget and palate. When selecting places to include, I limited my choices to eating establishments within the Circle Line on the London tube. Like many travelers, when I'm in a city for a short while, I don't want to spend my time and energy traveling to a restaurant on the outskirts of the city when I can eat just as well for the same price closer to my hotel or to particular neighborhoods of interest.

Great Eats London gives you straight-from-the-hip, no-nonsense information you can depend on. Because I personally have been to every address in this book, I write with firsthand knowledge. So that I receive the same service you can expect, I always dine anonymously and pay my own way. I never rely on advance-screening teams, hearsay, printed forms filled out by the restaurant, or local stringers. If I like a place, I consider it. If I'm rudely treated, or the food is poorly prepared or served, or the kitchen is dirty and the rest rooms terrible, then the restaurant is out, no matter what the food costs or how well known it may be. I wish I could include an entire section on some of the famous restaurants I think are rip-offs and tourist traps, but unfortunately, too many people would sue my publisher and me.

Great Eats London not only tells you what restaurants to go to, but also suggests what to order once you arrive. You will find a wide variety of ethnic cuisines, cheap and cheerful snack bars, historic pubs, cozy tearooms, fish-and-chips joints, sophisticated wine bars, and Big Splurges for those special occasions. The book also answers the important dining questions most London visitors have, such as: What is a "service charge"? Are you expected to tip? Is there a children's menu, a nonsmoking section, a special meal deal, a dress code? Which is the best table (and the worst)? Are reservations necessary?

The book is organized by postal code to help you find the restaurants closest to your hotel or to whatever tourist attraction you are visiting. You will find several indexes in the back of the book listing the restaurants alphabetically, as well as by the type of food served. There are lists of Big Splurges (for those with more flexible budgets), nonsmoking restaurants, and a glossary of English food and restaurant terms. Finally, there is a page soliciting your comments. I cannot overemphasize how valuable they are to me. They help me reconsider, investigate, question, and discover new places. If you agree with me, please let me know that, too. I have done my best to be accurate, but eateries often change faster than I can write. Therefore, I'm eager to hear any news you have about changes you find, or ideas you may have for future editions.

Dining out is meant to be pleasurable, but it does cost money. Of course, no one takes a trip to London in order to save money, but you don't want to waste it either. Revising this edition of *Great Eats London* reinforced my view that there is plenty of good food in London at affordable prices. I hope *Great Eats London* will take the guesswork out of London dining for you and will hold the key to a more enjoyable stay by leading you toward memorable dining experiences, saving you money, and inspiring you to return soon. Have a marvelous trip, eat well . . . and don't forget to write.

Tips for Great Eats in London

1. Always read the menu posted outside before going in. This avoids being seated and finding you don't like anything on the menu, or worse yet, that the prices are too high. If the menu is not posted (which by law it should be), ask to see one before deciding to stay. All menus must clearly state the prices, including the VAT (value-added tax is the British equivalent of sales tax); whether a service charge is included, and if not, how much it is; the cover charge; and the minimum if there is one. (See page 14 for an explanation of the cover charge.)

2. If you like haute cuisine without haute prices, consider making lunch your main meal. Many restaurants offer a set-price menu that includes two or three courses and the service charge. While these set-price two- or three-course meals may have limited choices, they represent great value for your money. Many of the more expensive restaurants in London have not only delicious, amazingly inexpensive set-price lunches but also different à la carte lunch and dinner menus, and the lunch prices on the à la carte menus are usually significantly lower than they would be for the exact same meal at dinner.

3. Two other bargain Great Eats for lunch are a pub or a picnic. At the pub, go early for the best and freshest selection and try to stick with the daily specials for the best results. For a picnic, shop the local markets and then take your feast to a park bench and watch the world wander by. (For a list of London markets, see page 31.)

4. Another Great Eat money-saver is to order something from a sandwich shop or a takeaway restaurant. Besides being cheap, ordering your food to go can save you service charges.

5. Order the restaurant's specialty. If you are in a fish-and-chips takeaway, opt for the deep-fried fish and save the hamburger for another time. Carefully consider the daily and house specials because they will be fresh and will represent the best efforts of the kitchen.

6. Afternoon tea can be a meal in itself, and it's a lovely experience that I encourage everyone to have at least once in London. If you are going to the theater or want an early evening meal, afternoon tea is a lifesaver. With a proper tea, you will enjoy dainty finger sandwiches, scones with clotted cream and jam, and rich tea cakes and tarts.

7. If you are dining with children, ask if the restaurant has a children's menu or reduced prices for kids (some restaurants offer up to half off a regular meal). This won't work for a sixteen-year-old half-back, but for the little ones, it is a Great Eats money-saving strategy.

8. If your waiter asks, "Would you like vegetables or a salad with your meal?" ask if they are included with the main course. If they cost extra, watch out: A round or two of vegetables and a side salad, at £3 to £6 extra per dish, per person, can turn a once-reasonable meal into a budget disaster.

9. Watch the fine print on your bill. A cover charge is per person; a minimum charge is also per person. A steep cover charge along with a hefty 12.5 percent service charge on top of a three-course meal with wine, dessert, and coffee could be hard to swallow. When the bill arrives, tally it up yourself and protest if it doesn't add up according to your calculations. Unfortunately, mistakes happen quite frequently.

10. The service charge, whether discretionary or added automatically, *is* the tip. You are not expected to pay a single extra pence, unless the service has been out of this world. Beware of the double-service-charge trick. See "Paying the Bill," page 14.

11. Never tip the bar staff in a pub. You can offer to buy them a drink, but never, never offer money (see "Pub Etiquette and Survival Techniques," page 25).

12. If reservations are recommended, take this advice seriously and make them. Remember, it costs nothing to reserve a table, and you will generally get a better table than the walk-in diner. When reserving a table, it is perfectly acceptable to ask about the average cost of a three-course meal with wine and service. Many restaurants overbook, so it is imperative that you arrive on time; otherwise, you risk losing your reservation. If you find you will not be able to go, please call and cancel so the restaurant can rebook your table.

13. Dress for success. If you are going to a nice restaurant, leave the jogging shoes and running outfits where they belong . . . in the hotel closet. Nothing brands you as a tourist more quickly and results in poor service faster than improper attire.

14. *Someone* has to sit in "Siberia" and be waited on by the new trainee, but it doesn't necessarily have to be you. Whenever you dine out, make sure you get what you are paying for. You should always treat the restaurant staff with the same courtesy you expect to receive from them. When you have a problem, however, it pays to complain quickly, although it seldom pays to get demanding.

Give the restaurant a chance to correct the situation for you and prevent it from happening to someone else.

15. Be patient. Relax. You are on vacation, remember? "Please" and "thank you" still go a long way toward getting good treatment and service. This is especially true in London. Even though you speak the same language (more or less), you are in a foreign city with its own culture and customs. Let your hosts do it their way—it's all part of the experience of traveling. If you insist on having things the same as they are at home, you may as well not even leave home in the first place.

How to Use
Great Eats London

Each listing in *Great Eats London* includes the following information: name and address; telephone number; fax, email, and Web address if available; general area or neighborhood; postal code; tube stop; days and hours of operation; whether reservations are needed; which credit cards are accepted; the average price for an à la carte and a set-price meal; whether service is included; and any special details about each establishment. A dollar sign ($) to the right of the name indicates a Big Splurge restaurant. In the listings, the map key number appears in parentheses to the right of each restaurant name; an entry without a number means it is beyond the parameters of the map.

At the end of the book is a glossary of English food terms, followed by a general index of all restaurants and indexes by category, such as Big Splurges, pubs, and tearooms and pâtisseries, and by type of food. Finally, there is the Readers' Comments page, which gives an address where you can send me your suggestions or share your experiences with *Great Eats London*.

These abbreviations indicate which credit cards are accepted:

American Express	AE
Diners Club	DC
MasterCard or Access	MC
Visa	V

Big Splurges

Restaurants that fall under the Big Splurge category are for people with more flexible budgets or for special-occasion dining to celebrate a birthday, anniversary, or just being in London. In the text, Big Splurges are marked with a dollar sign ($). Please refer to page 258 for a complete listing of all the Big Splurge restaurants in London.

Holidays

Many restaurants in London are now staying open on holidays, especially bank holidays (legal holidays) other than Christmas, New Year's Day, and Easter. However, this policy varies. To avoid disappointment, please call ahead to verify if a particular restaurant is open and what its holiday hours are. When December 25 and 26 fall on a weekend, extra holidays are given on the preceding Friday or following Monday. If New Year's Day falls on a weekend, the first Monday in January is a public holiday. Major holidays include the following:

New Year's Day	January 1
Good Friday	Friday before Easter
Easter Sunday	Varies, late March or early April
Easter Monday	Monday after Easter
May Day	First Monday of May
Spring Bank Holiday	Last Monday of May
Summer Bank Holiday	Last Monday of August
Christmas Day	December 25
Boxing Day	December 26

Hours

Mealtimes in London are similar to those in the United States: breakfast is served between 7 and 9 A.M., lunch is served between noon and 2:30 P.M., and dinner is served anytime from 6 until 11 P.M. If the last time given for a meal is 11 P.M., it means you will not be able to order after that time, but should be able to continue eating without feeling hurried. Between lunch and dinner, most restaurant managers want to let the waitstaff go home one hour after the last order has been taken. Restaurants with continuous food service usually like to stop serving about a half hour before closing.

Licensed and Unlicensed Restaurants

A surprising number of restaurants in London do not have liquor licenses. In many cases you can bring your own bottle of wine or beer (this is noted in the listings with the abbreviation BYOB), but you may be charged a nominal corkage fee by the restaurant. In a few cases, alcohol is prohibited altogether. If a restaurant is unlicensed, that should be clearly noted on the menu, along with any corkage fee. If nothing is said about licensing, that indicates the restaurant is licensed, and bringing your own liquor is not acceptable.

Maps

All of the postal codes covered in *Great Eats London* have an accompanying map and restaurant key, and in the text, these map key numbers appear in parentheses to the right of the restaurant's name. If a restaurant does not have a number, that means it is beyond the boundaries of the map.

Please note that the maps in *Great Eats London* are designed to help the reader locate the restaurants only; they are not meant to replace fully detailed street maps. If you plan on being in London for any length of time, even a day or two, I strongly suggest you buy the *London A–Z* street map (Z is pronounced "zed"), which comes in a handy booklet form or in an enlarged foldout version. This street map is a *must,* showing you everything you could ever want or need to know about the nooks and crannies of London. The maps you pick up at your hotel or at a tourist shop are virtually useless when it comes to finding anything more complicated than Buckingham Palace or Piccadilly Circus.

Nonsmoking Restaurants

Nonsmokers will quickly realize that there is no British surgeon general or multimillion-dollar ad campaign extolling the virtues of a smoke-free environment in eating establishments in London. However, more restaurants today are assigning small areas as smoke-free zones. During busy times in pubs, which are the last refuge of tobacco addicts, the gray haze can get as thick as London fog. *Great Eats London* notes in the write-ups those restaurants where smoking is prohibited or that contain a special nonsmoking section. Please see page 258 for a complete list of nonsmoking restaurants.

Paying the Bill

I am so far beyond my income that we could be said to be living apart.

—*e. e. cummings*

The bill can be confusing, even traumatic, for U.S. visitors to London because there are so many things on it that differ from U.S. restaurant billing practices. Armed with the following knowledge, you should be able to avoid the common traps and keep from being overcharged or confused when the bill arrives. It is important to go over the bill carefully before paying it. Unfortunately, mistakes are rampant and rarely favor the diner. If in doubt, always question.

Prices

There are two prices given in the restaurant listings in *Great Eats London*: the *set-price* menu and the *à la carte* menu. If a set-price menu is available, the listing will state what is served for this fixed amount of money. You may pay extra for the cover charge, wine, coffee, and service if they are not specifically included in the set-price. The à la carte menu prices represent the average cost of a three-course meal that includes a starter, a main course, and a dessert. Drinks, the service charge, and the cover charge, if there is one, will be extra. In determining the average prices of the restaurants in this book, I have avoided the cheapest and most expensive items on the menu, as well as the cost of beverages. Therefore, you could spend more or less depending on what you order and how much you drink. All prices quoted are in British pounds and were correct at press time. You should expect a certain margin of error in the prices attributable to inflation, the passage of time, and the whims of owners and chefs.

Cover Charge

The *cover charge* is not to be confused with the *service charge*. The cover charge is a great moneymaker. It's ostensibly charged to pay for the bread and butter (unless you do not intend to touch it, in which case you should have it removed from your table), any flowers on the table, the tablecloth and napkins, and who knows what else. All menus must state clearly the amount of the cover charge, though it usually appears in microscopic print at the bottom. If none is mentioned, none is imposed. The cover charge is *per person* and is listed separately on your bill, but it's added to the total to hike the amount of service you will pay. Thankfully, more and more restaurants are dropping this outlandish charge, but many Italian places are tenaciously hanging on, and even raising it. Pubs, takeaways, cafés, and less expensive restaurants never impose a cover charge.

Minimum Charge

Minimum charges are given in the text when applicable, and they are *per person,* not per couple, table, or group. These charges may be enforced during peak periods or in fancier eateries to discourage people from coming in only for a salad, thus occupying time and space that could be devoted to higher-paying customers. If the restaurant does not state a minimum charge, you are expected to order enough to add up to at least a main course. However, in cafés, pubs, tearooms, wine bars, sandwich shops, fish-and-chips shops, and takeaways, it doesn't matter how little you spend.

Service Charge

The service charge is the tip. You are not required or expected to leave one ha'penny more. That being said, trying to find out if the service is included on the bill is one of London's great after-dinner games. *Great Eats London* clearly states what you can expect in every listing.

No service charged or expected This means none has been charged and you are not expected to pay any at all. You will find this in all pubs (but not in a sit-down restaurant in a pub that has a waitstaff), in takeaways where you do not consume your food on the premises, and in casual cafés.

XX percent service charge This means the restaurant will add a service charge, usually 10 to 15 percent, to the total of your bill. Again, this represents the tip.

Service discretionary This means that the restaurant will not automatically add it but hopes you will, or that they will add it themselves, softening the blow by saying it is discretionary on your part to leave it (although at that point it is only technically up to you, since removing or reducing it might require explanation). If none has been added, you should leave at least 10 percent, or even better, 12.5 percent. If the evening has been extraordinary and you are feeling flush, give 15 percent. Anything more is excessive.

If the service or food is poor, the law says you do not have to leave any service charge, even if it is included and added onto your final bill. You must, however, make your complaint to the management and explain why you are deducting the service charge.

Service included This means that the service charge has been included in the price of the meal, and no other tip need be left. The service charge percentage may or may not be noted on the bill—watch out for the service charge scam if it's not (read on).

Important! Beware of the service charge/credit card scam. This is a gouging of the customer in no uncertain terms. If the restaurant has imposed a service charge and added it to your bill, but has left the space on your credit card signature slip for the "tip/gratuity" blank, they are trying to get you to pay twice. Often this happens in restaurants that say "service included" on the menu, but then make no other note of the service charge on your bill, hoping you'll forget and leave another tip. Watch out for this because it has been happening with increasing regularity. If it happens to you, you should definitely deduct at least a portion (if not all) of the original service charge to discourage such underhanded tactics. To avoid the double charge, draw a line through the space marked "tip/gratuity."

Remember: Only when *no* service charge has been added to your final bill (and you are not in a place where none is expected), and the food and service have been satisfactory are you expected to leave a tip at all.

VAT

The value-added tax is the British equivalent of a sales tax, and it is silently included in the price of any meal, no matter how big or small, simple or fancy. Some restaurants may note the VAT percentage on the menu or bill, but it is not an extra. At press time the VAT was 17 percent.

Reservations

When making a reservation you are, in fact, making a contract with the restaurant. Your part is that you will arrive at the right time, order a meal, and pay for it. The restaurant's part is that it will have a table for you at the agreed time and serve you food that has been prepared with reasonable skill and care. If you are told when booking that the table will be needed by a certain time, then that is also part of the contract. If you do not think you will have long enough to eat your meal, then go someplace else, because when your allotted time is up, you will have to vacate your table.

Takeaway Service

Many restaurants in London prepare food to go, which is called "takeaway service." Takeaway is a money-saver, because there is never a service charge on any food not consumed on the premises. For those of you with children or who need a fast bite on the go, this is a great convenience. If you don't want to queue for your food and are placing an order for more than one sandwich, it often pays to telephone or fax ahead with your order. Takeaway service is also important to keep in mind if you are going on a train trip anywhere in Britain. The food on British trains equals the service rendered passengers, varying from downright terrible to none whatsoever. Do yourself a favor . . . take your own food on any British train journey.

Transportation

You will see much more from the top deck of a London bus than you will by wearing yourself out walking miles to get to a restaurant (or taking a long and expensive cab ride) and then facing the same trip back after eating. Each listing in this book gives the closest tube stop (London underground railway). However, *close* is a relative term, because in all honesty, some of the walks are very long. Often you can do better by bus, or by combining the tube and the bus, arriving almost at a restaurant's doorstep. With a few exceptions, bus routes are not given because they do not always run at convenient hours or at night. My best advice is to purchase *The Guide to London by Bus and Tube*—and use it! It is available at most London news kiosks and bookstores, and it will save you not only time and energy but also money. To eliminate standing in line to purchase individual tickets, buy a Travel Card, which allows you to ride for less money than you would spend for single-fare tickets on both the tube and the buses. Depending on the type of card you buy, it will be good for one to thirty days and can be purchased at any tube station. All of the listings in *Great Eats London* are in Zone 1, central London, so unless you are planning trips to the suburbs, buy only a Zone 1 Travel Card.

Where to Sit

"Do you mind sitting upstairs, or downstairs in the basement?" Be wary if you're asked this. It invariably means being shunted to a large, unfriendly, and often deserted room that is used for catered groups or for seating unwary tourists. Unfortunately, these are often the nonsmoking sections of restaurants. When they don't refer to nonsmoking sections, "up or downstairs" can mean windowless rooms that get hot and unbearably smoky after one or two diners light up. If you are stuck in this Siberia, no matter how wonderful the food and service may be, you will lose something in the experience and probably won't enjoy your meal. That is why I have mentioned the most desirable places to sit in restaurants when it makes a difference.

General Information about Eating Establishments in London

Nearly everyone wants at least one outstanding meal a day.
—*Duncan Hines,* Adventures in Good
Eating, *1936*

Types of Restaurants

The following section covers the types of restaurants and major cuisines you'll find in *Great Eats London.*

American

Dining American-style in London may lose something in crossing the Atlantic, but for many homesick souls, a taste of home now and then feels mighty good, even if it isn't perfect in every respect. A number of American-themed restaurants have popped up that are a combination of amusement park, diner, souvenir stand, and museum. They lend themselves to family eating and are good places to stuff yourself on pancakes and waffles, burgers, slabs of ribs, Southwestern food, chili, apple pie, banana splits, and cheesecake. Menus are laminated and full of jokes and puns, there are things for the children to do and menus to color, and the decor is usually heavy on nostalgia, with ceiling fans, old advertisements, Western kitsch, and film posters of seasoned glamour-pusses and male heartthrobs from the thirties and forties.

British

A good dinner and feasting reconciles everybody.
—*Samuel Pepys's* Diary, *1660–1669*

Traditional British food can be as good as it is heavy and filling—and can contribute to your girth in record time if you aren't careful. For the best of Britain, start your day with a full English breakfast of bacon and/or sausage, eggs, beans, broiled mushrooms and tomato, fried bread, and tea or coffee. There are those hearty souls who feel that the best cure for any hangover is a large plate of grease-infused food, taken internally by way of a fried breakfast. If you agree, then a full English breakfast offers all the "healthy" eating you'll be able to stand in a twenty-four-hour period. At lunchtime, pop in to a pub for a hefty portion of steak and kidney pie or stop by a salt-beef bar and have a freshly sliced corned beef sandwich on rye that will put those made in most New York delis to shame. If you're in a hurry, join the queue at a busy fish-and-chips shop and munch your fish from a paper cone like the locals. In the mid-afternoon, stop for tea. The British love their tea, usually accompanied by an assortment of finger sandwiches and delectable pastries. If you are still hungry at dinnertime, dig into a succulent roast beef served with York-shire pudding and assorted vegetables and potatoes. Finish the feast with a warm treacle tart surrounded by soft custard. Who said British food wasn't filling . . . and good?

Modern British

The British have only three vegetables, and two of them are cabbage.
—*U.S. ambassador to London in the 1930s*

The land of fish-and-chips and roast beef with Yorkshire pudding now boasts more Michelin-starred restaurants than any city outside France. The London Tourist Board continues to polish a campaign promoting the city as a dining destination. This growing interest in food can be attrib-uted to the easing of the recession and the emergence of two-income families with disposable money and a lifestyle that lends itself to eating out on a regular basis. These Londoners have also adopted a somewhat healthier and lighter approach to eating, but it is nowhere close to the almost obsessive militancy witnessed in the States over grams of fat and sodium counts. This does not mean that bubble and squeak has given way to nouvelle anything. On the contrary, Britain has rediscovered its culinary past, favoring new twists on the hearty pies, stews, and puddings we all love.

British chefs are continuously reinventing themselves and their food, becoming high-paid media darlings, courted by competing restaurants and promoted aggressively by reviewers. Huge two- and four-hundred-seat "gastro-domes" have emerged that are geared toward stimulating every sensory nerve ending, sometimes including the palate. Between low-octane drinks and high-calorie desserts, diners can ogle one another behind designer sunglasses and banter with the tanned and toned waitstaff, who are often better dressed than the diners, but may or may not speak English. There is a financial catch to all this glamour and glitz, of course, and unless you go for lunch or opt for a set-price meal, you may feel more like a payer than a player in the modern British game of gourmet.

Central and Eastern European

These restaurants remain unconcerned with the current desire for lighter and healthier eating and are refreshingly oblivious to the craze for minimalist decor. Most Central and Eastern European restaurants keep their food traditions alive in cozy settings geared toward making every-one feel at home. Long live borscht, dumplings, roast pork and sauerkraut, strudels, pierogi, potato pancakes, dark grainy bread, slivovitz, and vodka! It is doubtful, however, that most patrons of these restaurants come just to eat their sturdy national cuisine ladled out in huge portions. In fact, many of the best of these restaurants are filled with old-timers reminiscing about their beloved homelands and the life and times they left behind.

Chinese

The ruling idea in a Chinese meal is the duality of yin and yang. This means a balance between a poached, a steamed, and a pickled dish along with a stir-fried one.

Chinese restaurants in London continue to change for the better. The interiors are getting brighter, the service is slightly more polite, and the quality of the ingredients and the cooking has improved. Many will argue that the best Chinese food is found in Chinatown, a maze of streets behind Leicester Square, where local Chinese live and gather to eat. Their demands for authenticity keep the quality good and the prices reasonable. The advantage to eating in Chinese restaurants, aside from the pleasing prices for most meals, is that they tend to remain open very late and all day on Sunday. Children are always welcome, and you are encouraged to share dishes, which is a boon for lighter eaters.

The best Chinese food is cooked quickly and simply to enhance natural flavors. Most of London's Chinese restaurants are Cantonese, which is considered China's gourmet cuisine, since delicacy and texture are prized over pungency. The Cantonese are known for quick-boiling a variety of vegetables, lightly steaming fish, and stir-frying chicken with cashews. They are also experts in making dim sum, those wonderful filled dumplings traditionally served with their morning tea. Years of experience and hours of skill go into the preparation of these popular Cantonese snacks, yet they sell for £1.75 to £3. Most come in portions of three or four; seven sets should be large enough for two for lunch. The only drawback to dim sum is that most restaurants stop serving it around 5 P.M.

French

French restaurants in London can be haute, haughty, and high priced— much more so than for the same quality and service in Paris. If you do decide you want a French meal in London, and if price is a consideration, go for lunch, when the set-price meals are usually available. Even if there is no set-price menu at lunch, the food will cost less than the same meal served at dinner. As in Paris, nouvelle anything is *out* and homey bourgeois cooking is *in*.

Greek

London's Greek community is largely made up of Greek Cypriots who immigrated after World War II, again in the early sixties, and after the Turkish invasion in the mid-seventies, when thirty thousand people arrived at London's doorstep. Largely unskilled, they found jobs in the garment industry and in restaurants in Soho and Camden. Over time they opened kebab joints and cafés that served as social gathering places where they could meet, eat, gossip, read, and speak their own language.

Greek food can be traced back to the second century. It has evolved through many influences and now has a newfound popularity, as the Mediterranean diet is a simple, healthy way of eating that emphasizes fruits and vegetables, pure spices and herbs, olive oil, grains, fish, and little meat. The *meze,* made up of cold and hot starters and a series of main dishes, is a good way to sample a variety of the most popular Greek cuisine.

Indian

A colleague of mine, Richard McIntyre, gave me the benefit of his wide knowledge and appreciation of Indian food in Britain. He pointed out that while one can enjoy Chinese and Italian cuisine in almost any city in the world, Indian cuisine is not so readily available. Therefore, when in Britain—especially in London, where there seem to be more Indian restaurants displaying Raj pomp than in India itself—visitors should take advantage. For most Americans, Indian food is exotic and different, but not for the Brits, who governed the subcontinent for hundreds of years. Having tandoori chicken for dinner is as normal for them as going out for pizza is for us. In London, Indian cuisine is becoming more sophisticated. Mouth-searing hot dishes have been replaced by those with subtle seasonings. Regional Indian dishes are becoming popular, proving that there is more to Indian food than curry. The one thing to watch out for is that there are still too many Indian restaurants that do not adhere to the same health and cleanliness standards that we do in the States.

Richard issued a word of warning about *balti,* which is an individual Indian dish cooked in a mini-wok and is currently all the rage because it is lighter and cooked to order. "Any decent Indian restaurant will cook an individual dish from scratch, so who needs a *balti?*" he said. "Forget them. They are a gimmick." He had one final piece of advice concerning Indian food in pubs: "Never touch it."

Indian restaurants have much to offer Great Eaters in London. They are open late, and the servings are plentiful for the money. Service is generally polite, and the waitstaff is accustomed to explaining various dishes to novices. When you have two or more in your group, it is best to order several dishes and share, as you would in a Chinese restaurant. Always try the bread and ask for yogurt to help put out the fire if you get something too hot. And remember, beer goes better with Indian food than wine does.

Italian

Italian cuisine remains the first choice of most Londoners, and one of the most fashionable. With the current emphasis on a high-carbohydrate diet, pasta has become a healthy alternative to heavier foods. In addition to pizza and pasta in every size, shape, flavor, and variety imaginable, you will find risotto, gnocchi, thick bean soup, fish, veal, and often wild game in season. Tiramisu still seems to reign supreme as the *dolce* darling. New-wave Italian cooking is making quite a splash with its focus on regional dishes.

Japanese

Bowls of Japanese noodles continue to be the food that has London talking and slurping. These one-bowl meals are easy to make and can be topped with a variety of ingredients, such as a single pork slice or a jumbo prawn. Sushi bars are becoming a growth industry, appealing to hipsters who watch their clothing and their banking figures. Some sushi bars are authentic, serving freshly prepared food. Others, eager to make a fast yen, have turned eating sushi into a three-ring circus, with quality and value definitely not in the center ring. At the other end of the scale are the restaurants catering to Japanese business and corporate people. These cost a fortune and are best left alone, unless someone else is paying the bill.

According to a Japanese proverb, "If you eat something you have never tasted before, your life will be lengthened by seventy-five days." The Japanese restaurants listed in *Great Eats London* offer suggestions for good-value lunches and dinners, and you are bound to find something you have never tasted before.

Southeast Asian

Authentic Southeast Asian food need not be expensive. It is an interesting dining experience because it offers well-flavored dishes using ingredients and spices most of us don't eat on a regular basis. As in Chinese restaurants, dishes are served all at once, thus it's customary for everyone at the table to share. If you order two or three starters and main courses with rice or noodles, you won't go away hungry. As with most Asian food, beer is a better accompaniment than wine.

Malaysian, Indonesian, and Singaporean food are closely related and often appear side by side on the menu. Ethnic Malaysians are Muslim, so pork is not served. Bali is Hindu, so beef is out. The principal flavorings are chili, coriander, lemongrass, coconut, tamarind, and fermented dried-shrimp paste. The simpler dishes and salads are often dressed with peanut sauce. While restaurants serving this food are not as widely known as Thai or Chinese, the cooking is good and the prices are much more reasonable.

Thai cuisine is tremendously popular in London, probably because so many people spend their holidays on package trips to Bangkok and at the beaches up-country. The nice thing about a Thai meal is that it isn't always a multicourse affair. Many Thai restaurants offer single-dish meals that can be eaten there or taken out. The food has a reputation for being fiery hot, so if you cannot handle lots of heat, ask to have the chili-pepper content reduced.

Vietnamese cooking has come into its own in London. Not too long ago, there was only one small noodle shop selling pho, the traditional Vietnamese breakfast of noodles and beef in broth. Now many more restaurants offer delicate dishes that in many cases are much more interesting than Chinese or Thai food. If you're not used to Vietnamese cuisine, go very easy on the nuoc mam, the pungent fish sauce that is served on the side with almost everything. For most Western palates, it is an acquired taste that may take a long while to develop.

Vegetarian

Vegetarians in London are no longer reduced to eating in dull restaurants that serve brown rice, lentils, and insipid veggies to a group of righteous, whacked-out health hippies grooving on an alternative lifestyle. Vegetarianism is now part of the mainstream, and it attracts a cross section of diners interested in a diet that is both delicious and healthy. Today, vegetarians, vegans, and even macrobiotics fare very well in London, and in a variety of price ranges. When reserving in any nonvegetarian restaurant, it is smart to mention how many in your party are vegetarians, thus alerting the chef ahead of time to make special preparations. If you wait until you are seated and ordering, the kitchen may be too rushed to do accommodate you. Ethnic cuisines also lean heavily toward a vegetarian diet, notably Italian, Indian, and Malaysian.

Pubs

No greater institution has ever been developed to further human happiness than that of a good public house.
—*Dr. Samuel Johnson*

What do you mean get rid of the pinball machines? They earn between £200 and £300 per week for the pub.
—*London publican*

Every traveler going to London considers a visit to a pub to be as important as seeing the changing of the guard at Buckingham Palace and the Crown Jewels at the Tower of London. As a visitor you can rely on being made welcome and enjoying yourself in a pub. In some, the welcome after a few pints will be more enthusiastic, and in only a few will you be politely ignored.

The word *pub* comes from *public house,* and in that phrase lies the essential character of this British institution. The British pub, licensed by the government, is a place where people can come together and talk freely. Pubs date back to Roman times, when they began as taverns

General Information about Eating Establishments in London **23** offering overnight accommodations and entertainment for travelers. In the thousand or so years since they were first introduced in Britain, people have talked about them, written about them, laughed and played in them, and relied on them for food, drink, and companionship. Pubs have been the haunt of highway robbers and smugglers, artists and writers, criminals and comics, and above all, ordinary people. Nowhere else in England can you find such a diversity of pubs as in London. Around almost every corner will be the welcoming door of a pub, and many of the city's pubs occupy some of its most ancient and historic buildings. In fact, there are more than five thousand pubs in greater London, and more per square yard in the City than in any other part of England.

Until the early twentieth century, pubs set aside different sections for different groups of customers. The tradesmen drank in the public bar and were shielded from the gentry, who drank in the lounge behind etched-glass "snob screens." Until 1970, few pubs were open to a woman alone, and those that were, were unsavory to say the least. Today, pubs still have a strong aura of masculinity, but a woman alone in a pub is no longer looked at in an unflattering light.

The Slug and Lettuce, Spotted Dog, Widow's Son, Dog and Duck, Sugar Loaf, Rose and Crown, Three Stags—what's with these names? It was the Roman invaders who first required innkeepers to display signs outside their premises to guide the illiterate masses. In 1393, Richard II introduced legislation that every inn should be clearly signed so travelers might swiftly find shelter from the robbers and murderers who stalked them. By pub signs you can identify loyalties and great events that date back to these early times. The Crown, for example, originated in the Middle Ages, when innkeepers felt it necessary to display their loyalty to the monarchy. The Rose and Crown commemorated the end of the conflict between the red rose of Lancaster and the white rose of York. The Stag was an early religious symbol, and the Sugar Loaf recalls the way sugar was sold many years ago.

English pubs are national institutions similar to cafés in Paris and coffeehouses in Vienna. As one pub owner aptly put it, "It's the pub people come to, to talk about things in the neighborhood." For millions of Londoners, their local pub is a home away from home, where they gather at the same time every day to meet their friends, catch up on local gossip, argue over politics, discuss the dreary weather, cheer their favorite sports team, and unfortunately for many a visitor, get boisterous around the pinball machines.

It isn't just the beer that defines a pub. A pub takes on the flavor of its neighborhood and location, and in many busy metropolitan pubs, the clientele changes almost hourly. Many regulars meet for lunch. Others get together in the afternoon for a game of cards or darts. In the evening, they stop by on their way home after work for a relaxing pint or two, and after dinner they come back to watch a sporting event on the "telly." The clientele in a pub represents a cross section of society, from the blue-collar workers in the East End to the aristocrats in Belgravia and Mayfair. In the City, expect to see lawyers in pinstriped suits discussing their cases. In Bloomsbury, known as literary London, you can mix with students and tweedy professors. The Hooray Henries (British yuppies) crowd the Chelsea pubs, and farther west along the banks of the Thames, writers, actors, and artists fill their favorites. Although the clientele doesn't change much in a pub, that does not mean that management is at a standstill. Most pubs are owned by huge breweries that require their employees to move from one pub to another as often as every two or three years if they want to climb the corporate pub ladder. The result is a constant change in pub practices, most notably in the kitchen. Whereas one manager may take a real interest in the food served, the next may scrap most of the hot food in favor of ready-made sandwiches.

Pub Etiquette and Survival Techniques

1. There is no service charged or expected in pubs. If, however, you eat in a pub that has a restaurant with table service, there will be some sort of service charge either levied or suggested as "discretionary."

2. You can offer to buy the bartender a drink, but never tip him or her or anyone else working behind the bar.

3. Be prepared for no-nonsense service. You order your food from the food area and drinks from the bar. You pay for each separately at the time of service. In busy pubs you are often given a number when you place your food order, and when it is called, you return to the food service area to get your plate. Otherwise you will be served cafeteria-style from a small food display area or will have your food brought to your table.

4. You must be eighteen years old to drink in a pub. Children under fourteen are not allowed in at all, but they may go into a pub restaurant.

5. If the English person next to you offers to buy you a drink, it is okay to accept, but you should offer to buy the next round.

6. Conversation is part of the reason people go to pubs. Bar-side chats are quick and easy ways to meet people, but don't expect an invitation to that person's home. The easiest way to start a conversation is to talk about the beer served in that particular pub. Then fall back on the weather and the latest sports scores before getting into heavier topics of the Crown and taxes.

7. The best pub food is usually in a pub that also has its own restaurant. The bar food will be less expensive than in the restaurant, even if some of the dishes are identical and come out of the same kitchen.

8. When pub food, or "pub grub," as it is called, is described in *Great Eats London* as "good," that means good by general pub standards. With only gastropub exceptions, the quality of pub food, which is often frozen and microwaved to order, must never be compared to that of restaurants, because it is aimed at clientele who want a quick, filling bite to go with their beer. Best bet is to stay with the daily specials.

9. Most pub desserts are terrible. Forget them.

10. If you want to relax in a pub in the afternoon and be assured of getting a good place to sit, arrive after 2 P.M. or before 6 P.M., but be aware that the hot meals may no longer be available, though cold sandwiches and snacks will be. Pubs will be least smoky at these times, as well. The flood of office workers who arrive around noon and after work prevents visitors from seating themselves or breathing any fresh, smoke-free air.

11. On the other hand, if you want to experience pub life at its fullest, go for lunch or around 6 P.M., when everyone stops by for a pint or two on their way home for the day. At lunch, don't expect to always get a seat. More often than not, your English neighbor will stand with a pint in one hand and a plate of food in the other and somehow manage to finish both without spilling either.

12. Pub hours are governed by Parliament. They are Monday to Saturday 11 A.M. to 11 P.M., Sunday noon to 10:30 P.M. Depending on the pub, its location, and its clientele, there are certain variations.

13. Ten minutes before closing time you will hear the closing bell, which signals that you have ten minutes to finish your drink before the pub closes and you are asked to leave.

Pub Food

If you want to eat without punishing your pocketbook, where do you go? To a pub, of course. For Great Eaters in London, pub food is a godsend, because it is so filling, so cheap, and so British. But you must be forewarned on two counts. One, at lunch most pubs are wall-to-wall people, and getting a seat requires either early arrival or a stroke of good luck. Two, generally, the food is filling and fattening: Don't even think of counting calories or monitoring your fat or cholesterol intake on your pub outings.

Even though all pub food tends to look, smell, and taste the same after a while, it is the soul and comfort food most British people grew up on. Several standbys you will find in most pubs are meat pies, the ploughman's lunch, and a roast joint served for Sunday lunch. The pies are usually steak and kidney or shepherd's, and they consist of diced meat and vegetables covered with gravy, topped with mashed potatoes, and baked in a casserole. The ploughman's lunch is a piece of crusty bread served with a large chunk of cheddar or Stilton cheese with chutney and a pickle on the side, and it's a good accompaniment to a pint of English bitter. On Sunday, you can expect to have some sort of roast served with potatoes, vegetables, and the appropriate trimmings. Beyond these staples, pub food varies from sandwiches to hot and cold buffet spreads, lasagna, chili, and in some instances, unimpressive attempts at dessert.

Despite its general mediocrity, food is considered a moneymaker in most pubs. In order to squeeze profits to the limit, many breweries now mass-produce their food in central kitchens, resulting in dull preparations with zero imagination. The food is then frozen and delivered to the pubs, which in turn cook it as needed. If you see a pub touting its food as "home cooked," that will usually mean made elsewhere, cooked here. If you see it advertised as "home made," someone in the pub kitchen is cooking over a hot stove and not just zapping your lasagna in the microwave.

Gastropubs

There is hope for better food in pubs, thanks to an increasing number of independently owned pubs that have been converted into "gastropubs." Young chefs on the rise are remaking pub kitchens and developing gourmet-inspired menus, which has caused an electrifying change that has taken London by storm. The demand for sausage and mash or steak and kidney pie dies hard, but now they share equal billing with seared tuna, smoked salmon, and pumpkin ravioli with sun-dried tomatoes downed with a glass or two of the house champagne rather than a pint of bitters. The decor in most gastropubs ranges from an assortment of spindly chairs and tables to sleek banquettes, designer tables with a spray of flowers, and skylighted roofs that can be rolled back in the summer. In all there is waiter service, and of course prices to match the upscale food and atmosphere.

English Beer

A large majority of pubs are "tied" to a particular brewery and sell only that brewery's ales. Free houses are not tied and can sell a wider range of brands. This doesn't really help visitors to England, who are often bewildered by the number of brews available in most pubs. In some, there are as many as two dozen ales alone. Every pub will have at least one bitter, plus stout, lager, and a range of bottled beers. One of the major attractions of English beer is its wide variety. No two are alike, and the taste of each depends on the techniques used by the brewery for that particular type of brew.

Asking for "a beer" will get you nowhere. You must specify not only the type and the brand but also the amount you want: a pint or half-pint. For the novice, the best thing to do is tell the bartender the type of beer you like: light, dark, heavy, loaded with the flavor of hops, low alcohol, and so on, and let him or her suggest something. Part of the fun is experimenting—try three or four before you settle on a favorite. Note that U.S. brands of beer are expensive in England, so "when in Rome . . ." Drink English beer in London, if only to save money. But if you don't want to drink beer, there are alternatives: soft drinks, hard liquor, wine, and cider, which is a potent alcoholic apple drink that's not for the kiddies.

It is beyond the scope of *Great Eats London* to present an in-depth discussion of English beer, but the following glossary should shed some light on this confusing subject.

A Beer Glossary

ABV Alcohol by volume. An ABV of 6 percent means that 6 percent of the beer is alcoholic.

Ale Ale is weaker and a little sweeter than bitter, though it is still much more robust than a typical American beer. Light or pale ale is bottled and served at room temperature.

Bitter If you want to drink what the locals do, order a pint of bitter, a clear, yellowish beer with a strong hops taste. This traditional British beer is the most popular, but it is hard for many Americans to get used to because it is never chilled—chilling it would ruin the taste. The best bitter is "real ale." Because of the real ale movement—a trend in British beer making toward a purer, more traditional sort of ale—most pubs serve brews that are still fermenting when they are delivered. Real ale is alive and continues to mature in the cask, and it must be pumped to the bar using a hand pump and served immediately. The taste of real ale is best at 56°F. It comes in two grades: ordinary and best or special, which is stronger.

Bottle-conditioned Beer that continues to ferment in the bottle, causing a slight amount of sedimentation.

Cask-conditioned Draught beer that leaves the brewery still fermenting in its cask.

Export ale Stronger than ale, and bottled as opposed to draught.

Keg beer As processed as you can get. All the yeast is killed off, and the brew is pasteurized, filtered, and heaven forbid, chilled. Most of the big American beers are made this way.

Lager If you want to drink what most Americans call beer, ask for a cold lager and stress the word *cold*. This brew is served in bottles or on draught, and there are more than twenty-five varieties.

Shandy An equal mixture of bitter and lemonade or ginger beer. Definitely an acquired taste.

Stout A strong, dark, rich, creamy brew with the foam lasting from the first sip to the last. This is actually a very dark version of an ale, and it is always served at room temperature. Guinness is the most popular. If you want to go slowly with your first stout experience, order a "black and tan," which is half stout and half lager.

Pub Crawls

Guided pub walks, or pub crawls, meet in the early evening near tube stations and tour a neighborhood, visiting several typical pubs along the way. It is a good way to become better acquainted with London and have a party while doing it. Check with your hotel or the London Tourist Board for brochures on guided walking tours of London. There are several operating, but the best one is Original London Walks (Tel: 020 7794 1764; Internet: www.walks.com). The outings last two or three hours, are worth the nominal fee, and take place rain or shine, even if you are the only one going.

Tearooms, Pâtisseries, and Bakeries

Everything stops for tea.
—Popular English saying

Name one other drink which cools, which warms, which calms, and which cheers all at once. There aren't many drinks like tea.
—Anonymous

For three hundred years, tea has been part of every level of British society. In the seventeenth century it was so expensive that tea caddies had locks on them. Now it is the cheapest drink after tap water.

Teatime conjures up so many images, all very comforting and all very British. Whether served in Styrofoam cups or in fine, translucent bone china, tea is serious business in England, which is just as it should be for the nation's favorite drink. According to the British Tea Council, more than 171 million cups are consumed daily in Britain.

If tragedy should strike, the ultimate English cure is a cup of tea. It doesn't matter if you get hit by a truck or lose all of your money—a "cuppa" will make things right again and cure the ills of the world as well.

English tea was served during the Regency days by the Duchess of Bedford to fill the gap between lunch and dinner. Victorian ladies drank tea in the drawing room while nannies passed the scones and tarts to the nursery set. A century ago, tearooms were about the only public place a lady could venture unchaperoned and yet maintain her good reputation. In fact, the first recorded English tearoom was a woman's idea. In 1864, the manager of a bread shop near the London Bridge started serving tea to her favorite customers, and before long everyone wanted some. She then asked the bakery if she could sell pots of tea with scones. The result was a huge success. Tea shops became a part of the nation's heritage and part of every English person's childhood memories.

A proper English tea in a lovely setting is a pleasant and filling alternative to a big lunch or dinner. It is also theater at its best, complete with lovely tea dishes, special silverware, trays, and hovering waitstaff in fancy dress. Many London tourists associate sipping in high style at teatime with the elaborate offerings at Brown's Hotel or the Ritz. Tea at the Ritz Hotel on Piccadilly is as famous as dinner at Maxim's in Paris— and it's only slightly less expensive and almost as difficult to get a table. Men must wear ties, and women should arrive in pretty dresses. A *proper* tea should not be confused with a *high* tea, which is a light supper with a hot dish followed by dessert and tea. High teas are more common in Scotland and northern England.

Few Londoners regularly dress to kill and pay in excess of £25 to sip tea at a fancy address. Instead, they go to a neighborhood tearoom or pâtisserie. These informal places usually serve light lunches, followed by tea and fancy pastries until 6 or 7 P.M. They offer good value and a nice atmosphere in which to have a pot of tea and a little sandwich or a sinfully rich treat that will keep you going until dinner, or in many cases until after the final curtain call at the theater. If you are looking simply for bread or perhaps a pastry on the go, head to one of London's aromatic bakeries.

NOTE: For something interesting and out of the ordinary, treat yourself to a visit to the Bramah Tea and Coffee Museum. The museum tells the 350-year history of coffee and tea, two of the world's most important commodities, in a fabulous collection of ceramics, silver, and prints. The collection includes a thousand coffeemakers and teapots, including the world's largest teapot. The shop sells ground coffee and a range of Brach teas (but no tea bags), as well as tea caddies, strainers, tea towels, and coffeemakers. They also serve coffee and tea.

The Bramah Tea and Coffee Museum is on Butlers Wharf near Tower Bridge, on Maguire Street, SE1 (Tel: 020 7378 0222). It's open daily from 10 A.M. to 6 P.M.

Wine Bars

Wine, the plasma of life.
        —*Mary Gregg Misch*

There are just two reasons for drinking. One is when you are thirsty, to cure it; the other when you are not thirsty, to prevent it.
        —*Thomas Love Peacock*

Wine bars offer new dimensions to dining out in London. In order to survive the competition, wine bars have been forced to serve better food and a wider variety of wines than is found in many restaurants. In many wine bars, you can order anything from a smoked salmon salad to a three-course meal at lower prices than you would pay for the equivalent in a nice restaurant.

For many people, wine bars have become attractive alternatives to pubs. Not only is the food better, but there is usually a place to sit, and the pinstripe and black-pumps crowd is quieter and more upmarket than the typical pub clientele. Wine bars are busy during lunch and after work, but if you avoid these peak hours, you should find a relaxing setting in which you can go and drink a variety of wines and sample a selection of foods especially chosen to go with the vintages being served. Staff in wine bars are usually well-versed on their bar's particular wines.

Markets

Street Markets

London is famous for its street markets, and although many of them no longer sell fruits and vegetables (opting instead for a brisk trade in knickknacks, jewelry, leather goods, antiques, and other sundries), some food markets remain. The West End's cheapest fruits and vegetables are found at the Berwick Street Market. Borough Market has more than forty good-quality food stalls and has become the in spot for London's foodies. The Spitalfields Market has sellers offering everything from organic produce to coffee and doughnuts to chili pickles to Oriental noodles.

At any street market, keep your eyes open for pickpockets. They are fleet-footed pros who will snatch your wallet or purse before you know what hit you. Wear a money belt under your clothing, not strapped around your waist for all to see and dip into.

Berwick Street Market, Berwick and Rupert Streets, W1, Tube: Leicester Square, Piccadilly Circus; Mon–Sat 8 A.M.–6 P.M.

Borough Market, between Borough High Street, Bedale Street, Winchester Walk, and Stoney Street, SE1, Tube: London Bridge; Fri noon–6 P.M., Sat 9 A.M.–4 P.M.

Spitalfields Market, Commercial Street between Lamb Street and Bushfield Street, E1, Tube: Liverpool Street; Sun 10 A.M.–5 P.M.

Department Stores and Supermarkets

You can find gourmet food markets at some of London's popular department stores. Two of London's best supermarkets are Waitrose and Sainsbury's. For fabulous organic produce, there's Planet Organic.

Harrods, 87–135 Brompton Road, SW1, Tube: Knightsbridge; Mon–Sat 10 A.M.–7 P.M.

Harvey Nichols, 109–125 Knightsbridge, SW1, Tube: Knightsbridge; Mon–Sat 10 A.M.–7 P.M. (Wed–Fri until 8 P.M.), Sun noon–6 P.M.

Marks & Spencer, 458 Oxford Street, W1, Tube: Bond Street, Marble Arch; Mon–Fri 9 A.M.–8 P.M., Sat until 7 P.M., Sun noon–6 P.M., open bank holidays.

Planet Organic, 42 Westbourne Grove, W2, Tube: Bayswater; Mon–Sat 9:30 A.M.–8 P.M., Sun noon–6 P.M. A second location is in WC1, opposite the Googe Street tube.

Sainsbury's. Branches are located throughout London.

Selfridges, 400 Oxford Street, W1, Tube: Bond Street; Mon–Wed, Sat 10 A.M.–7 P.M., Thur–Fri until 8 P.M., Sun and bank holidays noon–6 P.M.

Waitrose. Branches are located throughout London.

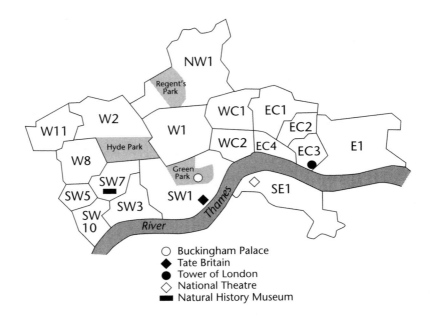

NW1

Regent's Park

W11　W2

W1

WC1　EC1

EC2

W8

Hyde Park

WC2　EC4

EC3　E1

Green Park

SW7

SW5

SW1

Thames

SE1

SW3

SW 10

River

○ Buckingham Palace
◆ Tate Britain
● Tower of London
◇ National Theatre
▬ Natural History Museum

RESTAURANTS IN LONDON
BY POSTAL CODE

London is chaos incorporated.
> —*George Mikes,* Down with Everybody, *1951*

Greater London has a population of more than seven million people and covers an area of more than six hundred square miles. But it is one of the world's easiest cities to get around, if you know what to do. First, arm yourself with a good map that shows all the streets and tube stops. The best is the *London A–Z* street map, available at most news kiosks and large bookstores. There are two types: the foldout version, which gives a good perspective about where you are and where you are going, and the book version, which is easier to use when you are in a particular area.

Just as Paris is divided into arrondissements, London is divided into postal districts. The postal code prefixes, made up of letters and a number, appear on London street signs and in every street address. The letters stand for compass directions in reference to the central district, and the numbers increase the farther you get from the center. If you are in London W1, you are in the middle of things, probably standing in Piccadilly Circus, dining in Soho, or shopping along Oxford or Regent Streets. If you are in London SW3, you are in Chelsea, and if you're in London WC1, you are in the Bloomsbury area, perhaps wandering through the British Museum. A London address followed by NW8 means it's far from the action.

W1

The West End

TOURIST ATTRACTIONS
Piccadilly Circus, Marble Arch,
Soho, Mayfair, Chinatown,
Marylebone, Wellington Arch,
Royal Academy of Arts,
Spencer House, Regent Street,
Oxford Street, St. James's
Church

Marble Arch was modeled after the Arch of Constantine in Rome, and it originally stood in front of Buckingham Palace. It was moved to its present site in 1851 and is now marooned on a traffic island, hardly noticed by frazzled motorists and inaccessible to pedestrians. Today, only royalty and the King's Troop Royal Horse Artillery may pass through its central gates.

The upmarket area known as Mayfair is between Piccadilly, Regent Street, Oxford Street, and Hyde Park. This includes New and Old Bond Streets and South Moulton Street, all of which are lined with designer boutiques, prestigious jewelry stores, art galleries, and elegant shops with a quiet assuredness only old money can buy (Sotheby's is here, too). Some of the most expensive real estate in London is in Mayfair: Grosvenor Square, the American Embassy, and the famed Savile Row, where the man in your life can order his excessively priced bespoke (custom) tailored wardrobe. Mayfair's posh residential neighborhoods are filled with beautiful eighteenth-century apartments. The Rolls-Royces and Jaguars quietly parked by the curb remind you that unless you have just won the lottery or inherited a vast sum of money, the lifestyle of the rich and famous may not yet be yours.

Both sides of Oxford Street have a dizzying variety of shops and department stores and impossible crowds, especially on Saturday. The large department stores are worth visits if you like mass merchandising and intensive power shopping. The smaller stores are generally full of the fashion fads of the moment and are fun to browse if you are a size two, or under thirty, or are with someone who is. Intersecting the middle of Oxford Circus is Regent Street, lined with many quality stores, including Jaegar, Liberty, Aquascutum, and the fabulous toy store Hamley's.

Piccadilly Circus is alive day and night with crazy traffic, waves of tourists, neon lights, and the largest Tower Records store on the planet. Piccadilly Street runs from the circus to Hyde Park Corner and is home to the Royal Academy of Arts, Fortnum and Mason, the Ritz Hotel, and entrances to Green Park.

34

Soho has a cosmopolitan atmosphere, with crowded streets full of bistros, cafés, avant-garde shops, galleries, first-run cinemas, and famous theaters in buildings that once housed massage parlors, porn shops, and shady hotels. In the 1950s, Soho was a beatnik stomping ground and the home of London jazz. In the 1960s, the Rolling Stones and the Who headlined its clubs. In the 1970s, punk moved to King's Road, and Soho became commercialized and fashionable. Soho is also the site of many Italian restaurants (on Old Compton Street), and it's a major gathering center for the gay community. On Berwick Street, look for the lively street market selling the season's best produce.

To the North of Soho, bordered by Bloomsbury, is Fitzrovia, an area populated by students and the hideous British Telecom Tower.

Gerrard Street is the main street of Chinatown. It is a pedestrian walkway framed by massive, scrolled dragon gates. The area is loaded with restaurants and Asian markets selling everything imaginable.

Marylebone (pronounced MAR–lee–bun) stretches between Regent's Park and Oxford Street. Britain's finest doctors have their offices on Harley Street, the beautiful Wallace Collection is here, and so is Madame Tussaud's and the London Planetarium.

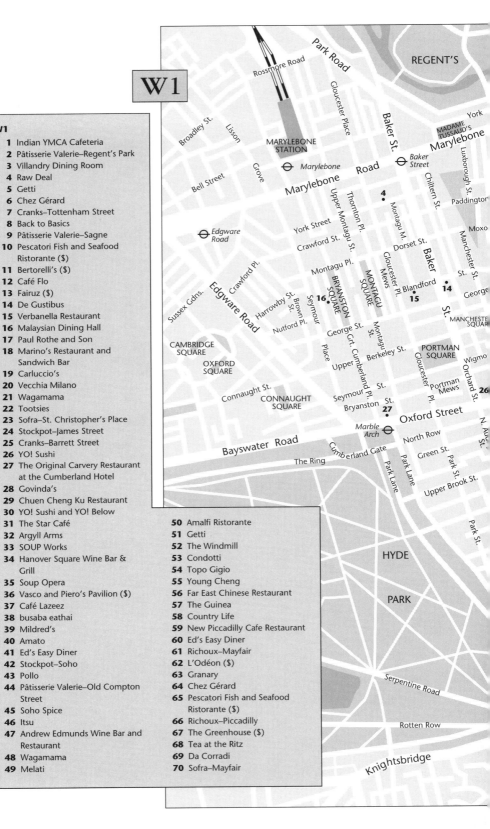

W1

W1

1 Indian YMCA Cafeteria
2 Pâtisserie Valerie–Regent's Park
3 Villandry Dining Room
4 Raw Deal
5 Getti
6 Chez Gérard
7 Cranks–Tottenham Street
8 Back to Basics
9 Pâtisserie Valerie–Sagne
10 Pescatori Fish and Seafood
   Ristorante ($)
11 Bertorelli's ($)
12 Café Flo
13 Fairuz ($)
14 De Gustibus
15 Verbanella Restaurant
16 Malaysian Dining Hall
17 Paul Rothe and Son
18 Marino's Restaurant and
   Sandwich Bar
19 Carluccio's
20 Vecchia Milano
21 Wagamama
22 Tootsies
23 Sofra–St. Christopher's Place
24 Stockpot–James Street
25 Cranks–Barrett Street
26 YO! Sushi
27 The Original Carvery Restaurant
   at the Cumberland Hotel
28 Govinda's
29 Chuen Cheng Ku Restaurant
30 YO! Sushi and YO! Below
31 The Star Café
32 Argyll Arms
33 SOUP Works
34 Hanover Square Wine Bar &
   Grill
35 Soup Opera
36 Vasco and Piero's Pavilion ($)
37 Café Lazeez
38 busaba eathai
39 Mildred's
40 Amato
41 Ed's Easy Diner
42 Stockpot–Soho
43 Pollo
44 Pâtisserie Valerie–Old Compton
   Street
45 Soho Spice
46 Itsu
47 Andrew Edmunds Wine Bar and
   Restaurant
48 Wagamama
49 Melati

50 Amalfi Ristorante
51 Getti
52 The Windmill
53 Condotti
54 Topo Gigio
55 Young Cheng
56 Far East Chinese Restaurant
57 The Guinea
58 Country Life
59 New Piccadilly Cafe Restaurant
60 Ed's Easy Diner
61 Richoux–Mayfair
62 L'Odéon ($)
63 Granary
64 Chez Gérard
65 Pescatori Fish and Seafood
   Ristorante ($)
66 Richoux–Piccadilly
67 The Greenhouse ($)
68 Tea at the Ritz
69 Da Corradi
70 Sofra–Mayfair

RESTAURANTS IN W1

($) indicates a Big Splurge

Restaurants

AMALFI RISTORANTE (50)
29–31 Old Compton Street, Soho, W1
Tube: Piccadilly Circus, Leicester Square,
Tottenham Court Road

Amalfi has been an upscale Great Eat on the Soho dining scene for more than three decades. The manager, Mr. Ramos, who has been there almost that long, shows no sign of slowing down, and neither does his Italian-speaking waitstaff. Clad in blue shirts, they laugh, joke, and kibitz with the regulars, who vie for seats in the upstairs dining room, which has a ceiling brightly painted with clouds and tiled tabletops hand-painted with scenes from the Amalfi coast. Just off the entrance is a pâtisserie and a takeaway counter. Downstairs are four arched grottoes that can seat a combined total of 140 people. One of the grottoes is papered with photos

TELEPHONE
020 7437 7284
OPEN
Daily
CLOSED
2 days at Christmas, New Year's Day
HOURS
Mon–Sat noon–11:15 P.M., Sun noon–10 P.M., continuous service
RESERVATIONS
Advised
CREDIT CARDS
AE, DC, MC, V

PRICES
À la carte, £9–18; set-price,
£7–9 for pasta and a salad;
January regional menus from
£16, 2 courses, dessert, and
coffee
SERVICE
12.5% service charge

of well-known Italian stage and screen stars; another is romantically candlelit with Chianti bottles hung above.

The best meal deal, upstairs or down, is the £7–9 pasta plate. For this price you have a choice of six types of pasta topped with any of their thirteen homemade sauces accompanied by a house salad. Or, you can enjoy cannelloni, lasagna, tortellini, risotto with mushrooms, or one of seven pizzas, all of which also come with a tossed green salad. For two weeks in January they feature special set-price menus and wines from various regions of Italy. Priced at less than £18, they offer very good value and plenty of delicious food.

Amalfi also offers some wonderful veal and chicken dishes and a small selection of fresh fish. All desserts are homemade and are seductively displayed in the window by the takeaway counter. Try to save room for dessert. You won't be sorry when you taste your first bite of *torta della nonna,* a short crust pastry filled with lemon cream and topped with pine nuts and a dusting of powdered sugar, or the rich tiramisu.

NOTE: Takeaway is available.

BACK TO BASICS (8)
21A Foley Street, Fitzrovia, W1
Tube: Goodge Street

TELEPHONE
020 7436 2181
FAX
020 7436 2180
INTERNET
www.backtobasics.uk.com
OPEN
Mon–Fri lunch and dinner
CLOSED
Sat, Sun, Christmas through
New Year's
HOURS
Noon–10 P.M, continuous
service
RESERVATIONS
Advised for lunch
CREDIT CARDS
AE, DC, MC, V
PRICES
À la carte £25–30
SERVICE
10% added to the bill

Fresh fish and plenty of it is the drawing card at the popular neighborhood green-and-white corner site known as Back to Basics. Inside, plain wooden tables are set with linens in a room hung with fish mobiles and plants, and in the summer tables are placed outside. Service is friendly. Keeping pace with diners who demand healthy food preparation, fish and chips are nowhere to be seen on the lengthy daily menu of fresh catches, which is written on two blackboards. Instead, look for innovative ways with lobster, salmon, wild sea bass, swordfish, skate, tuna, cod, scallops, halibut, and smoked haddock. Of course, please remember that some items may not be available because of weather, season, and fishermen's moods and luck, as well as that of the chef.

I like to start with the soup of the day or a bowl of mussels in white wine with lots of garlic and herbs. As a main course, the tuna steak with marinated tomatoes and grilled goat cheese is wonderful, and so is the fillet of halibut with celeriac vinaigrette and a crab-caraway butter. On a warm day, the fresh lobster served with a pesto mayonnaise is a delight, as is the poached-salmon salad or the king scallops paired with sweet chili sauce and sour cream. In an attempt to be well-rounded, there are a few non-briney menu items, but they are best avoided.

The portions here are so generous I have never had room for much beyond cheese and biscuits for dessert, but I am always tempted by the rich bread-and-butter pudding with a whiskey sauce.

BERTORELLI'S ($, 11)
19–23 Charlotte Street, Fitzrovia, W1
Tube: Goodge Street

Eat upstairs and splurge. Eat downstairs at the café-bar and pay half the price, but have all the upstairs quality in both food and service. The downstairs menu focuses on substantial Italian food that is well prepared and presented. A cornucopia of seasonal antipasti aims to please, with a lusty minestrone of seasonal vegetables served with basil-flavored oil, caramelized pear, rocket (arugula), watercress, and freshly shaved Parmesan salad with a balsamic-lemon dressing, or grilled asparagus with sun-dried tomato dressing. Five pizzas compete for attention with as many pastas and two kinds of risotto. Substantial main courses of honey-roasted duck with roasted winter vegetables, corn-fed chicken with a crisp fennel and mozzarella risotto cake, and salmon fish cakes served with herb mayonnaise should fill gourmands and still leave room for one of Bertorelli's ice-cream creations doused with a shot of Amaretto or the devilish chocolate brownie with pistachio cream.

NOTE: There is a second Bertorelli's in Covent Garden, WC2. Please see page 132.

TELEPHONE
020 7636 4174

OPEN
Mon–Sat

CLOSED
Sun, holidays (call to check)

HOURS
Café: Mon–Sat noon–11 P.M., continuous service; restaurant: lunch Mon–Fri noon–3 P.M., dinner Mon–Sat 6–11 P.M.

RESERVATIONS
Advised

CREDIT CARDS
AE, DC, MC, V

PRICES
À la carte: café £20–25; restaurant £30–40

SERVICE
Restaurant £2 cover charge; restaurant and café 12.5% service charge

busaba eathai (38)
106–110 Wardour Street, Soho, W1
Tube: Piccadilly Circus

The introduction on the menu tells you that *busaba* is a Thai flower and that the word *eathai* is a fusion of the words *eat* and *Thai*. It replaces the word *restaurant,* which often connotes a formal experience. The emphasis here is on casual dining with a minimum of fuss so that you can enjoy and take pleasure in what you are eating. Comfort while doing so, however, has never been mentioned. The futuristically stark interior, with black slab-cement flooring, is composed of hard backless benches around large square tables designed for communal eating. Each table is lighted by a shaded overhead lamp and dressed

TELEPHONE
020 7255 8686

INTERNET
www.busaba.com

OPEN
Daily

CLOSED
Christmas

HOURS
Mon–Sat noon–11 P.M, Sun until 10 P.M, continuous service

RESERVATIONS
Not accepted

CREDIT CARDS
AE, MC, V

PRICES
À la carte: £7–12
SERVICE
Discretionary

with two bottles of soy and hot sauce. If you want to dine alone, you sit at a window bench. The coed waitstaff is dressed in black sarong skirts. The only soft notes are the orchids and floating candles at the entrance and the aroma of incense. Even the bathrooms are something from the another world—or mind-set. Both the men and women share the same sink, but all you see of one another are your hands. Predictable Thai dishes of noodles, rice, curries, stir-frys, and deep-fried or grilled selections dominate the menu. The only dessert is lemongrass tea.

NOTE: No smoking is allowed.

CAFÉ FLO (12)
13–14 Thayer Street (off Marylebone High Street), W1
Tube: Bond Street

TELEPHONE
020 7935 5023
OPEN
Daily
CLOSED
2 days at Christmas
HOURS
Breakfast: Mon–Sat 10 A.M.– noon; brunch: Sat–Sun 10 A.M.– 3 P.M.; lunch: noon–5 P.M.; dinner: 5–10:30 P.M.; continuous service
RESERVATIONS
Not necessary
CREDIT CARDS
AE, MC, V
PRICES
À la carte: breakfast £3–8, lunch and dinner £8.50–20; set-price: lunch only, 2 courses chosen from menu or daily specials £12, 3 courses £15
SERVICE
12.5% service charge

Most of the Café Flo restaurants in London have a sleek look defined by the use of chrome, wood, and multicolored china, but not this one, which is the last with the look and feel of a traditional French bistro. The menu varies slightly with each location, changing seasonally and offering all the recognizable French dishes: *soupe de poisson* (traditional fish soup topped with *rouille,* croutons, and Gruyère); *fromage de chèvre* on a bed of rocket (arugula) and sun-dried tomatoes; *cuissede canard à l'orange* (roasted leg of duck in an orange sauce); *filet de cabillaud poêle au choux* (pan-sautéed cod fillet served on a bed of cabbage and roast garlic); *saucisses de Toulouse* (Toulouse sausages in a red-wine sauce served with deep-fried onion rings); *moules marinières* (mussels cooked in with white wine and shallots); and of course, *steak frites.* For dessert, order a rich crème brûlée, a *fondant au chocolat,* or a fresh fruit tart. On Saturday and Sunday, brunch is served at some branches of Café Flo, but here, any day, you can have either a full English breakfast or *le petit déjeuner* (coffee and croissants) from 10 A.M. until noon.

NOTE: There is a nonsmoking section and a children's menu. Other Café Flo branches are in Notting Hill (see page 99), Covent Garden (see page 132), Piccadilly (see page 157), and Kensington (see page 200).

CAFÉ LAZEEZ (37)
21 Dean Street, Soho, W1
Tube: Leicester Square, Tottenham Court Road

The Lazeez restaurants in London exemplify the definition of the word *lazeez:* delicate and aromatic; pleasing to the senses; delicious to taste. Indian food still holds the most-favored-nation status among ethnic-food lovers in London, but Americans often consider this unfamiliar food to be exotic and mysterious. A visit to any of the Lazeez restaurants is the perfect way to change your attitude about this multifaceted cuisine. Historically, Indian fare has been perceived as hot, spicy, and saturated in *ghee* (clarified butter). At Lazeez, the use of chili as a hot spice is moderated, and sunflower oil is substituted for the *ghee,* which does not compromise either your health or your palate. The menu presents a choice of either traditional dishes using authentic recipes or evolved dishes representing style and taste that have grown in Britain over the last thirty years. None of the food will be masked with curry, a word that does not even appear on the lengthy menu. *Curry* is an English derivative of the Tamil word for sauce, *karhi,* and it has been used as a catchword for all Indian cuisine.

The latest Café Lazeez, in Soho, is a dramatic open restaurant with low, indirect lighting in a burnt-adobe setting. Downstairs is the formal restaurant, and upstairs is the brasserie, which offers the better value for the money. The set brasserie menu offers two courses, selected from three appetizers, three main courses, and two desserts. While hardly out of the mainstream, they are nice introductions to modern Indian cuisine. Start with either the vegetarian soup of the day served with fresh naan, or *paneer pakora,* which is deep-fried cheese in a chickpea batter flavored with mint, or chicken *tikka*—tandoor grilled chicken pieces in a tangy marinade served with a small salad. For the main course, you can choose from lamb, cubes of chicken braised in tomato and garlic sauce (both served with rice), vegetables and a salad, or a stir-fry of mixed vegetables served with lentils and aromatic basmati rice. Dessert is either ice cream with nuts or rather heavy condensed-milk dumplings served warm in a sugary syrup.

Downstairs in the restaurant, the food becomes more complicated and expensive. However, all the main courses are served with basmati rice, the vegetable of the day, and naan, and the food is filling, so for most of us,

TELEPHONE
020 7434 9393

FAX
020 7434 0022

OPEN
Daily

CLOSED
Christmas

HOURS
Mon–Sat noon–1:30 A.M., Sun 6–10:30 P.M, continuous service

RESERVATIONS
Advised on weekends

CREDIT CARDS
AE, DC, MC, V

PRICES
Brasserie: Mon–Fri and Sun set-price lunch and pre-theater dinner, 2 courses £8, 3 courses £11; à la carte £10–18; restaurant: à la carte £20–25

SERVICE
12.5% service charge

one dish will be enough. The most popular dish on the international menu is the house specialty, the frontier burger, which pairs grilled, minced beef cured in crushed spices with pomegranate, served over naan, with red onions and fries. It is not my favorite, but it might be yours. I would rather order the chicken *dum pukht*, tender pieces of chicken breast flavored with cardamom, saffron, and cream and cooked slowly in a sealed pot. Another favorite for two is the half leg of spring lamb that has been marinated in a piquant combination of green herbs.

NOTE: There is another Café Lazeez in South Kensington (SW7), and City Lazeez is in Clerkenwell (EC1). Please see pages 201 and 224.

CARLUCCIO'S (19)
8 Market Place, Fitzrovia, W1
Tube: Oxford Circus

TELEPHONE
020 7636 2228

FAX
020 7636 9650

EMAIL
marketplace@carluccios.com

INTERNET
www.carluccios.com

OPEN
Daily

CLOSED
2 days at Christmas, New Year's

HOURS
Mon–Fri 8 A.M.–11 p.m., Sat 10 A.M.–11 P.M, Sun 11 A.M.–10 P.M

RESERVATIONS
Advised

CREDIT CARDS
AE, DC, MC, V

PRICES
À la carte £7–15

SERVICE
Discretionary

Antonio Carluccio is a household name among London's Italian-food lovers, many of whom regularly watched his cooking series on television and paid high prices to eat at his Neal Street restaurant. Now his new cooking shop/deli/café/restaurant is hot on the lips of these London cognoscenti as the perfect place to shop and eat the Italian way—at prices anyone can afford. During the day it is an Italian deli and café; by nightfall it has turned into a big, open, noisy restaurant. I found the food impressively consistent, well prepared, and nicely served by a waitstaff that handles the crowd with aplomb. The tin of savory assorted breads, served with either butter or extra-virgin olive oil, will keep you content until your antipasti arrive. If there are several of you, order one or two antipasti to share, and be sure to include the Sicilian *arancini di riso*—two rice balls, deep fried until crisp, one filled with melted mozzarella and the other with a meaty ragout, served with a piquant red-pepper sauce. Salads, pastas, eggplant and zucchini parmigiana, calzones, and daily specials complete the picture, until it is time for a *dolci*. All desserts are made here, and they are seriously decadent, especially the *tartufi di cioccolato*—a rich chocolate-truffle pudding. For something equally as good but less caloric, order the soothing *affogato*—homemade vanilla ice cream served in a tall glass with strong espresso poured over it. *Buon appetito!*

NOTE: Smaller portions are available for children. There are two other Carluccio's in W1, one in the basement of Fenwick on Bond Street (Tel: 020 7629 0699), open daily 10 A.M. to 6 or 8 P.M., depending on store hours, and one on St. Christopher's Place, off Oxford Circus (it was under construction at press time).

CHEZ GÉRARD (6)
8 Charlotte Street, Fitzrovia, W1
Tube: Goodge Street

For years, the Chez Gérard restaurants have been little patches of London that signified France. Francophiles, off-duty French chefs, and red-blooded carnivores have been drawn to the group's restaurants to revel in an atmosphere straight from Boulevard St-Germain and to savor the best *steak frites* this side of the Channel. Today the *steak frites* are as good as ever, but diners whose idea of gourmet heaven is not a juicy steak will appreciate the lighter touch of some of the menu selections. Grilled fresh salmon, a plate of roasted vegetables drizzled with fine olive oil and garnished with roasted garlic and *pistou* (a sauce of basil, garlic, cheese, and olive oil), or a simple grilled fish or roast chicken will please. To start, there are always escargots baked with garlic butter, onion soup gratinéed with croutons and Gruyère, and the plats du jour, featuring French faves such as *boeuf bourguignon* and *filet de sole farci*. The set-price menu, which varies slightly with each location, offers top-notch value when you consider that it is available Monday to Saturday evenings and Saturday or Sunday lunch (depending on the location), and that it offers choices from four starters, four main courses (including a vegetarian option), and three desserts.

The Charlotte Street location features an authentic Parisian zinc bar and chrome railway-carriage luggage racks for coats and bags in a light room with scrubbed tile floors. Upstairs, where smoking is prohibited, the atmosphere is almost antiseptic, with white walls and a marble bar separating a dozen or so tables from a line of banquettes.

NOTE: In addition to the one next listed, there are five other Chez Gérards: two in WC2 (see page 135), one in EC1 (see page 224), one in EC2 (see page 230), and one in EC3 (see page 234). There is a nonsmoking section upstairs at this branch.

TELEPHONE
020 7636 4975

FAX
020 7636 4975

INTERNET
www.santeonline.co.uk

OPEN
Mon–Fri and Sun lunch and dinner; Sat dinner only

CLOSED
Sat lunch, holidays

HOURS
Lunch: noon–3 P.M.; dinner: Mon–Sat 6–11:30 P.M., Sun 12:30–11:30 P.M.

RESERVATIONS
Essential

CREDIT CARDS
AE, DC, MC, V

PRICES
À la carte: £25–35; set-price pre- and post-theater menu: Mon–Sat dinner 6–7 P.M. and after 10 P.M., Sun lunch £17–28, 3 courses

SERVICE
£1 cover charge includes freshly baked French bread and butter, anchovy butter, marinated olives, and toasted salted nuts; 12.5% service charge

CHEZ GÉRARD (64)
31 Dover Street, Mayfair, W1
Tube: Green Park, Bond Street

See Chez Gérard above for full description. All other information (including a nonsmoking section) is the same.

TELEPHONE: 020 7499 8171
FAX: 020 7491 3818
OPEN: Mon–Sat lunch and dinner; Sun dinner only
CLOSED: Sun lunch, holidays
HOURS: Lunch: daily noon–3 P.M.; dinner: Mon–Sat 6–11 P.M., Sun 6–10:30 P.M.

CHUEN CHENG KU RESTAURANT (29)
17 Wardour Street, Chinatown, W1
Tube: Oxford Circus, Tottenham Court Road

TELEPHONE
020 7437 1398

FAX
020 7434 0533

OPEN
Daily

CLOSED
2 days at Christmas

HOURS
11 A.M.–midnight, continuous service

RESERVATIONS
Advised, especially for Sun lunch

CREDIT CARDS
AE, DC, MC, V

PRICES
À la carte £10–20; set-price £14–28, 2-person minimum

SERVICE
10% service charge

The functionally impersonal Chuen Cheng Ku in London's Chinatown is the place to have dim sum, the Asian treat of bite-size appetizers. This meal provides one of the best opportunities to sample a wide range of tastes. The hardworking waitstaff wheels dim sum carts around the tables, chanting the names of their offerings in Chinese. Diners then take their pick of the exotic mouthfuls wrapped in leaves or delicately arranged in willow baskets. Since most of the waitstaff knows only the Chinese names of the dishes, your only help in deciding is the picture menu on each table. But actually, it is much more fun and adventurous to just point as the cart passes and enjoy the surprise. This is, of course, if you wouldn't balk at a chicken foot doused in black-bean sauce.

In addition to dim sum, the long menu lists almost every other Cantonese dish you have ever heard of, and some you probably wish you hadn't. The best advice is to stick with the dim sum, which is served daily until 6 P.M. The most interesting time to go is for Sunday lunch, when you can observe extended Chinese families happily indulging in their favorite dim sum delicacies.

NOTE: Takeaway is available. There is a second branch at 20 Rupert Street, W1. The same hours, menu, telephone number, and prices apply.

CONDOTTI (53)
4 Mill Street (off Conduit Street), Mayfair, W1
Tube: Oxford Circus, Bond Street, Piccadilly Circus

Delicious pizza served in upscale surroundings is exactly what you can expect at the classy Condotti, near Regent Street. It looks and feels expensive, with a good-looking crowd sitting around well-spaced tables with starched linens and fresh flowers. The walls are hung with an interesting collection of the owner's contemporary art, and the service is polite and professional. But is pizza all that they serve? That's right, along with starters, assorted salads, desserts, and Italian wines.

Of their many pizzas, favorites include the Pizza Veneziana, with onions, capers, olives, pine nuts, and sultanas. (The Venice in Peril fund, which is raising money to save Venice from sinking, gets 40 pence for every Veneziana sold. So far, the total amount collected exceeds $1.5 million.) I also like the Pizza King Edward, with four cheeses and extra tomatoes, and La Reine, with ham, olives, and mushrooms.

Dessert decisions are never easy, but I am always partial to the dense chocolate fudge cake slathered in cream or ice cream. A light Italian wine or a bottle of Peroni beer makes a perfect accompaniment to the meal, and a bracing espresso is the best ending.

TELEPHONE
020 7499 1308
FAX
020 7491 2122
OPEN
Mon–Sat
CLOSED
Sun, holidays
HOURS
11:30 A.M.–midnight, continuous service
RESERVATIONS
Advised for lunch
CREDIT CARDS
AE, DC, MC, V
PRICES
À la carte £12–18
SERVICE
Discretionary; 12.5% service charge for 7 people or more

COUNTRY LIFE (58)
3–4 Warwick Street, Piccadilly Circus, W1
Tube: Piccadilly Circus

For a healthy vegan meal in London, Country Life will fill your plate starting at the philanthropically low price of £3 for a bowl of soup and a roll, and charging a mere one pence per gram for lunch. Average cost: £5, and there is a ceiling price of £6 on this meal. Country Life is run by the Seventh-Day Adventist church, whose friendly members are eager to spread their message, so you can expect to see their brochures and magazines prominently displayed. Monday to Friday, lunch is cafeteria-style, with a featured soup, main course, vegetable, and side dish. No time to sit down and eat? Then they will pack it for takeaway. In the evening, cloths cover the tables, waitstaff replace the cafeteria chow line, and everything is à la carte, with symbols on the dishes indicating whether each is gluten-free, yeast-free, or honey-free. In addition to the restaurant, Country Life operates a health food shop, which doesn't begin to compare with those we have in the States, but for London,

TELEPHONE
020 7434 2922
FAX
020 7434 2838
EMAIL
info@countrylife-restaurant.co.uk
INTERNET
www.countrylife-restaurant.co.uk
OPEN
Mon–Thur and Sun lunch and dinner; Fri lunch only
CLOSED
Fri dinner, Sat, holidays
HOURS
Buffet lunch: Sun–Thur 11:30 A.M.–5 P.M., Fri 11:30 A.M.–2:30 P.M. (till 3:30 P.M. in summer); dinner: Sun–Thur 5:30–10 P.M.; shop: Mon–Wed 9 A.M.–6 P.M., Thur 9 A.M.–7:30 P.M., Fri 9 A.M.–2:30 P.M., Sun 1–5 P.M.

RESERVATIONS
Advised for dinner
CREDIT CARDS
V
PRICES
Lunch buffet one pence per gram—cannot exceed £6; dinner £9 1 course, £11 2 courses, £14 3 courses
SERVICE
10% service charge

it passes. They also have cooking classes, and medical, nutrition, and dietary experts to help and give advice on a variety of topics.

NOTE: No smoking or alcohol allowed.

CRANKS RESTAURANT (25)
23 Barrett Street (off St. Christopher's Place), W1
Tube: Bond Street

TELEPHONE
020 7495 1340
FAX
020 7409 0671
OPEN
Mon–Sat
CLOSED
Sun, holidays
HOURS
Mon–Fri 8 A.M.–7:30 P.M., Sat 9 A.M.–7 P.M., continuous service (December hours are Mon–Sat 11 A.M.–4 P.M.); hours vary slightly with each location
RESERVATIONS
Not necessary
CREDIT CARDS
None
PRICES
À la carte £4.50–8
SERVICE
Discretionary

Given their menus and determination to prepare fat-free dishes, they generally live up to their motto: "Food for Vitality and Health." The chain of inexpensive vegetarian restaurants was one of the first on the London natural-food scene, introducing whole grains, free-range eggs, and vegetable casseroles as healthy alternatives to the British staples of sausage, beans, fried eggs, and creamy snacks. It now is blazing another new trail in vegetarian food by becoming a fast-food canteen with all dishes prepared in a central kitchen and dispatched daily to Cranks locations. The food caters to all types of vegetarians, including vegans, with only a slight nod to macrobiotic diners. I think some of the dishes are a little old hat, considering the innovations in vegetarian cuisine over the past few years, but one cannot fault their wholesomeness. Nor should one forget that this is food for the masses, and sophisticated creativity is not part of anyone's job description, least of all the chef's. The food is displayed cafeteria-style, allowing diners to choose from a daily selection of hot and cold dishes, salads, fresh fruit, soups, sweets, and hot and cold drinks, including fruit and vegetable juices. Go early for the freshest selection, and concentrate on the daily specials. Light breakfasts, including porridge, are also served.

NOTE: Patio seating is available on warm days on charming St. Christopher's Place. No smoking or alcohol allowed. Takeaway is available in all branches. In addition to the two listed below, there are two other Cranks Restaurants in WC2 (see page 136).

CRANKS–TOTTENHAM STREET (7)
9–11 Tottenham Street, Bloomsbury, W1
Tube: Goodge Street

This location is one of the more attractive. See Cranks above for full description. All other information is the same.

TELEPHONE: 020 7631 3912
FAX: 020 7636 6113
OPEN: Mon–Sat
CLOSED: Sun, holidays
HOURS: Mon–Fri 7:30 A.M.–7:30 P.M., Sat 10 A.M.–6 P.M., continuous service

DA CORRADI (69)
20–22 Shepherd Market, Mayfair, W1
Tube: Green Park

Da Corradi is a regular lunchtime hangout for local Mayfair office workers who enjoy the low-key atmosphere and good, affordable Italian cooking in the rustic, two-floor, Shepherd Market surroundings. A line often forms in front around noon, when the aroma of the lusty sauces float to the sidewalk. The freshly prepared food is worth the brief wait, especially the daily specials of homemade soup, lasagna, tortellini, or the chef's weekly creations. All the pastas and sauces are made here by owner Guiseppe Corradi and his family. They even go so far as to pick their own mushrooms for the wild mushroom pasta sauce. When I asked Guiseppe where he picked the mushrooms, he told me it was a secret spot that even the Pope couldn't squeeze out of him.

If you aren't in the area for lunch, stop by for a morning cappuccino and a bowl of real porridge—the kind that is slow-cooked with milk, not zapped in the microwave; it's served with brown sugar. This is also a handy spot if you want an early dinner before the theater, or if you don't want to be fashionably correct and eat after 8 or 9 P.M. If you just want a sandwich on the run, go to Da Corradi's sandwich bar next door and order a Hot Italian Job: toasted ciabatta or focaccia bread piled with mozzarella, ham, avocado, tomato, and basil.

New to the menu are the pizzas, but a strong warning is in order: They are made outside of England (!), shipped to the restaurant each week, stacked in a pile in a display case, and reheated as ordered. I cannot imagine what the thinking is here; this is a pizza travesty that should be outlawed and definitely avoided by you!

TELEPHONE
020 7499 1742
OPEN
Restaurant: Mon–Fri breakfast, lunch, and dinner, Sat breakfast and lunch only; sandwich bar: Mon–Fri
CLOSED
Sat dinner, Sun, holidays
HOURS
Restaurant: 7–11:30 A.M., noon–10 P.M., continuous service; sandwich bar: 7 A.M.–5 P.M.
RESERVATIONS
Advised during peak hours
CREDIT CARDS
AE, DC, MC, V (£10 or more)
PRICES
Restaurant: à la carte £12–18; sandwich shop: £3.50–5
SERVICE
10% service charge

DE GUSTIBUS (14)
53 Blandford Street, Marylebone, W1
Tube: Baker Street, Marble Arch

TELEPHONE & FAX
020 7486 6608

INTERNET
www.degustibus.co.uk

OPEN
Mon–Fri

CLOSED
Sat–Sun, holidays

HOURS
7 A.M.–4 P.M., continuous service

RESERVATIONS
Not accepted

CREDIT CARDS
None

PRICES
À la carte £3.50–7

SERVICE
Discretionary

"No sandwich is ever complete unless it is made with De Gustibus bread." Quite a claim, and true when you consider that De Gustibus was voted the baker of the year for two years in a row and also has received the best bread in Britain award. All of their robust sandwiches can be made on your choice of nineteen freshly baked breads with your choice of spread and hot and cold fillings that include meat, sausage, dairy, seafood, fowl, and vegetarian. Every combination you can imagine is available, from a traditional English cheddar to smoked salmon or turkey, Mexican tuna, and six oversize tripledeckers. Things get going at 7 A.M., when local office workers pop in for toast spread with homemade jam, a freshly baked danish or croissant, and a steaming latte or cappuccino. By 11 A.M., the backless, painted wicker stools and green metal garden chairs at the window counter are full of happy munchers, and by noon, the place is chockablock with regulars ordering a takeaway sandwich and one of the restaurant's brownies or a slice of chocolate-raisin crunch cake, which is so rich it could qualify as a candy bar. If you don't want a sandwich (which I cannot imagine, if you are here), there are daily hot specials, salads, quiches, pizzas, and homemade soups served with a basket of bread.

NOTE: No smoking allowed. Now there is a second location at the Borough Market. Please see Markets, page 31.

ED'S EASY DINER (41)
12 Moor Street, Soho, W1
Tube: Leicester Square, Tottenham Court Road

TELEPHONE
020 7439 1995

OPEN
Daily

CLOSED
Christmas Day

HOURS
Mon–Thur, Sun 11:30 A.M.–11:30 P.M. (till midnight in summer), Fri–Sat till 1 A.M.; deliveries: Mon–Fri 11:30 A.M.–9 P.M., Sat noon–6 P.M.

RESERVATIONS
Not accepted

CREDIT CARDS
AE, MC, V (minimum charge £10)

"If you can find a better diner, eat there!" says one of the many signs in Ed's American-style diners in London's Soho and Chelsea (see also page 181). This is the original one, and now there are five others where the eating is as good as the people-watching, which provides an up-close look at the latest fads for teenyboppers and nubile fashion groupies. Seating is on stools around a circular counter, from which you watch the cooks prepare mainstream American fast food that will take you back to the days when expanding waistlines, high cholesterol, and fat levels were not on the top of our worry lists. Even the menu warns: "Healthnicks . . . Eat your heart out. Don't blame us, we're only doing our job."

All the favorites are here: pure beef burgers served with five types of fries and three kinds of onion rings; kosher hot dogs smothered in cheddar cheese; tuna melts; grilled cheese sandwiches with bacon or tomato; chicken served four ways; and five salads, from Caesar to fresh fruit. Wash it all down with a thick malt or milkshake in one of seven flavors, including banana and peanut butter, a Pepsi, or a bottle of beer. On Saturday and Sunday the Chelsea branch is open for breakfast. If you're in the neighborhood and starving, stop by and order the Lumberjack: two eggs any style, hash browns, bacon, sausage, tomato, toast, butter, and jelly. More delicate appetites will like the French toast with maple syrup or Belgian waffle with a side of fruit, syrup, or chocolate sauce. In the mood for sinful sweets? Consider a slice of pecan pie with whipped cream or the Kit-Kat choco-lat sundae. And don't forget the Cracker Jacks, Atomic Fire Balls, and Reese's Pieces: Ed sells them all. The gum-chewing staff is friendly, and the original Seeburg juke-box (circa 1948) plays popular fifties and sixties tunes. It all adds up to a wonderfully nostalgic experience.

NOTE: Takeaway is available. If you can't get to Ed's in person but are within his two Soho delivery areas, call the Diner Line, place your order (it must be over £15), and sit tight until one of his Waiters on Wheels brings your meal to your door (no deliveries on Sunday). There is also an Ed's Easy Diner in Chelsea, SW3 (see page 181).

PRICES
À la carte £4–8; minimum charge at peak times £4

SERVICE
Discretionary

ED'S EASY DINER (60)
Pepsi Trocadero, Shaftesbury Avenue at Piccadilly Circus, W1
Tube: Piccadilly Circus
See Ed's Easy Diner above for a full description. All other information is the same.

TELEPHONE: 020 7287 1951

TUBE: Piccadilly Circus

FAIRUZ ($, 13)
3 Blandford Street, Marylebone, W1
Tube: Baker Street, Bond Street
Fairuz is named after a famous Arabic singer, and also means the color blue. The restaurant consistently draws a steady stream of regulars who swear by the kitchen's competent renditions of healthy Lebanese cuisine. The interior is cozy, with beams and brick archways creating little alcoves and Arabic music adding an air of authenticity.

TELEPHONE
020 7486 8108/8182

FAX
020 7935 8581

OPEN
Daily

CLOSED
2 days at Christmas and New Year's

HOURS
Mon–Fri noon–11 P.M., Sat
until 11:30 P.M, Sun until
10:30 P.M, continuous service

RESERVATIONS
Advised

CREDIT CARDS
AE, DC, MC, V

PRICES
Set-price mezza £18 per person;
set-price hot and cold mezza,
mixed grill or vegetarian main
course, fresh fruit, beer, herbal
tea or coffee £26 per person; à la
carte £25–35

SERVICE
£2 cover charge per person for
bread, vegetables, and olives;
service discretionary

The wooden tables are set with linen napkins and a big bowl of raw vegetables and olives. When you sit down, a basket of warm bread arrives to tide you over during the menu selection. This is the sort of place it is fun to visit with three or four people, so that all can order something different and everyone share. The choices are almost limitless and include forty-two hot and cold starters, seven charcoal grills, not to mention fish and the two house specialties: stuffed lamb and grilled boneless chicken cooked with onions and pepper.

Service is good, the food fresh and appealing, and the prices right, considering the choice and quality of the food. In sum, it is a Great Eat in London.

FAR EAST CHINESE RESTAURANT (56)
13 Gerrard Street, Chinatown, W1
Tube: Leicester Square

TELEPHONE
020 7437 6148

OPEN
Daily

CLOSED
4 days mid-January

HOURS
Bakery: 7 A.M.–7 P.M.;
restaurant: 7 P.M.–1 A.M.

RESERVATIONS
Not accepted

CREDIT CARDS
MC, V

PRICES
À la carte £.90–1.60

SERVICE
No service charged or expected

The Wu family runs this friendly hole-in-the-wall restaurant, tearoom, and bakery in the heart of Chinatown. A few years ago, you would see the senior Mr. Wu holding court daily at the table in the back, chatting with his friends, reading the paper, and generally keeping an eye on things. When I asked about him recently, his son Richard told me he now reads his paper at home. It is clear, however, that he still has a firm grip on things, because Richard's modern ideas—expanding the menu, redecorating and modernizing the interior— have been met with his father's continuing disapproval. Yet the food remains as it has been for almost forty years: delicious. Offerings include Chinese cakes and pastries, such as sticky glazed *char-siu* buns, lotus-seed moon cakes with egg yolk, curry beef puffs, and coconut butter buns. These delicacies don't keep particularly well, so plan to eat your booty within a few hours if you buy takeaway.

From 7 P.M. to 1 A.M. daily, the Wus convert their bakery into a restaurant; that is, they add a few tables. Frankly, I wasn't impressed with the restaurant side of this operation and recommend that you stick with the bakery items.

GETTI (51)
74 Wardour Street, Soho, W1
Tube: Piccadilly Circus

Getti founder Stefano Fraquelli explains: "Certainly there are many restaurants providing Italian food, and many doing it authentically, but none have attempted to capture the essence of Italian style. There is more than food, ambience, and service to our restaurant. We are a way of life, a place to relax, meet friends, and to celebrate. In Italy, it is called *dolce vivere*, which means 'sweet living.'"

The three Getti (pronounced *jetti,* with a soft "g") restaurants are joined in spirit and execution, but each is individually managed and reflects the neighborhood in which it is situated. The style is classy, intimate, and high quality, with fairly priced meals. "Part of the concept of *dolce vivere* is to avoid nasty shocks to the system," says Fraquelli. The modern restaurants are bright and airy, with bold blues offset by cherry wood tables with frosted glass insets and ergonomically sculpted banquettes and chairs. The style may be cool, but the service is warm. The menu of Italian favorites highlights risotto, with updated interpretations of Italian classics and wines by the glass or bottle. Depending on the time of year, the distinctive seasonal menu may offer a salad of poached octopus on a julienne of fennel, celery, and rocket; baked polenta with a Gorgonzola and red-onion chutney; or thin slices of raw tuna marinated with lemon, red peppercorns, black olives, and olive oil. The risotto with red-wine-marinated strawberries is as innovative as it is delicious, and so is the ravioli filled with goat cheese and served with a warm red-pepper coulis. Fish plays heavily on the main course selections; otherwise, look for a tender duck breast served with wild mushrooms, or lamb baked in a parsley crust. A selection of Italian cheeses makes an authentic ending, but for a sweeter finish, the mascarpone and raspberry crème brûlée is wonderful.

Other Getti restaurants are 42 Marylebone High Street, W1 (see next listing) and on Jermyn Street, SW1 (see page 159).

TELEPHONE
020 7437 3519

FAX
020 7434 2336

OPEN
Daily

CLOSED
Christmas Day

HOURS
Mon–Fri: lunch noon–3 P.M, dinner 6:30–11 P.M; Sat–Sun: noon–10:30 P.M, continuous service

RESERVATIONS
Advised

CREDIT CARDS
AE, DC, MC, V

PRICES
À la carte £22–28

SERVICE
Discretionary

GETTI (5)
42 Marylebone High Street, W1
Tube: Baker Street, Bond Street

See Getti above for description. All other information is the same.

TELEPHONE: 020 7486 3753
FAX: 020 7486 7084
OPEN: Daily
HOURS: Noon–3 P.M., 6–10:30 P.M.

GOVINDA'S (28)
9 Soho Street, Soho, W1
Tube: Tottenham Court Road

TELEPHONE
020 7437 4928
OPEN
Mon–Sat; Sun for "love feast"
CLOSED
Sun in the restaurant, holidays
HOURS
Noon–8 P.M., continuous service; love feast Sun 4:30 P.M.
RESERVATIONS
Not necessary
CREDIT CARDS
MC, V (minimum £5)
PRICES
Buffet: £5 noon–7 P.M., £4 7–8 P.M.; à la carte: £3–8; love feast: by donation
SERVICE
No service charged or expected

Govinda's is a cafeteria-style restaurant where there is no smoking, no booze, no service charged or expected, and no garlic, onion, meat, fish, or eggs served. What you will find at this Hare Krishna–run buffet mecca for vegan and vegetarian diners is all the food you can eat for under £6, served on an oval metal platter. The especially hungry will appreciate the huge casseroles or the veggie burger with cheese served with a side salad. Also watch for pizza, lasagna, jacket potatoes with all sorts of toppings, and some run-of-the-mill desserts. Budget-minded Great Eaters with only a few pence in their pockets can show up between 7 and 8 P.M. to take advantage of what's left of the buffet for only £4.

On Sunday the restaurant is closed, but at 4:30 P.M. a "love feast" is held in the temple/restaurant next door. Everyone is welcome and the food is free, but you are expected to leave a donation.

GRANARY (63)
39 Albemarle Street, Mayfair, W1
Tube: Green Park

TELEPHONE
020 7493 2978
OPEN
Mon–Fri; Sat–Sun lunch only
CLOSED
Sun, holidays
HOURS
Mon–Fri 11:30 A.M.–7:30 P.M., Sat–Sun noon–3:30 P.M., continuous service
RESERVATIONS
Necessary for 6 or more
CREDIT CARDS
MC, V

Celebrating a half century in the business, and now joined by his son Julian, John Shah told me, "After this time, we should get it right. We don't sell *posey* food, nothing is frozen, everything is made here, and compromises are not part of the kitchen's mandate." Shah's Granary is an all-day lunch buffet in which there are always twelve hot dishes, six salads, and ten luscious desserts available. The nice part is that you can arrive any time, be assured of a full lineup of food, and order as much or as little as you want. The inside is attractive, with green plants, and the food is appealingly arranged along the glassed-in buffet line. There is room for a hundred, and every seat is occupied during the lunch crunch from 1 to 2 P.M. If you aren't counting fat grams or calories, fill up on the roast loin of pork; the ever-popular avocado stuffed with prawns, spinach, and cheese; or chicken potpie. Virtuous diners will be happy with the vegetable-stuffed eggplant, lemon chicken, a pasta loaded with roasted veggies, or an assortment of the salads. All hot main courses are garnished with potatoes-of-the-day or rice, and portions are large, so you shouldn't fear hunger pangs later on in the afternoon. I always save room for the dessert specialty—banana layer cake—or a slice of the chocolate mousse cake. Never mind the calories . . . every single one is worth it.

PRICES
À la carte £9–16

SERVICE
No service charged or expected

THE GREENHOUSE ($, 67)
27A Hay's Mews, Mayfair, W1
Tube: Green Park, Hyde Park Corner

The renovation of London's culinary landscape is no more evident than at the Greenhouse. The setting, on a back street in the ground floor of a block of Mayfair apartments, is a bit dull, but once you walk along the tree-lined entranceway, which offers a peek into the kitchen on the left, you will be in a pleasantly formal room surrounded by businesspeople at lunch and smartly attired couples in the evening. The food is modern, imaginative, and pleasing. From Monday to Friday there is a remarkably well priced set menu with starters such as rare-roasted carpaccio of peppered veal and porcini mushrooms served with a crostini of roasted tomatoes, goat cheese ravioli perched atop warm Provençale vegetables, or a moist slice of char-grilled tuna on a mix of peppers. Next might be roasted breast of guinea fowl, spicy lamb stew with white beans, or roasted salmon with a lemon-dill and tomato fondue.

In the evening, the lights are turned down and the à la carte menu expanded to include a parfait of chicken livers with red-onion jam, smoked haddock fish cakes with a smooth egg and parsley sauce, or a rabbit terrine with an apple and mustard *rémoulade*. The wild mushroom risotto with Parmesan *beignets* makes a delicious vegetarian main course. Carnivores will appreciate the pot-roasted breast of pheasant with a sage and mushroom stuffing or the grilled *pavé* of Scotch beef served with pan-fried foie gras. Desserts are a delight and include dense chocolate fondant, a silky crème brûlée, and an old-fashioned bread-and-butter pudding.

TELEPHONE
020 7499 3331/3314

FAX
020 7499 5368

OPEN
Daily

CLOSED
Sat lunch, holidays

HOURS
Mon–Fri: lunch noon–2:30 P.M., dinner 7–11 P.M.; Sat: dinner 7–11 P.M.; Sun: lunch 12:30–3 P.M., dinner 7–10 P.M.,

RESERVATIONS
Essential

CREDIT CARDS
AE, DC, MC, V

PRICES
À la carte: £30–38; set-price lunch: Mon–Fri £17 2 courses, £22 3 courses, Sun £25 3 courses

SERVICE
12.5% service charge

NOTE: Please don't confuse this Greenhouse with the Greenhouse vegetarian restaurant in Bloomsbury, WC1—they are unrelated.

INDIAN YMCA CAFETERIA (1)
41 Fitzroy Square, Regent's Park, W1
Tube: Warren Street

TELEPHONE
020 7387 0411
OPEN
Daily
CLOSED
Some holidays for lunch, call
to check
HOURS
Breakfast: Mon–Fri
8–9:15 A.M., Sat–Sun, holidays
8:30–9:30 A.M.; lunch: Mon–
Fri noon–2 P.M., Sat–Sun,
holidays 12:30–1:30 P.M.;
dinner: daily 7–8 P.M.
RESERVATIONS
Not accepted
CREDIT CARDS
AE, MC, V
PRICES
À la carte £3–5
SERVICE
No service charged or expected

For the nearest thing to Indian home cooking, eat at the Indian YMCA Cafeteria, where you will rub elbows with students at breakfast and dinner and with budget-conscious office workers and neighborhood residents at lunch. While certainly not the place to entertain your boss, it is good to keep in mind if you like very simple Indian food.

The philanthropically priced meals are geared toward Indian students and other guests who stay at this YMCA while studying in London. Naturally, any attempt at decor is out, and the choices for each meal are limited. The breakfasts are usually English style, but once a week an Indian dish is added. One of the most popular Indian breakfast dishes is *upma,* a southern Indian dish made from cereal and vegetables. It is nice once in a while, but something I do not yearn for often. At lunch three main dishes are offered: a vegetarian, meat, and fish curry. Each is served with rice or chapati. Dal and condiments are on the shared tables. The dinner selections vary among tandoori chicken, mutton stew, and spicy prawns, as well as a vegetarian selection. Desserts are forgettable, mostly canned fruit or ice cream. Tea, coffee, and fruit juice are included with breakfast and lunch; coffee is included with dinner.

NOTE: No smoking or alcohol allowed; the cafeteria is unlicensed.

ITSU (46)
103 Wardour Street, Soho, W1
Tube: Piccadilly Circus, Leicester Square

TELEPHONE
020 7479 4794
INTERNET
www.itsu.co.uk
OPEN
Daily
CLOSED
2 days at Christmas, New
Year's
HOURS
Mon–Thur noon–11 P.M., Fri–
Sat until midnight, Sun until
10 P.M., continuous service

Sushi bars are one of the dining phenomena of London. Starting a few years ago with YO! Sushi (see page 75), the concept of sitting at a shared table or on a stool around a conveyor belt and helping yourself to bits and bites of raw food wrapped in seaweed caught on with the baby boomers looking for not only healthy food, but also convenience, spontaneity, and informality when eating out. The dishes at Itsu have a creative twist to them, especially the "inside out" sushi, with the seaweed wrapper enveloped with rice and a decorative sliver of fish adorning the top. Your bill is tallied according to color coding on the plates of food you have selected. Itsu lives up to its promise: "Eat well with us. Feel well with us. Leave us and look well."

NOTE: No smoking allowed. There is another Itsu in Chelsea. Please see page 183.

RESERVATIONS
Not necessary

CREDIT CARDS
AE, MC, V

PRICES
À la carte £10–15

SERVICE
Discretionary

L'ODÉON ($, 62)
65 Regent Street, Piccadilly Circus, W1
Tube: Piccadilly Circus

In the last few years, London has experienced a rash of ultra-trendy restaurants that offer a see-and-be-seen atmosphere in which dressing to the nines and eating out is more about posing than dining. Some of these gastronomic palaces work, offering a culinary energy matched by few. Others provide more style than substance and are wildly expensive, quite beyond the spirit of *Great Eats London*. But there are some notable exceptions, and L'Odéon is one of them. At L'Odéon the food is superb and the setting a knockout. The 280-seat restaurant occupies a dazzling space, with half-moon windows overlooking Piccadilly Circus and Regent Street. Despite its size and minimal interior, there is an intimate feel, largely achieved by the blue banquette seating that ebbs and flows throughout the room. A jazz piano player in the evening adds just the right touch of romance to it all.

The international menu is innovative and seasonally inspired. The only difficult thing about it is trying to decide what to order. The selections change frequently, but if the seared foie gras served with roasted honey-drizzled pears and a toasted brioche, or the butternut squash and lemon-thyme soup are listed, please consider these two special winter starters. For the main course, the hearty osso buco, slowly cooked with sage, tomato, and orange and garnished with saffron mashed potatoes, or the duck confit served with braised lentils and a peppery rocket and turnip salad with a fruit tea dressing, are stellar choices. Vegetarians are not left behind, especially with the herb gnocchi tossed with roasted tomatoes, baby artichokes, and sprigs of wild rocket. You can see what I mean by imaginative and unusual.

For dessert, I love the *tarte tatin* topped with rosemary ice cream or the orange and Grand Mariner parfait with a caramelized orange sauce. If these seem too formidable, order a delicate chestnut honey *panacotta,* served with a

TELEPHONE
020 7287 1400

OPEN
Mon–Sat

CLOSED
Sun, holidays

HOURS
Lunch: noon–2:45 P.M.; dinner: 5:30–11:30 P.M., pre-theater dinner menu served until 7 P.M.; bar menu: 11 A.M.–2:45 P.M. and 5:30 P.M.–1 A.M.; bar closes at 3 A.M.

RESERVATIONS
Essential; request a window seat

CREDIT CARDS
AE, DC, MC, V

PRICES
À la carte: £30–35; set-price: lunch and pre-theater menu £17 2 courses, £21 3 courses, bar menu £5–9 1 course

SERVICE
£1.50 cover charge; service not included for parties of 5 or less; 12.5% service charge for 6 or more

winter fruit compote. A selection of sorbets makes for just the right light finish.

The bargains at L'Odéon are hard to beat for the set-price lunch and pre-theater dinner, or from the bar menu, which is available 11 A.M.–2:45 P.M. and 5:30 P.M.–1 A.M.

MALAYSIAN DINING HALL (16)
44 Bryanston Square (in the basement), Marylebone, W1
Tube: Marble Arch

TELEPHONE
020 7723 9484
OPEN
Daily
CLOSED
Christmas Day, 2 Muslim holidays that vary each year
HOURS
Breakfast: 8–10 A.M.; lunch: noon–3 P.M.; dinner: 4–9 P.M. During month of Ramadan, open noon–9 P.M.
RESERVATIONS
Not accepted
CREDIT CARDS
None
PRICES
À la carte £3.50–5; set-price £3–4
SERVICE
No service charged or expected

When was the last time you had rice slowly simmered in coconut milk and topped with anchovies and chili peppers for breakfast? Or how about fish head curry, *mee bandung* (spicy soup with noodles), or fried *kway teow* (a mix of seafood, eggs, and noodles)? All this plus a daily vegetarian dish, a fish plate, and one or two curries (registering mild, medium, and searing) are yours for the taking at the Malaysian Dining Hall, a little-known basement student canteen subsidized and overseen by the Malaysian government. Technically, you must be Malaysian or a guest of one to eat here, but for years, this rule has existed in theory, not in practice. Open for breakfast, lunch, and dinner every day except Christmas and two Muslim holidays, this haven for Malaysians far from home serves some of the most authentic Malay and Indonesian food in London. And if you ordered every-thing in sight, you still would have trouble spending more than £5. The menu changes daily, the standards are high, the food is fresh, and the cafeteria has a well-worn atmosphere. For an unusual and mighty inexpen-sive dining experience, this one is hard to top. But hurry, because rumor has it that the cafeteria may close, or move to smaller quarters.

NOTE: There is a nonsmoking section. No alcohol allowed; the dining hall is unlicensed.

MARINO'S RESTAURANT AND SANDWICH BAR (18)
31 Rathbone Place, Bloomsbury, W1
Tube: Tottenham Court Road

TELEPHONE
020 7636 8965
OPEN
Mon–Sat
CLOSED
Sun, holidays

I would use the term *restaurant* in Marino's case rather loosely. This sandwich pit stop looks like almost every other quickie takeaway shop in London: the front counter is staffed by two or three fast-working sandwich makers, and in the back are a few tables on which blue-plate specials and plates of pasta, pizza, and oversize omelettes fill the nutritionally naive during lunch. Early birds duck into a full English breakfast in the morning, and cappuccino-and-cake eaters hang out here later in the afternoon. The difference at Marino's is not necessarily the sandwich fillings themselves, which are good, but the bread they are on. Warm, crusty, freshly baked baguettes hold tuna, bacon, turkey, egg salad, and more, lifting otherwise ordinary sandwiches way out of the doldrums. I was told Marino's sells more than five hundred sandwiches a day. Keep it up, Marino; you have a good thing going.

HOURS
Mon–Fri 7 A.M.–7 P.M., Sat 8:30 A.M.–4:30 P.M., continuous service

RESERVATIONS
Not accepted

CREDIT CARDS
MC, V (minimum £5)

PRICES
À la carte £5–9

SERVICE
No service charged or expected

MELATI (49)
31 Peter Street, W1
Tube: Piccadillly Circus

"We wish you Selamat Makan [good eating]." This is the ritual toast at the beginning of a meal in Indonesia and Malaysia.

Smart new colors of lavender and turquoise, and modern, light-colored chairs around plain tables dressed with fresh flowers, set the casual tone at Melati. The food served is inspired by the Chinese, Indians, and Dutch who settled in Indonesia, Singapore, and along the Malay Peninsula. These dishes will provide unusual, exciting eating for those willing to experiment, and bear in mind that most hot dishes can be tailored to individual tastes. The menu is long, and the choices could quickly bewilder the novice. When in doubt, ask your waiter to help you put together a typical meal. Beef, fish, seafood, rice, noodles, and vegetables all figure prominently on the menu. The good-value lunch specials revolve around rice or noodle dishes with a huge variety of toppings. For dessert there is a pancake stuffed with coconut and surrounded by coconut milk, *rambutas* (Malaysian fruits similar to litchi), or a banana fritter dusted with sugar. Having lived in the Far East, I have eaten many a meal there, and I can say that the food at Melati is as good as anything I had in Kuala Lumpur or Jakarta.

NOTE: Takeaway is available.

TELEPHONE
020 7437 2011, 7734 1996

OPEN
Daily

CLOSED
2 days at Christmas

HOURS
Mon–Sat noon–11:30 P.M., Sun until 10:30 P.M., continuous service

RESERVATIONS
Advised on weekends

CREDIT CARDS
MC, V (£10 minimum)

PRICES
À la carte: £12–19; set-price: lunch £5.50–6.50 1 course (one noodle or rice plate, or fresh Chinese greens), lunch and dinner £16.50 8 courses and coffee or £13.50 vegetarian, 2-person minimum

SERVICE
Discretionary, 10% service charge for 5 or more

MILDRED'S (39)
58 Greek Street, Soho, W1
Tube: Tottenham Court Road

If you don't already believe it, a meal at Mildred's will convince you that well-conceived vegetarian food is a dining experience to savor and repeat. The owners, Jane Muir and Diane Thomas, became friends while

TELEPHONE & FAX
020 7494 1634

EMAIL
mildreds@vegetarian58. freeserve.co.uk

OPEN
Mon–Sat
CLOSED
Sun, holidays
HOURS
Mon–Sat noon–11 P.M.,
continuous service
RESERVATIONS
Not accepted
CREDIT CARDS
None
PRICES
À la carte £6–10
SERVICE
Discretionary 10% service
charge for 6 or more

working together in various restaurants in London. During that time they decided that they could run a better restaurant. The result is Mildred's, which they named after the Joan Crawford film *Mildred Pierce,* because both Joan (in her early years), and Mildred were waitresses. The usually friendly service can get harried during the lunch rush, and the hard seats can be slightly uncomfortable. I also wish the waitstaff would wear more than a tank top, which allows a full display of their tattoos and body piercing. Those quibbles aside, the nourishing menu, which changes weekly, offers a variety of vegetarian and vegan specials, soups, salads, casseroles, homemade desserts, organic wines, champagne, beer, and milk. Always served are a daily soup and pasta, white-bean falafel in a flour tortilla with a side salad, stir-fried veggies with assorted add-ins, and a detox salad with a half dozen ingredients. The portions are enormous and basically guilt-free, unless you succumb to the double chocolate pudding with mocha sauce, or a slice of banoffee (banana and toffee) pie.

NOTE: No smoking allowed. Takeaway is available.

NEW PICCADILLY CAFE RESTAURANT (59)
8 Denman Street, Piccadilly Circus, W1
Tube: Piccadilly Circus

TELEPHONE
020 7437 8530
OPEN
Daily
CLOSED
Several days at Christmas, New Year's Day, Easter Sunday
HOURS
Noon–9 P.M., continuous service
RESERVATIONS
Not accepted
CREDIT CARDS
None
PRICES
À la carte £6–10
SERVICE
Discretionary

As you walk down short Denman Street, only a block from Piccadilly Circus, you can't possibly miss this budget diner's dream: It is the only restaurant with the big red neon sign flashing "EATS" in the front window. There is nothing even remotely interesting about the restaurant's interior. In places the floors are worn through to the bare boards, and the aging booths, with their yellow Formica tables, have obviously held many a hungry soul. There is a wall lined with postcards sent by longtime customers to owner Lorenzo Marioni and his sister Rosita, who has held court at the cash register since her father opened the restaurant in 1951. In the evening, Dina, the other sister, is in charge. Service by waiters wearing starched white jackets can be good or downright rude. If you get one with a flippant attitude, complain to one of the bosses, since they want to know which waiters need to mellow out. Despite this infrequent service drawback, do not pass up this oasis of economy, which is filled throughout the day with locals, fringe showbiz people, and thrift-minded tourists who fill up on the heaping portions of chicken, steak, veal, spinach and ricotta cannelloni, omelettes, salads, the all-day breakfast, and desserts. Definitely try the homemade apple pie with custard sauce.

NOTE: The restaurant is unlicensed, but you can bring your own alcohol (no corkage fee). Takeaway is available.

THE ORIGINAL CARVERY RESTAURANT AT THE CUMBERLAND HOTEL (27)
Marble Arch, W1
Tube: Marble Arch

"Help yourself, and eat as much as you like, but please . . . no doggie bags" is the motto at the Carvery restaurant, where traditional English food can be had for a modest financial investment. This is genuine value for the money, especially when you consider that you are encouraged to eat as much as you can, that children under sixteen pay only half price, and early-bird diners pay only £16. Plan to arrive with a giant-size appetite to properly tackle the dazzling buffet tables laden with hors d'oeuvres, salads, and succulent roasts of beef, lamb, pork, turkey, and ham with all the trimmings, along with a wide selection of vegetables and potatoes. Vegetarians are not ignored; there are always two or three hot dishes without meat available. To round it all off, the dessert trolley has fruit, pastries, cakes, trifle, hot puddings, ice cream and sorbets, and a selection of English cheeses. Seconds and thirds are allowed, but remember—no doggie bags.

The restaurant is big and bright in the best hotel-style, with large, well-placed tables properly set. Sunday lunch seems to be the busiest time, so book ahead on that day. Also, watch for seasonal holiday promotions and two-for-one vouchers.

The first Original Carvery opened at the Regent Palace Hotel in 1959, but unfortunately, the space was sold and is now the mega-restaurant Titanic, which rapidly sank to the bottom of London dining popularity. The Carvery idea was introduced by Christopher Salmon after a stay in a small farmhouse hotel where guests served themselves. The original Carvery was open from Monday to Saturday for lunch only, and the price of the meal was ten shillings and six pence. The first menu had a choice of four starters, three roasts, and five desserts. Guests were allowed to carve their own meat, and a chef was on hand to teach them how. A bottle of claret to accompany the meal was an extra twelve shillings. Times and prices have certainly changed.

TELEPHONE
020 7262 1234

FAX
020 7724 5620

OPEN
Daily

CLOSED
Never

HOURS
Lunch: Mon–Sat noon–2:30 P.M., Sun noon–3 P.M.; dinner: Mon–Sat 5–10 P.M., Sun 6–10 P.M., early bird Mon–Fri 5–7 P.M.

RESERVATIONS
Advised for Sunday lunch

CREDIT CARDS
AE, DC, MC, V

PRICES
Set-price: lunch £18, Sun lunch £18–20, dinner £20, early bird £16; children under 16 half price; all prices are for 3 courses, all you can eat

SERVICE
Discretionary

PAUL ROTHE AND SON (17)
35 Marylebone Lane, Bond Street, W1
Tube: Bond Street

TELEPHONE
020 7935 6783
OPEN
Mon–Fri, sometimes Sat (call to check)
CLOSED
Sat, Sun, holidays
HOURS
8 A.M.–6 P.M., continuous service
RESERVATIONS
Not accepted
CREDIT CARDS
None
PRICES
À la carte £3.50–6.50
SERVICE
No service charged or expected

Paul Rothe and Son specializes in sandwiches—and oh, what sandwiches they are! For more than a hundred years, nothing much has changed in this grocery-lined deli within a short walk of the Wallace Collection and shopping on New Bond Street. The Rothe family is on hand every day, making all of the sandwich spreads—including chopping the liver, cooking the fresh salmon, roasting the meats, and using the bones for some of the best soup you've ever had from a Styrofoam cup. As you can tell, formality is out, but good lunchtime food is in at this citadel of bargain eating, where the queue begins around noon. The homemade potato salad or coleslaw goes well with any sandwich order. Ask which desserts are homemade, and hope they have jam tarts and mince pies at Christmastime. Prepare to take your order to go unless you get a seat at one of the few tables or the three seats at the bar.

NOTE: Call in your order by 11 A.M. for noon pickup.

PESCATORI FISH AND SEAFOOD RISTORANTE ($, 10)
57 Charlotte Street, Fitzrovia, W1
Tube: Goodge Street

TELEPHONE
020 7580 3289
FAX
020 7580 0539
INTERNET
www.pescatori.co.uk
OPEN
Mon–Fri; Sat dinner only
CLOSED
Sat lunch, Sun, holidays
HOURS
Lunch: noon–3 P.M.; dinner: Mon–Tues 6–11 P.M., Wed–Sat 6–11:30 P.M.
RESERVATIONS
Essential
CREDIT CARDS
AE, DC, MC, V
PRICES
À la carte £35–40; set-price lunch, starter, and daily special £25 (£35 includes a dessert, glass of wine, half-bottle of mineral water, and coffee); seafood festival 3 courses, wine, and coffee, price on request (depends on type of fish served)

Since it first opened in 1961, Pescatori (Italian for "fisherman") has been known for the excellence of its cuisine, its friendly Italian welcome, and its impeccable service. Marinated, char-grilled, barbecued, and roasted fish was a culture shock to many British diners when this style of cooking was introduced, since it was so different from the usually overcooked, richly sauced British approach to fish. With the gradual emergence of a healthier diet, now termed "the Mediterranean diet," fish is heralded as one of the best foods around, and as a result, fish restaurants such as Pescatori have come into their own.

The menu at Pescatori offers an unusual and delicious range of fresh fish dishes cooked the Italian way. These include regional specialties such as seared swordfish with marinated roast peppers; flash-grilled tuna on a bed of crushed sweet potatoes with artichoke, black olives, a red onion, and tomato salsa; and the famous *Grigliata Mista di Crostacei*—a platter of well-seasoned shellfish grilled with olive oil, garlic, and herbs. Pescatori is also famous for its *cacciucco,* the Italian version of bouillabaisse. This dish is so special it is not on the menu and must be ordered in advance. Eating *cacciucco* (with five Cs in its name to match the standard five types of fish and shellfish in it: scallops, prawns, mussels, clams, and salmon, plus monkfish, red snapper, and whatever else may be in season) is more of a ritual than just sitting down to a plate of food. You need to take your time, use your hands if necessary, and ask for plenty of napkins and finger bowls.

Pescatori features seafood festivals in the summer. These are of special interest to Great Eaters in London because the set-price menus include a glass of *prosecco* with crostini (small toasts with a variety of toppings); a selection of bread, olive oil, and butter; three courses; and coffee. They are offered Monday to Saturday evenings and usually feature a menu based around oysters, shellfish, or lobster, depending on the particular festival being held. Please call the restaurant to check on dates and the menu being offered.

It is important to note that non–fish eaters also can be assured of a delicious meal at Pescatori. While the selection is limited, there are always three or four starters, a veal or beef entrée, and a pasta dish.

The restaurant includes three dining areas: a main section, a bar for more casual, light dining, and a private room for parties. The eclectic feel is imparted by a collection of traditional and aquatic antiques, hanging fishnets, a suspended skiff overhead, an iced fresh-fish display, whitewashed walls, strongly accented colors, natural stonework, and metal art. The overall look is airy and comfortable. Because a meal at Pescatori can be over some budgets, it is smart to save this as a Big Splurge dining destination.

NOTE: Customers can book ahead to have their own catch cleaned and cooked at Pescatori. There is another location at 11 Dover Street in Mayfair (see below). The same menu is served.

PESCATORI FISH AND SEAFOOD RISTORANTE ($, 65)
11 Dover Street, W1
Tube: Green Park

See Pescatori Fish and Seafood Ristorante above for full description. All other information is the same.
TELEPHONE: 020 7493 2652

SERVICE
12.5% service discretionary

POLLO (43)
20 Old Compton Street, Soho, W1
Tube: Leicester Square

TELEPHONE
020 7734 5917/5456

OPEN
Daily

CLOSED
Christmas Day, Easter Sunday

HOURS
Noon–midnight, continuous service

RESERVATIONS
Not accepted

CREDIT CARDS
None

PRICES
À la carte £4–8

SERVICE
Discretionary

Prices are low and portions more than satisfying at Pollo, a low-cost hot spot near Leicester Square in Soho. The specialties of the house are chicken fixed a dozen ways and the eighty-plus pastas, more than forty of which are geared toward vegetarians, and all are priced to sell at less than £4. It is a virtual mob scene at lunchtime, with the famished regulars occupying every red Naugahyde seat and booth on both floors. Service can get rushed and pushy if you linger at all. Aside from the chicken and pastas, the menu covers all the bases, from meat and fish to omelettes, salads, and even a banana split. There is also a page of daily dishes that deserves careful attention. The only dessert made here is the tiramisu.

RAW DEAL (4)
65 York Street (off Baker Street), Marylebone, W1
Tube: Baker Street

TELEPHONE
020 7262 4841

FAX
020 7258 1131

OPEN
Mon–Sat

CLOSED
Sun, holidays

HOURS
Mon–Fri 8 A.M.–10 P.M., Sat until 9 P.M., continuous service

RESERVATIONS
Advised for lunch

CREDIT CARDS
None

PRICES
À la carte: £8–14; set-price: lunch £12, 3 courses and coffee; minimum charge at peak times £2

SERVICE
Discretionary, 10% service charge for 5 or more

Cozy, clean, cheap, and above all, good for you! This is the unbeatable combination awaiting you at Raw Deal, a vegetarian restaurant that has thrived in this location for more than a quarter century. Every day, bountiful salads, unusual soups, hot and savory main dishes, and seasonal specials are dished out to the health-conscious regulars, who are served cafeteria-style for lunch and waited on for breakfast and in the evening. Desserts that tempt even the most rigorous dieter include fruit crumbles and several great cakes—carrot, coffee, pecan, chocolate, and apple. I like to arrive just ahead of the lunch rush, order a half portion of the daily special main course, which comes with a selection of two or three salads, and then splurge on a dessert.

The light orange interior walls combine with big picture windows to create an open atmosphere. In the evening, candles add a nice touch, and on sunny days, two tables on the sidewalk offer ringside seats for the passing parade.

NOTE: No smoking allowed.

SOFRA–MAYFAIR (70)
18 Shepherd Market, Mayfair, W1
Tube: Green Park

For high-quality Turkish food served in stylish, pleasant surroundings, you won't find anything better than the Sofra restaurants, bistros, and cafés dotted around London. Affable owner Hüseyin Ozer offers continuous service 365 days a year in all locations. His philosophy is simple and to the point: "If you are not entirely happy with your choice, we shall immediately replace it with another dish without hesitation. We guarantee that you will leave your table completely satisfied." Can't beat that.

The original Sofra Bistro is at 18 Shepherd Market in Mayfair. It is a two-story corner location at which you can choose from thirty starters and almost as many main courses, which are divided into grills, casseroles, and vegetarian items. The Sofra concept is to offer snacks and small meals throughout the day, bargain set-price lunches, dinners, and hot and cold mezes aimed to pull in an attractive crowd, eager to sample food. It is easy to see why Sofra was voted one of the best ethnic restaurants and why it continues to be one of London's favorite cheap eats, when you can dine on such mouthwatering specialties as *midye tava* (lightly battered mussels deep fried and served with a sauce of garlic oil, bread crumbs and yogurt), *hellim* (white sheep and goat cheese served hot from the grill), homemade dolmas (grape leaves stuffed with rice, onions, pine nuts, and herbs), *humuz kavurma* (diced lamb with pine nuts and hummus), or *imam bayildi* (eggplant cooked with tomatoes, peppers, onions). The healthiness of the food is another selling point: It's high in fiber, with fresh vegetables, herbs, olive oil, and yogurt, and low in greasy meats and saturated fats.

NOTE: Takeaway is available. A second branch of Sofra is just off Oxford Street (see next listing), and a third is in Covent Garden, WC2 (please see page 148).

TELEPHONE
020 7493 3320, 7499 0399
FAX
020 7499 8282
OPEN
Daily
CLOSED
Never
HOURS
Noon–midnight, continuous service
RESERVATIONS
Advised
CREDIT CARDS
AE, DC, MC, V
PRICES
À la carte £22–28; set-price 2-course lunch £7, dinner £8; 11-dish hot and cold mezes for 2 people £10 per person for lunch, £12 per person for dinner
SERVICE
12.5% service charge

SOFRA–ST. CHRISTOPHER'S PLACE (23)
1 St. Christopher's Place, Oxford Street, W1
Tube: Bond Street

See the preceding entry for Sofra–Mayfair for a description. All other information is the same.
TELEPHONE: 020 7224 4080
FAX: 020 7224 0022

SOHO SPICE (45)
124–126 Wardour Street, Soho, W1
Tube: Leicester Square, Tottenham Court Road

TELEPHONE
020 7434 0808
FAX
020 7434 0799
EMAIL
Info@sohospice.co.uk
INTERNET
www.sohospice.co.uk
OPEN
Daily
CLOSED
Christmas Day
HOURS
Mon–Thur 11:30 A.M.–
12:30 A.M., Fri–Sat till 3 A.M.,
Sun 12:30–10:30 P.M.,
continuous service
RESERVATIONS
Advised for dinner, especially
on weekends
CREDIT CARDS
AE, DC, MC, V
PRICES
À la carte: £25–30; set-price
lunch daily or pre-theater Mon–
Sat 5–7 P.M.: £8.50 3 courses;
lunch or dinner monthly
regional menu: £18 3 courses;
both include tea or coffee
SERVICE
10% service charge for 8 or
more, discretionary otherwise

Soho Spice is a red-hot, fast, fresh Soho Indian restaurant offering zest, color, and rich taste sensations in bright, cool, relaxing surroundings. Featuring a "Cuisine of the Month" menu, the restaurant invites diners to tour the regional menus of the Indian subcontinent. Your dining travels will take you to Kashmir, known as the Switzerland of the East and famous for its flaming-red, yet mild-tasting, chilies. Punjab, called the granary of India, is known for its earthy food, while Kerala, the Venice of the East, provides you with hot and spicy cuisine. From the exotic holiday paradise of Goa the food will also be red-hot, but from the Northwest Frontier, made famous by the Khyber Pass and warrior tribesmen, you will dine on red meat dishes. In addition to the regional menus, Soho Spice offers a set-price three-course lunch with both vegetarian and meat choices. All main courses are served with rice, naan, dal, and seasonal vegetables.

NOTE: There is a nonsmoking section.

SOUP OPERA (35)
2 Hanover Street, Mayfair, W1
Tube: Oxford Circus

TELEPHONE
020 7629 0174
OPEN
Mon–Sat
CLOSED
Sun, holidays
HOURS
Mon–Fri 7:30 A.M.–5 P.M.,
Sat 11 A.M.–5 P.M.
RESERVATIONS
Not accepted
CREDIT CARDS
None
PRICES
£3.50–10
SERVICE
Discretionary

London soup bars have revolutionized on-the-run office lunches and now represent somewhat of an underground growth industry in the parts of the city filled with big office buildings and the workers who toil in them. The Soup Opera in Mayfair is virtuous for its austere simplicity. The antiseptic interior consists of a room wrapped in blond wooden bars with tall silver metal stools meant for precarious perching and a counter filled with bubbling soup vats kept hot by thermostatic temperature controls. Every day there are a dozen or more vegetable, meat, and seafood soups served in three sizes: 12 ounce (peckish), 16 ounce (hungry), and 32 ounce (ravenous). Each one is rated to show if it is vegetarian, contains nuts, or is gluten or dairy free, low-fat, or spicy. Can't choose between the sweet potato, chickpea and red pepper, vegetable, or the New England clam chowder? Ask for a sample taste. All soups come with a chunk of white, wheat, or ciabatta bread, or a baguette and a piece of fruit. Drinks consist of coffee, tea, soft drinks, and fruit smoothies. Other Soup Opera locations are opening throughout London. For the branch in the City at 56–57 Cornhill, EC3, see page 236.

NOTE: No alcohol allowed; the restaurant is unlicensed.

SOUP WORKS (33)
9 D'Arblay Street, Soho, W1
Tube: Oxford Circus

In London, soup bars are the hottest craze for voguettes who have abandoned sandwiches as their mid-day meal. SOUP Works features ten or more interesting and flavor-packed liquid meals on a menu that changes daily. The queue is out the door by noon for the chicken, sweet potato, and coconut; tomato, eggplant, and roast pepper; English root vegetable; and cream of shiitake mushroom soups. Each soup comes in four sizes and lists its vegetarian, fat, nut, gluten, and dairy particulars. Soup toppings are available, as are specialty breads, assorted desserts, and cold drinks. Arrive between 8 and 11:30 A.M. during the week and order the breakfast special: porridge with a choice of toppings that includes dark chocolate bits, maple or golden syrup, raisins, cinnamon, bananas, or just plain sugar and cream.

NOTE: To have their soups on your side of the Atlantic, buy the book *SOUP*, which is for sale in most of their locations. Other locations in W1 are at 58 Goodge Street and 15 Moor Street. No alcohol allowed; the restaurant is unlicensed.

TELEPHONE
020 7439 7687

FAX
020 7287 5574

INTERNET
www.soupworks.co.uk

OPEN
Mon–Fri

CLOSED
Sat–Sun, holidays

HOURS
Mon–Fri 8 A.M.–5 P.M.

RESERVATIONS
Not accepted

CREDIT CARDS
None

PRICES
À la carte £1.75–9, breakfast porridge special £3 (includes coffee)

SERVICE
Discretionary

THE STAR CAFÉ (31)
22 Great Chapel Street, Soho, W1
Tube: Tottenham Court Road, Oxford Circus

The Star has been on the same site and under the same family ownership for more than seventy years. The owners pride themselves on having the oldest café in Soho. The food served is designed to inspire confidence in these hard economic times, and the café offers a concise, no-nonsense menu that is a varied catalog of pasta, meat, and fish dishes, omelettes, made-to-order sandwiches, and an all-day breakfast. Aside from the daily specials, I think the sandwiches, all piled on bagels, freshly baked baguettes, or toasted ciabatta bread, are the real stars.

TELEPHONE & FAX
020 7437 8778

INTERNET
www.TheStarCafeSoho.co.uk

OPEN
Mon–Fri

CLOSED
Sat–Sun, holidays

HOURS
Breakfast 7 A.M.–noon, lunch noon–4 P.M.

RESERVATIONS
Advised for 2 or more at lunch

The selection seems endless, ranging from a simple peanut butter and jam or Marmite, to steak and sautéed onions, to a triple-decker layered with hot smoked bacon, roasted chicken, avocado, tomatoes, fresh basil, lettuce, and pesto dressing. The area is full of film and photo labs, and the employees from these offices make up the backbone of the clientele. The best seating is amid the action on the main floor, which contains tables covered with red-and-white-checked oilcloths; you also can see (or hear) the television, which is always on for news in the morning and sports in the afternoon. Here you can also enjoy the impressive collection of pre–World War II enamel advertising signs that cover the walls. Service is swift, the food is reliable, and the prices are well within all budgets.

NOTE: Takeaway is available.

CREDIT CARDS
None
PRICES
À la carte £7.50–9
SERVICE
Discretionary

STOCKPOT–SOHO (42)
18 Old Compton Street, Soho, W1
Tube: Leicester Square, Tottenham Court Road

TELEPHONE
020 7287 1066
OPEN
Daily
CLOSED
Christmas Day
HOURS
Mon–Tues 11:30 A.M.–11:30 P.M., Wed–Sat 11:30 A.M.–11:45 P.M., Sun noon–11 P.M., continuous service
RESERVATIONS
Not accepted
CREDIT CARDS
None (no traveler's checks either)
PRICES
À la carte £5–8; set-price £4–6, slightly more on weekends
SERVICE
Discretionary

There are several Stockpots in London, and each is individually managed, but all operate on the same theory—volume. Stockpot diners fill up on lumberjack-size portions of international and British standards in areas of the West End and Chelsea where getting even a snack for less than £15 can be a challenge. The Basil Street location (page 187), around the corner from Harrods in Knightsbridge, is a welcome relief for shoppers who have spent a bundle at the famed department store. The Panton Street (page 166) and James Street restaurants (see below) are Great Eats near the theater district, and the King's Road site (page 187) offers respite from the many fast-food bars and cafés that infest this popular cruising ground in Chelsea.

The interiors of all the Stockpots are bare and somewhat harsh, with green plants, black-and-white photos or prints accenting the pine tables, and hardwood chairs. The staff seem jolly and efficient, even when put to the test with a full house and a queue waiting to be seated. Daily mimeographed handwritten menus offer something for everyone, from pastas, dishes of the day, fish (mostly fried), omelettes, and salads to desserts with calories but little imagination. The best advice I can give is to stick with the daily specials or anything that must be cooked to order and served immediately. Stay away from any dish that sounds complicated, odd (such as

Mexican stew), or seems clearly beyond the scope of the place. Please note that every cheap eater in London knows about the Stockpot's food bargains, so expect a wait and don't plan to linger over coffee if there is a crowd.

STOCKPOT–JAMES STREET (24)
50 James Street, W1
Tube: Bond Street

See Stockpot–Soho above for full description. There is a nonsmoking section at this location.

TELEPHONE: 020 7486 9185
OPEN: Daily
CLOSED: Christmas Day
HOURS: Breakfast 7–11 A.M., lunch 11 A.M.–5 P.M., dinner 5–10 P.M.
RESERVATIONS: Not necessary
CREDIT CARDS: None
PRICES: Breakfast £2–4, lunch £5–7, dinner £6–9
SERVICE: 10% service charge

TOOTSIES (22)
35 James Street, W1
Tube: Bond Street

Tootsies restaurants offer honest, good-value meals geared toward families on a budget. They are all-purpose family Great Eats with three locations in London (see also pages 114 and 206) and several outside the city, serving the type of predictable American food that welcomes ketchup. Their main claim to fame is their hamburger, which comes three ways: single, double, or vegetarian. It is served with lettuce, tomato, mayonnaise, french fries, and a dill pickle. For a few pence more you can dress it up with cheddar cheese, baked beans, a fried free-range egg, mesquite barbecue sauce, Mexican hot sauce, mushrooms, blue cheese sauce, or guacamole. Hearty breakfasts include a glass of fresh orange juice and two cups of tea or coffee to go with your sausages and eggs or waffles, which are served with maple syrup and bacon. There are also salads, sandwiches, milk shakes, and desserts, of which the dark and deadly sticky chocolate pudding cake is my favorite. Children under ten have their own "Tots at Tootsies" menu, which they can color at the table with the crayons supplied.

NOTE: There are nonsmoking sections in some Tootsies, but not this one.

TELEPHONE
020 7486 1611
OPEN
Daily
CLOSED
Christmas Day, New Year's Eve
HOURS
Mon–Thur noon–11 P.M., Fri–Sat noon–midnight, Sun 10 A.M.–11 P.M., continuous service
RESERVATIONS
Not necessary
CREDIT CARDS
MC, V
PRICES
À la carte £9–16
SERVICE
12.5% service charge

TOPO GIGIO (54)
46 Brewer Street, Soho, W1
Tube: Piccadilly Circus

TELEPHONE
020 7734 5931, 7437 8516
OPEN
Mon–Sat
CLOSED
Sun, 2 days at Christmas
HOURS
Noon–11:15 P.M., continuous service
RESERVATIONS
Advised, especially for pre-theater dining
CREDIT CARDS
AE, DC, MC, V
PRICES
À la carte £22–28
SERVICE
Discretionary

I found Topo Gigio because I did not have any other choice. So many visitors to London had told me about it that despite my impression that it was too touristy and I wouldn't like it, I finally gave in and had dinner here—and was happily surprised. Everyone was right; this is a good, family-owned, family-run Soho restaurant with modestly priced food. And it's not touristy.

Giuseppe and his older brother Maurizio are continuing the gracious traditions started by their father, who opened the restaurant almost forty years ago. The waiters in red vests and black pants are attentive without being condescending, and service is brisk without feeling rushed. The tables, covered in bright red cloths, are turned several times an evening. The busiest times are just before the theater and just after the last curtain call. You will find a mixture of visitors and regulars, most of whom are served their favorite Italian dishes without ever consulting the menu. Management frowns on ordering just pasta and encourages you to ask questions if you don't see what you want on the menu. If the ingredients are in the kitchen, the chef will make the dish. The portions are modest, so you can safely have several courses plus dessert and not feel too full. When ordering, consult the long list of specialties, and for dessert, try the *tartufo,* which is a scoop of creamy ice cream bathed in a dark-chocolate coating.

VASCO AND PIERO'S PAVILION ($, 36)
15 Poland Street, Soho, W1
Tube: Oxford Circus, Tottenham Court Road

TELEPHONE
020 7437 8774
OPEN
Mon–Fri; Sat dinner only
CLOSED
Sat lunch, Sun, holidays
HOURS
Lunch noon–2:30 P.M., dinner 6–11 P.M.
RESERVATIONS
Advised
CREDIT CARDS
AE, DC, MC, V
PRICES
À la carte £25–35; set-price dinner *only,* £20 2 courses, £24 3 courses

You don't have to splurge to eat dinner at Vasco and Piero's Pavilion, a solid Soho Italian choice in which the hospitality is warm and the Italian food is well prepared. It was recommended to me by another restaurant owner in the neighborhood as his favorite Soho Italian eatery—and let me assure you, there are scores of them. The family-run restaurant has a long track record . . . more than thirty-five years on this corner with a devoted following, who appreciate not only the good food value, but also the warm, refined atmosphere and great selection of Italian wines. If it is on the menu, one of the best starters for both lunch and dinner is the grilled polenta served with fat asparagus spears and Parmesan cheese shavings, or the roast peppers accenting a plate of fresh tomatoes and bufala mozzarella. If you like calf's liver and onions, you won't be sorry you ordered it. It is said to be the best in London. The homemade spinach and ricotta tortelloni in a buttery sage sauce, or the tagliatelle with mushrooms, are only two of the pasta standouts. As for the desserts, I always order the lemon tart or dark-chocolate mousse for the perfect finish to this special Great Eat in London.

SERVICE
12.5% service charge

VECCHIA MILANO (20)
74 Welbeck Street (north of Oxford Street), W1
Tube: Bond Street

TELEPHONE
020 7935 2371

FAX
020 7224 5471

OPEN
Mon–Sat

CLOSED
Sun, holidays

HOURS
Noon–11 P.M., continuous service

RESERVATIONS
Advised during peak hours

CREDIT CARDS
AE, DC, MC, V

PRICES
À la carte £25–35; set-price lunch or dinner £11 2 courses, £15 3 courses

SERVICE
10% service charge

"What, another pasta place?" moaned my dining companions as we arrived at Vecchia Milano, an old-time Italian restaurant close to the shopping crowds surging along Oxford Street. "Trust me," I said. "This is one you are going to like and want to return to often!" Once our order of *bruschetta* (toasted bread with garlic and olive oil piled high with fresh tomatoes) arrived, along with the trio of roasted peppers marinated with fresh anchovies and black olives in a garlicky dressing, return visits were already being envisioned. Further seduction wasn't needed as we tucked into a warm goat cheese salad surrounded by roasted plum tomatoes and grilled marinated zucchini, followed by the heavenly *panzerotti alla ricotta* (huge pockets of fried ravioli stuffed with ricotta cheese and spinach, set off by a spicy tomato sauce). Other main course pastas included the *pennette vegetariane* (a light mixture of zucchini, goat cheese, sun-dried tomatoes, and arugula tossed with olive oil and garlic), a creamy tortelloni with wild mushrooms, and *garganelli al salmone,* fresh egg pasta with a light salmon sauce.

Certainly the fish and meat dishes do not take a backseat to any of the wonderful pastas, especially not the grilled tuna steak served with lemon, olive oil, and a sprinkling of fresh herbs, or the grilled lamb chops served with potatoes and red onions. As for desserts, you are on your own here—all we could manage was a glass of sweet wine with a plate of crisp almond *biscotti* for dipping.

VERBANELLA RESTAURANT (15)
15–17 Blandford Street, Marylebone, W1
Tube: Baker Street, Marble Arch

TELEPHONE
020 7935 8896

FAX
020 7935 7675

OPEN
Mon–Sat

CLOSED
Sun, holidays

HOURS
Lunch noon–3 P.M., dinner
6–10:30 P.M.

RESERVATIONS
Advised

CREDIT CARDS
MC, V

PRICES
À la carte: £16–25; set-price for
lunch or dinner: all starters
£3.50, all main courses £6.50

SERVICE
12.5% service charge

Verbanella is not the kind of chic watering hole that bursts on the scene and suddenly fades away when the glitz wears off. This is a two-room, family-owned neighborhood place that has a pleasant, unhurried atmosphere, service that comes with a smile, and a contented clientele who appreciate realistic prices for homespun Italian back-burner food. One page of the menu is devoted to pasta, another to Italian wines, which are very reasonably priced. Salads are also featured, and I think the best is the Insalata Verbanella, filled with artichoke hearts, bufala mozzarella, and both fresh and sun-dried tomatoes. In addition, there is the New Style Menu, which lists five starters, all at £3.50, and ten main courses for £6.50 each. Depending on the season and market availability, you can look forward to mixed grilled vegetables with Gorgonzola cheese, herb-and-cheese-stuffed mushrooms, or a bowl of steamed mussels to start, followed by roast suckling pig, rabbit casserole, grilled salmon, or sautéed veal with peppers, fresh tomatoes, and onions in a white wine sauce. For dessert I have only one recommendation, and that is the rich zabaglione—don't miss this, please!

VILLANDRY DINING ROOM (3)
170 Great Portland Street (corner of Weymouth Street), Marylebone, W1
Tube: Great Portland Street

TELEPHONE
020 7631 3131

FAX
020 7631 3030

INTERNET
www.villandry.com

OPEN
Restaurant and shop daily, bar
Mon–Sat

CLOSED
Christmas Eve in the evening,
December 25 and 26,
New Year's Eve in the evening,
New Year's Day; bar only
on Sun

HOURS
Restaurant: breakfast
8–10:30 A.M., lunch noon–
3 P.M., dinner 7–10:30 P.M.;
shop: Mon–Sat 8 A.M.–10 P.M.,
Sun 11 A.M.–4 P.M.; bar: Mon–
Fri 8 A.M.–10:30 P.M.,
Sat 10 A.M.–10:30 P.M.

The Villandry Dining Room has moved from its quirky, cramped quarters on High Street and now occupies a huge one-block-deep space in the northern tip of Marylebone, not too far from Regent's Park. Frankly, I think a great deal of the restaurant's charm and appeal have been lost in the transition. Before, this French *épicerie*/deli/takeaway/bistro served dinner only two nights a month, and reservations for these eagerly awaited dining events were essential as far in advance as possible. Because the Villandry was primarily a grocery store selling French cheeses, pâtés, fruit tarts, bread, and some fresh produce, the dinner seating, which filled the front and back rooms, was makeshift at best. You were definitely crammed in at tables positioned with jigsaw-style precision to allow as many places to be set as was humanly possible. The proximity allowed you to literally rub elbows with your neighbors, a well-heeled group clad in designer dresses and Savile Row suits with whom you wound up acquainted by the end of the evening. Now the intimacy has given way to a barnlike space divided into a very expensive grocery, deli, meat, and produce section and, beyond it, a bar, florist, and cavernous dining hall served by a serious waitstaff clad in black.

But the food, which covers the bases from breakfast through dinner, is hard to fault. The chefs continue to be inspired by seasonal products, and the creations are always memorable and seldom repeated. The menu clearly reminds guests that food made to order takes time to prepare, so plan accordingly. I don't know if that is an excuse for slow service or a ploy to get you to drink more wine between courses, but I can say that the food is worth the wait on most occasions. One of the best times to experience the new Villandry is on Saturday or Sunday for breakfast, when many regulars combine it with a shopping trip to the market. You can begin with a glass of fresh orange juice while deciding between buttermilk fruit pancakes, French toast made with brioche and served with maple syrup, or a full English breakfast. Lighter appetites will appreciate a bowl of Greek yogurt with fresh fruit and honey, Villandry's own granola, or an almond croissant and a cappuccino. For a quick, gourmet bite anytime, settle in at the bar, where you can order plates of *charcuterie* or cheese, a lovely dessert, roasted vegetable *bruschetta* with herb dressing, grilled polenta with baby spinach, a bowl of homemade soup, or a char-grilled chicken breast with new potatoes, braised cabbage, and pancetta.

The daily changing lunch and dinner menus are more serious affairs, yet always imaginative. All main courses are nicely garnished, and baskets of homemade breads are replenished throughout the meal. Depending on the time of year, you might find seared venison salad with poached pears, marinated duck and shredded-vegetable salad with soy and ginger dressing, or seared tuna with a spicy aubergine puree dressed in an herb and chili vinaigrette. Follow this with grilled monkfish with peppers and roast zucchini, a grilled organic rib eye with chips and béarnaise sauce, roast breast of goose with root-vegetable gratin and cranberry sauce, or for a vegetarian change of pace, herb-crusted goat cheese served with artichokes, sweet potatoes, olives, and cherry tomatoes. Forget trying to be virtuous or counting dessert calories and zero in on the moist chocolate cake.

CLOSED
Sun

RESERVATIONS
Essential

CREDIT CARDS
AE, MC, V

PRICES
À la carte: breakfast £8–12, bar £8–15, lunch and dinner £25–30

SERVICE
12.5% service charge

Otherwise, it is a toss-up between the fruit tart or the cheesecake topped with fruit compote.

NOTE: Smoking allowed in the bar only.

WAGAMAMA (48)
12–26 Lexington Street, Soho, W1
Tube: Piccadilly Circus

TELEPHONE
020 7292 0990

INTERNET
www.wagamama.com

OPEN
Daily

CLOSED
Christmas Day through New Year's Day

HOURS
Mon–Sat noon–11 P.M., Sun 12:30–10 P.M., continuous service

RESERVATIONS
Not accepted

CREDIT CARDS
AE, DC, MC, V

PRICES
À la carte £8–12

SERVICE
Discretionary

Welcome to Wagamama, where the philosophy is "positive eating, positive living." What is Wagamama? It's a Japanese noodle bar based on the ramen shops that have been popular in Japan for two hundred years. Ramen are Chinese-style thread noodles served in soups with various toppings, and they can't be eaten without slurping noises. It is said that the extra oxygen the slurping creates adds to the taste of the dish. Wagamama also specializes in fat white noodles called *udon,* and in addition, it offers a few rice dishes for those who aren't interested in noodles. Reservations are not taken, and dining is at long communal tables in a basement dining room with all the charm of a high school gym. Despite the spartan surroundings, the atmosphere is lively, especially at peak lunch and dinner hours, when the hordes queue to get in. The menu contains thorough explanations of each dish and reminds diners that quality is the first priority at Wagamama. The menu boasts that fresh noodles and produce are delivered daily and that "everyone concerned with Wagamama is actively involved in suggesting and implementing small improvements to the operation." The friendly waitstaff punch your order into handheld electronic keypads, which send it via radio signal to the appropriate station in the kitchen. When each dish is cooked, it is served immediately, meaning that individual dishes are delivered at different times to a group of diners. If your server has a red letter *L* on his or her badge, this means he or she is a new recruit in training, and the management asks, "Please be gentle with this person."

For most people, one bowl of noodles is enough with a side order of *gyoza,* the typical accompaniment to ramen: grilled dumplings containing a mix of cabbage, carrots, water chestnuts, and garlic, with a chili and garlic sauce on the side for an extra kick. The final plus for eating a nutritious, healthy meal at Wagamama is that they enforce a strict nonsmoking policy. And dishes can be prepared without MSG on request.

Great Eaters at the Lexington Street Wagamama arrive in a linear space from which they can view the kitchen before going into the basement restaurant. This branch seats 176 people and offers a range of *yakitori* and tempura dishes in addition to Wagamama's usual soup noodles and pan-fried noodles.

NOTE: There are currently five Wagamamas in central London (see pages 105, 124, and 167).

WAGAMAMA (21)
101 Wigmore Street, Marylebone, W1
Tube: Bond Street, Marble Arch

See Wagamama above for full description. All other information is the same.

TELEPHONE: 020 7409 0111

YO! SUSHI and YO! BELOW (30)
52 Poland Street, Soho, W1
Tube: Oxford Circus

The first YO! Sushi opened on Poland Street in Soho in 1997. By the end of the first week, it was turning a profit, and the owner, Simon Woodroffe, has never looked back on his way to the bank. Now there are at least a half dozen YO! Sushi outlets in greater London, along with YO! To Go, a delivery service; and YO! Below, a Japanese bar that serves beer from a pipe to imbibers seated at sunken tables with smoke-extracting ashtrays, offers massages, and has a DJ and karaoke-singing waitstaff. Plans in the works for YO! Tel (a hotel), YO! Ganic, an organic grocery store, as well as outlets in the States. YO! Sushi is considered to be one of the coolest and grooviest sushi restaurants in London, where diners sit at an open counter, watch the food selections go by on a conveyor belt, and are served drinks by a self-propelled talking robot. What you see is what you get, and at the end of your meal, a server will count your color-coded plates and drinks and hand you the bill. The futuristic surroundings are unbeatable, but what about the food? YO! Sushi only seems to prove that raw fish and seaweed have never been so fashionable. In all, more than 150 dishes rotate throughout the week, each plate spending up to four hours on the belt. I think the food is marginal at best and downright terrible too much of the time. However, for a peek into what the dining future may hold, stop by and decide for yourself, but don't say I didn't warn you.

TELEPHONE
020 7287 0443

DELIVERY PHONE & FAX
020 7841 077 (phone), 020 7841 0799 (fax)

INTERNET
www.yosushi.com

OPEN
Daily

CLOSED
2 days at Christmas

HOURS
Noon–midnight, continuous service

RESERVATIONS
Not necessary

CREDIT CARDS
AE, DC, MC, V

PRICES
À la carte £6–16

SERVICE
YO! Sushi states, "If you appreciate the service, then you can leave a tip, which is shared between all kitchen and floor staff."

NOTE: The YO! Sushi boutique sells T-shirts, hats, watches, sushi plates, sushi aprons, and many more frivolous YO! items. In addition to the other W1 location following, please see pages 168 and 226 for YO! branches elsewhere in the city.

YO! SUSHI (26)
Selfridges Food Hall, 400 Oxford Street, W1
Tube: Bond Street

See YO! Sushi above for full description. All other information is the same.

TELEPHONE: 020 7318 3944
HOURS: Mon–Sat 10 A.M.–7 P.M., Sun noon–6 P.M.

YOUNG CHENG (55)
76 Shaftesbury Avenue, Soho, W1
Tube: Leicester Square

TELEPHONE
020 7437 0237, 7644 6666
OPEN
Daily
CLOSED
Christmas Day
HOURS
Noon–11:45 P.M., continuous service
RESERVATIONS
Not necessary
CREDIT CARDS
AE, MC, V
PRICES
À la carte £6–15; set-price £8–12, 3 courses and wine
SERVICE
Discretionary

For many people, some of the best ethnic food in London is Chinese. For all of us, it is one of the cheapest eats we will find. At Young Cheng's storefront restaurant on Shaftesbury Avenue in the West End theater district, a crowd of mainly Chinese diners turns up from noon until almost midnight. The chef stands in a tiny corner kitchen in the front window, chopping, boiling, and stir-frying as fast as he can. If he runs out of any ingredients, he dashes two doors down to the Chinese greengrocer and grabs what he needs. Not every dish works, but if you stay with the specialties—baked spareribs, barbecued meats, and tofu dishes—you will have a pleasant, satisfying meal. Bear in mind that all lunches come with rice or noodles, thus keeping your tab even lower.

The second location, on Lisle Street (see page 149), is larger and a little tonier, but definitely not as authentic or as full of interesting regulars as the Shaftesbury site. The abrupt service matches the atmosphere. The food, however, is just as good, and the three-course set-price menus for around £8–12 per person offer a good value. As with most Chinese restaurants, don't be overwhelmed by the compendium-style menu; usually the kitchen can make whatever you want, as long as they have the fixings.

Pubs

ARGYLL ARMS (32)
18 Argyll Street, Westminster, W1
Tube: Oxford Circus

Before the pub was built here in 1860, 18 Argyll Street was the home of the Duke of Argyll. A gold sign stating "In 1832 on this spot nothing happened" humorously reminds patrons that not much was going on here until the pub opened. Today the ivy-covered pub stands on a traffic-free pedestrian walkway by the Oxford Circus tube stop, and it's a large, lively example of the Victorian-era drinking house, with its separate bars, lovely acid-etched mirrors, and mahogany woodwork. It is also well known for its association with the theater world; in fact, the Palladium Theatre is just across the street. The pub is busy at lunch and packed in the afternoon, both inside and outside, with customers standing around the beer barrels out front. While hardly an oasis for fine dining, its pub grub is familiar, with the edge going to the hot salt-beef (corned beef) sandwich with mustard and pickles, made to order on malted wheat bread.

NOTE: There is a nonsmoking section in back.

TELEPHONE
020 7734 6117

OPEN
Daily

CLOSED
Christmas Day

HOURS
Mon–Sat 11 A.M.–11 P.M., Sun noon–10:30 P.M.; hot food served noon–4 P.M., sandwiches 11 A.M.–9 P.M.

RESERVATIONS
Not accepted

CREDIT CARDS
AE, MC, V

PRICES
À la carte £5–8

SERVICE
No service charged or expected

THE GUINEA (57)
30 Bruton Place, Mayfair, W1
Tube: Green Park

Everything about the Guinea pub is exceptional, including the loo, which is nicknamed "The Shrine." I will say no more; just see it for yourself.

Since the early 1400s there has been a pub on this site. In the early days it catered to the servants and stable hands from the nearby mansions. Today the pub is run by Carl Smith and his wife, Pauline, who also run the Windmill (see the next listing), and it's one of the most successful in the city thanks to its award-winning food. After one or two meals in a pub you will no doubt agree that the food isn't much to write home about, unless you want to bemoan the fact that it is basically boring, tasteless, and totally uninspired. Not so at the Guinea, where the food is the main draw. In fact, the pub won the best steak and kidney pie in Britain award three years in a row. It also nabbed the best pub sandwich award one year and placed second in the same competition the next.

TELEPHONE
020 7499 1210

FAX
020 7491 1442

OPEN
Mon–Sat

CLOSED
Dinner in the bar, Sat lunch, Sun, holidays

HOURS
Bar: Mon–Fri 11 A.M.–11 P.M., Sat 6:30–11 P.M., lunch Mon–Fri 11:30 A.M.–2:30 P.M.; restaurant: Mon–Fri lunch 12:30–2:30 P.M., Mon–Sat dinner 6:30–11 P.M.

RESERVATIONS
Accepted in restaurant only

CREDIT CARDS
AE, DC, MC, V

PRICES
Bar: à la carte £7–9; restaurant: à la carte £20–30

SERVICE
In restaurant only: £1.25 cover charge for dinner, 12.5% service charge

If you want one of the limited daily editions of their famed pies, the best plan is to arrive at 11:30, when they come out of the oven. Otherwise you will be milling around ten deep outside, waiting for your lunch. Not having the pie? Then order the Mirabeau, the 1991 winner of the best pub sandwich award. This creation is a triple-decker on grilled ciabatta bread featuring char-grilled Angus steak, lettuce, tomatoes, tarragon, anchovies, olives, and a dollop of mayonnaise. The 1992 best sandwich runner-up was presented to the Guinea for its Chicken Siciliano: grilled free-range chicken, smoked bacon, cream cheese, fresh parsley, oregano, black olives, and sun-dried tomatoes piled on ciabatta bread. Because the sandwiches are made to order, allow twenty to thirty minutes to be served.

NOTE: If you wander through the pub's lounge to the formal restaurant, the Guinea Grill, you will be in for a Big Splurge meal in one of London's most exclusive grill rooms.

THE WINDMILL (52)
6–8 Mill Street (off Conduit Street), Mayfair, W1
Tube: Oxford Circus

TELEPHONE
020 7491 8050
OPEN
Mon–Fri; Sat afternoon
CLOSED
Sat dinner, Sun, holidays
HOURS
Bar: Mon–Fri 11 A.M.–11 P.M., Sat noon–4 P.M., Mon–Fri lunch noon–3 P.M., Sat lunch 12:30–3:30 P.M., Mon–Sat dinner 6–9:30 P.M.; restaurant: Mon–Fri lunch noon–2:30 P.M., dinner 6–9:30 P.M.
RESERVATIONS
Not accepted
CREDIT CARDS
AE, DC, MC, V
PRICES
Bar: à la carte £4–8; restaurant: £12–18, minimum charge £5
SERVICE
No service charged or expected in the pub, service discretionary in the restaurant

The Windmill, a pub managed by Carl and Pauline Smith (who also run the Guinea, see preceding listing), is what most visitors to London are hoping to find and never do. As with the Guinea, the food is the main reason to be here. The Windmill serves the same award-winning dishes, featuring steak and kidney pie and char-grilled sandwiches. In addition, watch for such British favorites as black pudding with mash, fried cabbage, and bacon; a mixed grill; fat sausages with onion gravy; and liver and bacon. Also, you don't have to belly up to the bar for your meal; you can actually get table service in a nonsmoking area downstairs, or sit upstairs in the more formal dining area, where Oriental rugs dot the hardwood floors and interesting prints adorn the walls.

From Monday to Friday between noon and 3 P.M. you can sample bar snacks and sandwiches downstairs. Also Monday to Friday, the restaurant upstairs is open, serving a proper full-course dinner, starting with an avocado, smoked salmon, and prawn salad, or the smoked chicken Caesar salad. Then try their sausage from the National Sausage Champion Muffs of Bromborough, or the shepherd's pie made with minced lamb with a potato topping. The curries are another of the chef's specialties, but be forewarned: They are hot and require *at least* two beers to put out the fire.

NOTE: The upstairs is nonsmoking.

Tearooms, Pâtisseries, and Bakeries

AMATO (40)
14 Old Compton Street, Soho, W1
Tube: Leicester Square, Tottenham Court Road

If you are looking for a slice of heaven, go directly to Amato, where everything is baked on the premises in a basement kitchen the size of the restaurant. All the pastry temptations are here and beckoning. You only have to look in the magnificent case and try to decide what will keep you off the diet for today. If you want a light bite to go with your sweet, Amato serves sandwiches, a two-egg omelette with a choice of fillings, a daily quiche, three salads, two daily hot dishes, and filled croissants.

TELEPHONE
020 7734 5733

FAX
020 7287 2086

EMAIL
cakes@amato.co.uk

INTERNET
www.amato.co.uk

OPEN
Daily

CLOSED
2 days at Christmas, New Year's, and Easter

HOURS
Mon–Sat 8 A.M.–10 P.M., Sun 10 A.M.–8 P.M.

RESERVATIONS
Not necessary

CREDIT CARDS
AE, DC, MC, V (minimum £5)

PRICES
Pastries £1.30–2.50, light meals £6–8

SERVICE
Discretionary

PÂTISSERIE VALERIE (44)
44 Old Compton Street, Soho, W1
Tube: Piccadilly Circus

The tearooms under the Pâtisserie Valerie umbrella are considered to be the best in London, and after one or two visits, you will see why. This original one in Soho first opened its doors in 1926, when Belgian-born Madame Valerie decided to introduce continental pastries to the English. It was an instant success and remains popular to this day. When the Germans bombed the shop during World War II, the management moved around the corner to the present location. The impossibly crowded downstairs room, with renditions of Toulouse-Lautrec posters painted on the walls, has shared

TELEPHONE
020 7437 3466

INTERNET
www.patisserie-valerie.co.uk

OPEN
Daily

CLOSED
2 days at Christmas, New Year's Day, Easter Sunday

HOURS
Mon–Fri 7:30 A.M.–8 P.M., Sat 8 A.M.–8 P.M., Sun 9:30 A.M.–7 P.M.

RESERVATIONS
Not necessary

CREDIT CARDS
AE, MC, V
PRICES
À la carte £3.50–12
SERVICE
Discretionary

tables, people standing in the aisles, and rushed waitresses reaching over diners' heads and under their noses. The new room upstairs is less hectic, but lacks spirit. This shop is known for its wedding and birthday cakes.

No matter which location you visit, you will mix in the early morning with a group of regulars sipping cups of coffee and enjoying the warm danishes being brought from the kitchen. During the noon rush, creamy omelettes, salads, club sandwiches, and other light fare are the choices. Everyone knows to save ample room for the best part: dessert. The fresh fruit tarts, heavenly macaroons, mousse- and whipped-cream-filled cakes, and éclairs will quickly force you to give up the intention to be virtuous with your diet. And don't forget teatime, which is considered a must and worth queuing for.

NOTE: The pastries are available for takeaway. In addition to the two branches listed below, see Café Valerie in Covent Garden, page 151, and Pâtisserie Valerie in Knightsbridge, page 191.

PÂTISSERIE VALERIE–SAGNE (9)
105 Marylebone High Street, Marylebone, W1
Tube: Baker Street, Bond Street

Pâtisserie Valerie at Sagne, Marylebone, has been an elegant tearoom for decades. It was established in 1921 by a famous chocolatier and pâtissier, M. Sagne, from Verlay, Switzerland. The café is magnificent, with its original mural documented in the book *Discovering London's Period Interiors*. Pâtisserie Valerie took over in 1993, extending the main room but maintaining the glorious 1930s atmosphere. Everyone agrees that the most beautiful cakes of all the Pâtisserie Valerie shops are here. See Pâtisserie Valerie above for a full description. All other information is the same.

TELEPHONE: 020 7935 6240

OPEN: Daily

CLOSED: 2 days at Christmas, Easter Sunday, some holidays (call to check)

HOURS: Mon–Fri 7:30 A.M.–7 P.M., Sat 8 A.M.–7 P.M., Sun 9 A.M.–6 P.M.

CREDIT CARDS: AE, MC, V

PÂTISSERIE VALERIE–REGENT'S PARK (2)
66 Portland Place, Regent's Park, W1
Tube: Great Portland Street

See Pâtisserie Valerie above for a full description. This branch is on the first floor of the Royal Institute of British Architects (RIBA) building and has a large terrace that is lovely in the summer. All other information is the same.

TELEPHONE: 020 7631 0467
OPEN: Mon–Sat
CLOSED: Sun, 12 days at Christmas, a week at Easter, all holidays
HOURS: Mon–Fri 8 A.M.–6 P.M., Sat 8 A.M.–5 P.M.
CREDIT CARDS: AE, DC, MC, V

RICHOUX–MAYFAIR (61)
41A South Audley Street (off Grosvenor Square), Mayfair, W1
Tube: Bond Street, Green Park

These three rather old-fashioned tearooms have been owned and operated by the same family for thirty-five years. The detailed menu has something for every taste, every time of day, and every budget. Whether it's breakfast, morning coffee, lunch, afternoon tea, dinner, or late supper, if you are hungry, Richoux will serve you. Richoux occupies key locations across from Harrods in Knightsbridge (see page 192), near Piccadilly Circus (see next listing), and in the heart of Mayfair near the American Embassy, making them even more attractive for shoppers, cinema-goers, and sightseers who want a dignified place to relax over a full meal or just a simple cup of herbal tea. The restaurants began in 1909 as pâtisseries and candy shops, with the exception of the Piccadilly location, which originally was a Chinese restaurant. If you look, you will still see some of the remnants of this early beginning.

NOTE: Takeaway is available for pastries, candies, and preserves. There are nonsmoking sections in all restaurants.

TELEPHONE
020 7629 5228
OPEN
Daily
CLOSED
2 days at Christmas
HOURS
Mon–Fri 8 A.M.–11 P.M., Sat 8 A.M.–11:30 P.M., Sun 9 A.M.–11 P.M.
RESERVATIONS
Not necessary
CREDIT CARDS
AE, DC, MC, V
PRICES
À la carte £6–20; set-price lunch or dinner £14 2 courses, £17 3 courses
SERVICE
Discretionary, 10% added for 5 or more

RICHOUX–PICCADILLY (66)
172 Piccadilly, W1
Tube: Piccadilly Circus, Green Park

See Richoux–Mayfair above for a description. All other information is the same.

TELEPHONE: 020 7493 2204

OPEN: Daily

CLOSED: Never

HOURS: Mon–Fri 8 A.M.–11 P.M., Sat 8 A.M.–11:30 P.M., Sun 9 A.M.–10:30 P.M., afternoon tea 3–6 P.M.

TEA AT THE RITZ (68)
150 Piccadilly, Green Park, W1
Tube: Green Park

TELEPHONE
020 7493 8181

FAX
020 7493 2687

INTERNET
www.theritzlondon.com

OPEN
Daily

CLOSED
Never

HOURS
Unreserved seating 2 P.M., reserved seatings at 3:30 and 5 P.M.

RESERVATIONS
Required, and at least a month ahead for weekends and as far in advance as possible (at least a month or more) for Christmas, Easter, and Mother's Day

CREDIT CARDS
AE, DC, MC, V

PRICES
£28

SERVICE
Discretionary

Tea at the Ritz represents a step back in time, reminding us that in this world of uncertainty, some things never change. The Ritz was opened in May 1906 by famed hotelier César Ritz, and in 1995 it was fully restored at a cost of more than £25 million pounds. Throughout the course of its illustrious history, no other hotel has been more synonymous with elegance, sophistication, and sheer luxury than the fabled Ritz. The gracious seven-story building has an imposing French-chateau-style facade, an interior as magnificent as its exterior, and a guest-to-staff ratio of two to one. While the price of even the most modest double room at the Ritz (which is around $500 for two, breakfast and 17.5% VAT extra) is beyond most budgets, Tea at the Ritz is an affordable luxury everyone should treat him- or herself to at least once.

Tea is served in the Palm Court, an impressive Louis XVI space with a gilded trellis and widely spaced marble columns framed by archways and deep steps, which have ornate rails that were installed for the Queen Mother. In the back of the room is a sculptured female figure flanked by floor-to-ceiling mirrors. Lighting comes from a central glazed roof framed by two shell windows, a pair of wrought-iron lamps resembling birdcages, and an ornate chandelier. Tea is served in silver teapots with silver milk pitchers and tea strainers. The food is presented on fine bone china that features the gold, pale green, and rose colors of the room. Freshly made sandwiches of smoked salmon, cucumber, egg salad with cress, turkey, and cream cheese are served on the base of a three-tier stand. The middle tier has freshly baked scones with jam and clotted Cornish cream, and the top tier a selection of tea cakes. During the week a pianist adds background music, and on the weekends, a harpist plays. The ritual has become a London institution, enjoyed by kings, queens, presidents, media personalities, and the general public, who now know the meaning of "putting on the Ritz." Proper dress is required, which means a jacket and tie for the men, and no jeans, T-shirts, or athletic shoes for anyone. Reservations are mandatory for the sittings at 3:30 and 5 P.M., but there is an option to arrive at 2 P.M., when free seating is available.

Wine Bars

ANDREW EDMUNDS WINE BAR AND RESTAURANT (47)
46 Lexington Street, Soho, W1
Tube: Piccadilly Circus

Andrew Edmunds is billed as a wine bar, but if you arrive at mealtime, you are expected to order a meal, not just a glass of wine with an appetizer.

But don't worry—the prices for lunch and dinner are as appealing as the food, and consequently, the place has a following and is usually full. The seasonally changing dishes are prepared with equal amounts of flair and care and with liberal amounts of imagination. Depending on the season, you might consider starting with the roasted fennel, artichoke, and bacon salad, the split-pea and cumin soup with feta cheese, or the Serrano ham with apple chutney and arugula salad. Main dishes might be free-range chicken with roasted vegetables; lamb served with new-potato salad, roast shallots, and mint pesto; or tagliatelle with artichoke hearts and tomato sauce. If you want a really sweet ending, go for the chocolate mousse cake or the tiramisu. Otherwise, order a plate of Neal's Yard cheeses and grapes. The varied wine list is reasonably priced and includes specially featured wines of the moment.

All the prints you see hanging in the restaurant are from the owner's print shop next door (open Mon–Fri 10 A.M.–6 P.M.), and they can be yours for the right price.

TELEPHONE
020 7437 5708

OPEN
Daily

CLOSED
Christmas Day, Easter Sunday

HOURS
Lunch: Mon–Fri 12:30–2:45 P.M., Sat–Sun 1–3 P.M.; dinner: Mon–Fri 5:30–10:45 P.M., Sat–Sun 6–10:30 P.M.

RESERVATIONS
Essential

CREDIT CARDS
AE, MC, V

PRICES
À la carte £16–22

SERVICE
Discretionary, but an optional 12.5% service charge added for bills over £50

HANOVER SQUARE WINE BAR AND GRILL (34)
25 Hanover Square, Mayfair, W1
Tube: Leicester Square

TELEPHONE
020 7408 0935

FAX
020 7636 1110

EMAIL
Don_Shiraz@hotmail.co.uk

INTERNET
www.donhewitsonlondon
winebars.com

OPEN
Mon–Fri

CLOSED
Sat, Sun, holidays

HOURS
Bar: 11a.m.–11 p.m., Grape
Dinners from 8 p.m.

RESERVATIONS
Advised for dinner

CREDIT CARDS
AE, DC, MC, V

PRICES
À la carte £10–20, Grape
Dinners £22 (includes
unlimited wine)

SERVICE
Discretionary

The popular Hanover Square Wine Bar and Grill is run by Don Hewitson, the well-known New Zealander who has popularized the concept of blending good wines and foods at realistic prices. As one review aptly put it, "What distinguishes Don Hewitson's wine bars is that he actually knows and cares about wines." Main course salads, pastas, daily bistro dishes, and grills are the call of the day for the business-clad lunchtime crowd. From Monday to Friday evenings, a quiet ambience pervades as regulars gather around the bar before sitting down to Don's successful Grape Dinners. These popular set-price meals include three courses from the Bistro-Rotisserie menu and unlimited glasses of three specially selected wines.

W2

Paddington and Bayswater

Bayswater runs along the northern end of Hyde Park and includes Paddington Station, a major train terminal with connections to the north as well as direct links to Heathrow for most major airlines. The area is full of cheap hotels and lots of Indian and Pakistani restaurants. Across Bayswater Road is Hyde Park, which joins with Kensington Gardens to form a 634-acre park, the largest in London. Speaker's Corner, on the northeast corner of Hyde Park, is a must. If you have an orange crate and something to say that is not obscene, or you have an urge to breach the peace, then you can do so at Speaker's Corner. The best time to see the real nutcases is on a Sunday around 2 to 3 P.M.

RESTAURANTS IN W2

Bistro Daniel	**88**
Hafez	**88**
Halepi	**89**
Kahn's	**90**
Kam Tong	**90**
Mandalay	**91**
Mawar	**91**
Nahar Cafeteria	**92**
New Culture Revolution	**92**
Poons	**93**
Royal China	**94**
Veronica's ($)	**94**

TEAROOMS, PÂTISSERIES, AND BAKERIES

Pâtisserie Française	**96**

($) indicates a Big Splurge

W2, W8, W11

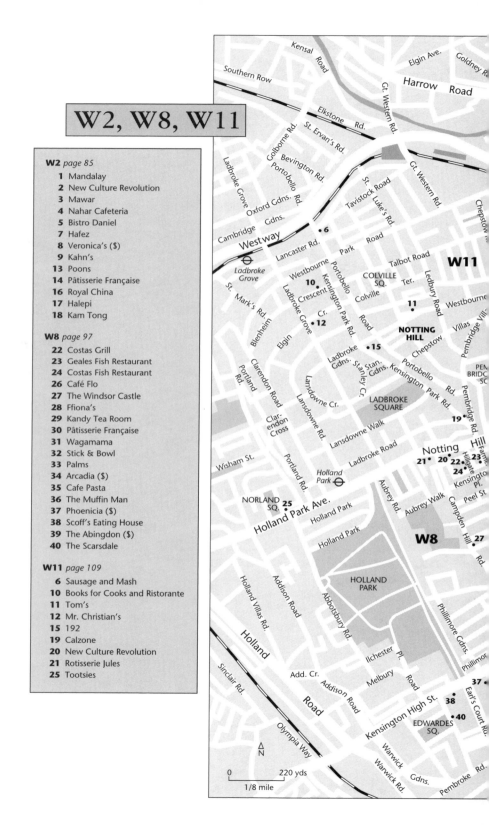

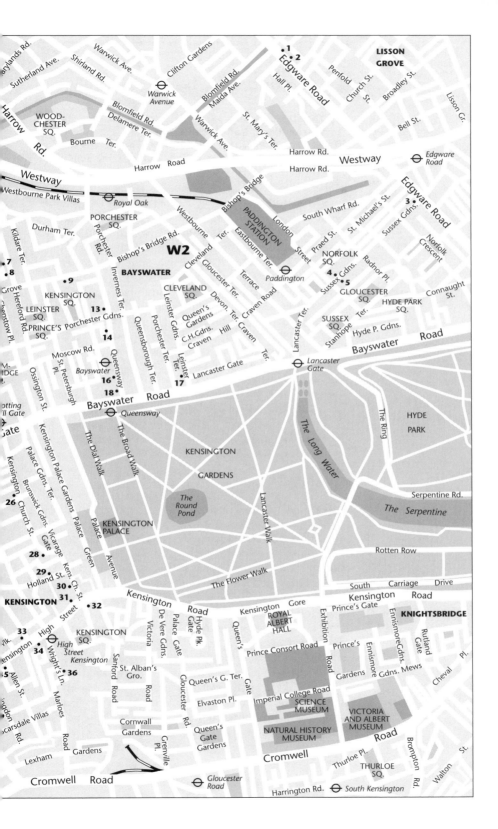

Restaurants

BISTRO DANIEL (5)
26 Sussex Place, Paddington, W2
Tube: Lancaster Gate, Paddington

TELEPHONE
020 7723 8395, 7262 6073
OPEN
Daily
CLOSED
Holidays
HOURS
Lunch noon–2:30 P.M., dinner
6:30–10:45 P.M.
RESERVATIONS
Advised
CREDIT CARDS
AE, MC, V
PRICES
À la carte: £25–28; set-price
lunch: £10.95 2-courses, £ 14
3 courses
SERVICE
12.5% added

For a taste of French Provençale cooking, Francophiles can count on Bistro Daniel. Owner and chef Daniel Gobet grew up in Lyon, where his father was a well-known *charcutier*. When he decided to open in London, he imported everything, including the blue ladder-backed chairs, Provençal paintings, and the staff to create this well-loved oasis of French dining not far from Hyde Park. Upstairs is the formal, more expensive restaurant, but you want to be downstairs in the arched bistro, where the food is of the same quality, but the dishes are less complicated and not as expensive. Everything on the seasonal menu is prepared here, including the desserts. At lunch, the value-packed set-price meal offers two or three courses from daily changing blackboard suggestions. I like Daniel's homemade duck sausage followed by a delicately roasted pheasant served with silky mashed potatoes. The pair of white and dark chocolate mousses wrapped up the delicious experience. À la carte choices have all the familiar standbys, including escargots, foie gras, duck confit with *lentils du Puy*, profiteroles, plus a good selection of French cheeses and wines.

NOTE: There is a nonsmoking section.

HAFEZ (7)
5 Hereford Road, Westbourne Park, W2
Tube: Bayswater, Queensway, Notting Hill Gate

TELEPHONE
020 7229 9398, 7221 3167
OPEN
Daily
CLOSED
2 days at Christmas
HOURS
Noon–midnight, continuous
service
RESERVATIONS
Advised
CREDIT CARDS
None
PRICES
£12–18
SERVICE
10% service charge

Fresh food, carefully cooked using quality ingredients and served at a fair price, never goes out of style, and certainly not at Hafez—a twenty-year-old standby not too far from Notting Hill Gate. It has a cast of regulars, including one elderly man who has eaten his lunch at the same table since the day they opened. It is a small place, dominated by a mosaic bread oven and a few well-set tables. The bread oven will play an important part in your meal, as you watch the chef roll out the dough, swing it like a pizza, stretch it over an oblong pillow, and toss it onto a stone slab inside the oven, in which it cooks for five minutes and is removed with foot-long tongs and brought piping hot to your table. Careful, don't fill up because there is more to come. If you're sharing plates, order the *mazah* (a selection of five start-ers), and follow it with the mixed grill of lamb fillet, lamb chops, minced lamb, and spring chicken. With the spring chicken you absolutely must have the fluffy, buttery-rich saffron rice, which could be an entire meal in itself for many people. Skip the fish—it is all frozen.

You might be able to save room for dessert, because, as the chef told me, "our portions are too big for the English, but just right for Americans." If you do, try the baklava.

HALEPI (17)
18 Leinster Terrace, Bayswater, W2
Tube: Bayswater, Queensway, Lancaster Gate

Halepi is not mentioned in many guidebooks or listed in London dining directories, and that is the way its loyalists want to keep it. Owned and run by the Kazolides family since 1966, Halepi offers typical Greek-Cypriot food in a rustic setting with long rows of closely placed tables covered with bright cloths. Greek bouzouki music plays in the background, and a native crowd arrives for both business lunches or long party evenings. The main difference between Greek mainland cooking and Greek-Cypriot food is that Cyprus has more Middle Eastern influences, thanks to its historic links with Tur-key and its proximity to Lebanon, Syria, and Israel. The emphasis is always on meats and grilled food.

If you are starved or are with a group prepared to share several dishes, start with an order of meze (assorted appetizers). Otherwise, concentrate on the grilled ke-babs of chicken, lamb, or beef, or perhaps one of the house specialties. If you like lamb, you'll be in heaven. Try the *klefticon* (oven-cooked baby lamb seasoned with aromatic spices), the minced lamb and eggplant moussaka layered with béchamel sauce, or the *afelia* (pork filet cooked in wine and spices served with both potatoes and rice). Not to be overlooked are the dolmas (grape leaves stuffed with lamb and rice). For dessert? Naturally you will have the homemade baklava, those melt-in-your-mouth layers of flaky pastry filled with honey and ground nuts. Halepi's, made by the owner's mother and touted as the best in London, are so big that one serving will feed two people.

NOTE: Takeaway is available.

TELEPHONE
020 7262 1070, 7723 4097

OPEN
Daily

CLOSED
2 days at Christmas

HOURS
Noon–1 A.M., continuous service

RESERVATIONS
Essential for dinner

CREDIT CARDS
AE, DC, MC, V

PRICES
À la carte £24–32

SERVICE
12.5% service charge

KAHN'S (9)
13–15 Westbourne Grove, Bayswater (west of Queensway), W2
Tube: Bayswater

TELEPHONE
020 7727 5420
FAX
020 7229 1835
EMAIL
info@kahnsrestaurant.com
INTERNET
www.kahnsrestaurant.com
OPEN
Daily
CLOSED
Christmas Day
HOURS
Mon–Thur: lunch noon–3 P.M.,
dinner 6–midnight; Fri–Sun:
noon–midnight, continuous
service; holy month of
Ramadan: noon–midnight
RESERVATIONS
Advised for large parties
CREDIT CARDS
AE, DC, MC, V
PRICES
À la carte £7–14; set-price £10
SERVICE
10% service charge

Kahn's still maintains its reputation for cheap, mass-produced Indian food served by a corps of waiters who have been called "diabolically rude" and who answer the criticism with, "Well, what do you expect when we are busy? Some guests even come because of us!" The jammed-together seating is uncomfortable, and there are long weekend queues, but despite all this, everyone seems to have a good time in this big, bustling, noisy restaurant, which can seat 350 diners at one time under a cloudlike ceiling mural.

A great deal of food is prepared ahead, which enables lightning service and encourages speed eating. The turnover is fast, so you are not likely to get something that has languished past its prime in a lukewarm pot on the back burner. The astonishingly cheap tandoori chicken is wonderful; so is the house specialty, butter chicken, prepared in a butter, cream, nut, and marsala sauce. Hardy taste buds should consider the chicken *jalfrezi,* a hot curry dish that requires an extra beer to put out the fire. In addition to the chicken dishes, look for those containing lamb, mutton, vegetables, fish, and seafood. Only Halal meat is served, so you won't find anything on the menu with beef or pork in it. Desserts here are a tough call, with the lemon or orange sorbet being the best of the lot.

NOTE: There's a children's menu, and takeaway is available.

KAM TONG (18)
59–63 Queensway, Bayswater, W2
Tube: Queensway, Bayswater

TELEPHONE
020 7229 6065
OPEN
Daily
CLOSED
Never
HOURS
Noon–11:15 P.M., continuous
service
RESERVATIONS
Advised for Sun lunch
CREDIT CARDS
AE (minimum charge £5)

When I first walked by Kam Tong on a wet Sunday around four in the afternoon, the place was packed with local Chinese, which is always a good sign. We aren't talking about a five-stool, mom-and-pop take-out joint, but an auditorium-size restaurant that is perpetually busy from noon until almost midnight. It would be a stretch to call it gourmet or posh, but it is a reliable cheap bet in London if you're in the mood for Chinese food or want to eat a meal at an odd hour, or at any time, for that matter.

If you have seen one basic Chinese menu, you have probably seen them all. This one is no different. There are 151 dishes, not counting eight more noodle offerings and three set-price meals. Dim sum is available daily from noon until 5 P.M. You name it and it is here, served with lightning efficiency.

NOTE: Takeaway is available.

PRICES
À la carte: £10–18; set-price: £14–17 2-person minimum, £25–28 5-person minimum; minimum charge for any meal £6

SERVICE
12.5% service charge

MANDALAY (1)
444 Edgware Road (near Lisson Grove), W2
Tube: Edgware Road, Bakerloo Line

If you are curious about Burmese food, Dwight Altaf Ally's Mandalay is a reliable Great Eat that is worth the schlep from the tube stop. Both he and his brother Gary speak excellent English and are eager and happy to explain their menu. Voted one of London's best budget meals, the restaurant is a family-run affair that feeds a mix of Burmese and smart cheap-eating locals who arrive with children in tow for the two set-price lunches served Monday through Saturday. For under £4 you will have your choice of chicken, meatball, vegetable, or shrimp and potato curry with rice. For less than £7 you will have the same curry choices plus a vegetable spring roll, banana fritters, and tea or coffee. If you decide on the à la carte menu, be sure to try the *calabash*—fritters made from squash strips rolled in a rice-flour batter flavored with turmeric and fresh ginger—or the coconut noodles and chicken, a Burmese staple.

While you are in the neighborhood, walk to the Church Street Market, which is an ethnic mix of food, flowers, clothing, watches, housewares, and piles of cosmetics sold for almost a third less than anywhere in the West End.

NOTE: No smoking allowed.

TELEPHONE & FAX
020 7258 3696

OPEN
Mon–Sat

CLOSED
Sun, holidays

HOURS
Lunch noon–3 P.M., dinner 6–11 P.M.

RESERVATIONS
Not necessary

CREDIT CARDS
AE, DC, MC, V

PRICES
À la carte £8–12; set-price lunch £4–7

SERVICE
Discretionary

MAWAR (3)
175A Edgware Road (corner of Sussex Gardens), Paddington, W2
Tube: Edgware Road

Enter through the green door and walk down the green carpeted stairs to this family-owned restaurant where the gentle owner told me, "We make our food like we do at home, and you are our valued guest." *Mawar* means "the red rose," and this seems to be about the only splash of color other than green in this spotless restaurant,

TELEPHONE
020 7262 1663

FAX
020 7262 7201

OPEN
Daily

CLOSED
Muslim new year's day (dates vary)

HOURS
Cafeteria-style fast food noon–
11 P.M.; restaurant service
6–10 P.M.

RESERVATIONS
Not necessary

CREDIT CARDS
MC, V

PRICES
Cafeteria fast food £5–6; à la
carte £10–15

SERVICE
10% added

which serves Malaysian and Indonesian food to contented locals every day except on the Muslim new year. The bargain Great Eats start with the cafeteria-style fast food served from noon until 10 p.m. For a modest increase in price and much wider choice, I like to go in the evening, when there is restaurant service from 6 until 11 p.m. and grilled meat and fish cooked to order are the best sellers. On the weekends, look for *nasi ayam,* their special chicken rice served with a hot chili sauce and a bowl of soup; *nasi lemak,* rice cooked with coconut milk and served with a choice of chicken or fish and accompanied by fried anchovies, peanuts, and cucumber; and on Sunday, *nasi minyak,* fried-rice pilaf with onion and ginger, vegetable curry, and lamb cooked with nuts and raisins. No liquor is served, but you are free to bring your own.

NOTE: Takeaway is available. No smoking. Restaurant is unlicensed, but BYOB (no corkage fee).

NAHAR CAFETERIA (4)
190 Sussex Gardens, Paddington, W2
Tube: Paddington, Lancaster Gate

TELEPHONE & FAX
020 7402 5111

EMAIL
marahouse@fsnet.co.uk

OPEN
Daily

CLOSED
1 week at Christmas through
New Year's (call to check)

HOURS
Mon–Fri: lunch noon–3 P.M.,
dinner 6–11 P.M., Sat–Sun:
9:30 A.M.–9:30 P.M., continuous
service

RESERVATIONS
Not accepted

CREDIT CARDS
None, cash only

PRICES
À la carte £3.50; set-price £4–5

SERVICE
No service charged or expected

Much to the delight of legions of London diners who went into a three-year culinary mourning period when it was closed, the Nahar Cafeteria is back in full form and better than ever. Open for breakfast, lunch, and dinner, it serves Halal Malaysian food to scores of devoted regulars, some of whom show up at the same time every day for the astoundingly cheap daily specials that range from £4 for plain rice, one main dish, and a vegetable, to £5 for two more main dishes. Weekend breakfasts are also popular, provided you can happily tuck into coconut rice, anchovies, chili sauce, egg, peanuts, and cucumber wrapped in a banana leaf, or the slightly less adventurous fried noodles or rice vermicelli served with hot sauce and a boiled egg.

NOTE: Cafeteria is unlicensed—BYOB (no corkage fee).

NEW CULTURE REVOLUTION (2)
442 Edgware Road (near Lisson Grove), W2
Tube: Edgware Road, Bakerloo Line

TELEPHONE
020 7402 4841

OPEN
Daily

CLOSED
Christmas Day

What is this revolution? At the New Culture Revolution it is "serving people's food and breaking away from high cholesterol dishes to give you a healthy and pleasurable experience of good eating." Chinese cooking has always placed an emphasis on the art of balancing the proper combination of ingredients to promote good health, long life, and energy. At the New Culture Revolution, northern Chinese food is served and reflects a delicate balance of starch, fiber, and protein. Wheat is a staple rather than rice, which does not grow in the region. Thus, there is a wide variety of dumplings and noodles. The fast-food menu is typically long, but each section carefully describes what a diner can expect. No MSG is used. Starters are light and appetizing and are chosen to stimulate good digestion and cleanse the palate. Vegetarian crispy dumplings are filled with wood ear mushrooms, glass noodles, Chinese leaves, water chestnuts, and bamboo shoots. Twelve noodle dishes mingle meat or seafood with varied accompaniments. Home-style northern Chinese dishes combine chilies, garlic, sesame, and other spices with lightly cooked ingredients that retain their natural flavors and qualities. The New Culture Revolution is a victory for you, allowing you to eat quickly and well, stay healthy, and still have a great Great Eat in London.

NOTE: Takeaway is available with a 10% discount. There's a nonsmoking section. There's also a branch in Notting Hill Gate (see page 112) and Chelsea (see page 185).

HOURS
Counter service for takeaway: noon–3 P.M., 5:30–11 P.M.; restaurant: daily 6–11 P.M., Sun lunch noon–3 P.M.

RESERVATIONS
Not necessary

CREDIT CARDS
MC, V

PRICES
À la carte £8–14

SERVICE
Discretionary

POONS (13)
205 Whiteleys Shopping Center, 151 Queensway, Bayswater, W2
Tube: Bayswater, Queensway

For the best Chinese food in London, most people go to Chinatown, where no fewer than thirty restaurants lie huddled in a maze of streets just behind Leicester Square. One of the most famous of these is Poons, which has branches in several other parts of the city. The location on Lisle Street in Chinatown is the original. It is still an unpretentious hole-in-the-wall that is a favorite with the old Chinese. On my last few visits I was shocked at the low level of cleanliness and food sanitation, and thus do not recommend it for any Great Eater in London. Ditto the location on Leicester Street. The other Poons—which are not in Chinatown but on Woburn Place (see page 123), in the City (see page 235), and here at Whiteleys Shopping Center—are modern, clean, and worthwhile.

At the City location, the menu goes beyond functional Chinese food, offering many dishes that have never been prepared in the U.S. In addition to a serene

TELEPHONE
020 7792 2884/2889

OPEN
Daily

CLOSED
3 days at Christmas

HOURS
Noon–11 P.M., continuous service

RESERVATIONS
Advised for dinner

CREDIT CARDS
AE, DC, MC, V (minimum charge £10)

PRICES
À la carte £12–22; set-price £17–25 2-person minimum

SERVICE
12.5% service charge

dining room, there is an eighty-seat fast-food section dedicated to nearby office workers who haven't time for a more leisurely lunch. The branch on Woburn Place is large and rather formal, while the one at Whiteleys is open and sleek, just like most mall restaurants in the U.S. The food at all three is good; the service is typically abrupt, and the prices won't kill the budget if you stick to the simple dishes, the set-price meals, or the dim sum served Monday to Friday from noon until 4 P.M. and Saturday and Sunday until 4:45 P.M. MSG is omitted on request.

NOTE: Takeaway is available.

ROYAL CHINA (16)
13 Queensway, Bayswater, W2
Tube: Bayswater, Queensway

TELEPHONE	020 7221 2535
FAX	020 7792 5752
OPEN	Daily
CLOSED	Never
HOURS	Mon–Sat noon–11 P.M., Sun 11 A.M.–10 P.M.
RESERVATIONS	Essential for Sunday lunch
CREDIT CARDS	AE, DC, MC, V
PRICES	À la carte £9–15; set-price £27–34 per person, 2-person minimum
SERVICE	12.5% service charge

Many restaurants in London serve dim sum, the snacks the Cantonese enjoy with their tea. When in Bayswater and in the mood for dim sum, Londoners all know that the best address is Royal China, at 13 Queensway. Served daily from noon until 5 p.m., these tasty steamed dumplings make the perfect light lunch. At other times watch for chef specials with fresh fish and seafood. Of course, the long menu lists three set menus and almost every Cantonese dish and its variations, but the Great Eats here are the dim sum and fresh fish, so follow the lead of the Chinese locals and order what they know is best.

VERONICA'S ($, 8)
3 Hereford Road, Westbourne Park, W2
Tube: Bayswater, Queensway, Notting Hill Gate

TELEPHONE	020 7229 5079 (24 hours), 7221 1452
OPEN	Mon–Fri; Sat dinner only
CLOSED	Sat lunch, Sun, holidays
HOURS	Lunch noon–2:30 P.M., dinner 6–11:30 P.M.
RESERVATIONS	Essential
CREDIT CARDS	AE, DC, MC, V

Since the end of the nineteenth century, a restaurant has occupied this historic Victorian building at 3 Hereford Road. Noted caterer Veronica Shaw took over in 1982 and began to experiment with English dishes when English food was far from fashionable. She emphasized a return to her British culinary heritage, introducing regional and historical themes to her food. The result is her award-winning restaurant, which definitely proves it is possible to eat British and eat well.

The inside reminds me of a charming country house, with its cozy, warm interior decorated with formally clad tables in the front room and a garden setting in back with church pews for seating and candlelight for romance. Local London artists are featured in changing exhibitions, and together with the hurricane candles, copper pots, and light classical music, they create an intimate atmosphere. Even the ladies' room is worth a trip to see the newspaper clippings of the many reviews Veronica has received, as well as the unusual light pull.

The menus change three or four times a year, and besides offering imaginative interpretations of unusual and classic favorites from early English cooking, they tell diners the history and background of each dish. The recipe for honeyed mushrooms with goat cheese and roast beet vinaigrette is two thousand years old, practiced by London's Roman ancestors. The double-roasted duck with thyme, oregano, and parsley combined with sorrel and garlic—or orange and Grand Marnier—has been a favorite of Veronica's guests since she opened, as is the oak char-grilled beef fillet served with creamed potatoes. Apple, potato, and onion cake with a mint, chervil, and tarragon dressing began as a "Lenten Pie" traditionally served for meatless days during Lent. Desserts such as hazelnut meringue and raspberry syllabub, adapted from an eighteenth-century recipe, or the twentieth century's love affair with chocolate as represented in the double-chocolate mousse and strawberries served with shortbread, encourage everyone to save a little room at the end of the meal. Veronica's also presents special holiday dinners, which may include a Victorian Christmas dinner or a traditional English meal with all the trimmings.

Another constant at Veronica's is the commitment to healthy eating. The fat in the sauces is reduced; honey and brown sugar replace white sugar; salt is kept to a minimum, with fresh herbs and lemon used instead. Appropriate dishes are marked low-fat, high fiber, or suitable for vegetarians or vegans. Only the freshest and best meats, produce, and cheese are used, and wherever possible, organic products are chosen. Wild produce, gathered by Veronica herself on countryside trips, is used abundantly in the summer, when dishes display the bounty collected and include a profusion of wild mushrooms, elderflowers, blackberries, daisies, and dandelions. There is a small, well-balanced choice of wines. The restaurant pioneered the inclusion of nonalcoholic wines

PRICES
À la carte: £30–35; set-price: Mon–Fri lunch £16, Mon–Thur dinner £22

SERVICE
10% service charge, £2 cover charge if no starter ordered

and beers on its list and has introduced a selection of organic wines.

From the start of your meal, when you are offered a complimentary nutty dip with fresh vegetables and homemade bread with sweet butter, to the finish, when you sip your coffee and nibble on homemade sweetmeats, you will have a wonderful dining experience that you will want to repeat often. I can't wait to go back.

NOTE: Catering is available.

Tearooms, Pâtisseries, and Bakeries

PÂTISSERIE FRANÇAISE (14)
127 Queensway, Bayswater, W2
Tube: Bayswater, Queensway

TELEPHONE
020 7229 0746

FAX
020 7221 0504

OPEN
Daily

CLOSED
2 days each at Christmas, New Year's, Easter

HOURS
Pâtisserie: Mon–Wed 7 A.M.–7 P.M., Thur–Sat 7 A.M.–8 P.M., Sun 7:30 A.M.–7 P.M.; restaurant: Mon–Wed, Sun 7 A.M.–6:45 P.M., Thur–Sat 6 A.M.–7:45 P.M., continuous service

RESERVATIONS
Not accepted

CREDIT CARDS
None

PRICES
Pâtisserie: £1.75 and up; restaurant: à la carte, £4–9

SERVICE
Discretionary

Pierre Péchon opened his Pâtisserie Française on this site in 1925, and in 1949, the year his son was born, he opened the second location on Kensington Church Street. At the Queensway shop you will be drawn to the tempting window display of all your favorite French goodies: big, buttery croissants, *pain au raisin, pain au chocolate,* brioche, glistening fruit tarts, and creamy mousse-filled cakes. Once inside, there is more: everything from apple strudel to scones and a variety of fabulous whole-grain and specialty breads, any of which can be ordered salt-free. In back is a dining section where you can sit and enjoy one of these bakery treats, or order breakfast from 7 A.M. to 3 P.M. They also serve quiche lorraine, hot soup, salads, a *plat du jour,* triple-decker sandwiches on their great bread, and savory and sweet crêpes. Given the high quality of the food, which is all made right here and is head and shoulders above almost everything else on this street, it is no wonder it is usually SRO every day from morning to night. Service can be abrupt when crowded.

NOTE: Takeaway is available for pastries. There is a second location at 27 Kensington Church Street (see page 108), but the selection is not as varied.

W8

Kensington

This is a gracious and sheltered residential area that includes Kensington Palace, where Queen Victoria was born and Princess Diana lived. When visiting the palace you can see the Royal Court Dress collection, which displays clothes worn to regal gatherings from 1750 until today; the State Apartments including the room where Queen Victoria was baptized; and the King's Gallery, which exhibits seventeenth-century paintings. Kensington High Street is regarded as one of London's major shopping areas, and Kensington Church Street is an important street for the antique collector with a platinum credit card.

TOURIST ATTRACTIONS
Kensington Palace and Gardens, shopping on Kensington High Street

($) indicates a Big Splurge

Restaurants

THE ABINGDON ($, 39)
54 Abingdon Road, Kensington, W8
Tube: High Street Kensington

TELEPHONE
020 7937 3339
FAX
020 7795 6388
OPEN
Daily
CLOSED
Christmas Day
HOURS
Restaurant: lunch Mon–Sat
12:30–2:30 P.M., Sun until
3 P.M., dinner Mon–Sat 6:30–
11 P.M., Sun 6:30–10:30 P.M.;
bar: Mon–Sat noon–11 P.M.,
Sun until 10:30 P.M.
RESERVATIONS
Advised
CREDIT CARDS
AE, MC, V
PRICES
À la carte: £25–30; set-price
lunch: Mon–Sat £12 2 courses,
Sun £14 2 courses, £16
3 courses
SERVICE
12.5% service charge

The Abingdon is a stylish addition to Kensington. Open seven days a week for lunch and dinner, it offers a small, thoughtful menu of daily changing, seasonal modern Continental food that's worth the higher prices. The interior has a coolly modern, big-city feel with a central bar, sanded pine tables, a line of striped banquettes, and booths in the back. When reserving a table, request a booth; if you are seated along the banquettes in front or at one of the round tables by the bar, the bar noise will drown out any table conversation you hoped to have.

A nice feature of the Abingdon is that the set-price lunch menus include many of their best dishes. For instance, for Sunday lunch you could start with a roasted tomato wrapped in smoked salmon and dressed with dill and honey. Follow this with the roast leg of lamb—pink, juicy, and very tender. For dessert, the white-chocolate parfait is the hands-down winner. If you are doing lunch during the rest of the week and thinking vegetarian, the asparagus, celery, and courgette risotto is delightful, and so is the marinated vegetable salad with goat cheese and a tangy balsamic dressing. Dessert treats are the raisin sponge cake with hot toffee sauce or a Baileys-infused almond *mille-feuille*. With a view to circumventing the beef crisis, smoked ostrich breast is an unusual starter that is surprisingly good, but available only for dinner. A quartet of fresh fish offerings, duck breast casserole, and a vegetable *feuillette* round out the evening mains.

ARCADIA ($, 34)
35 Kensington High Street, Kensington, W8
Tube: High Street Kensington

TELEPHONE
020 7937 4294
OPEN
Mon–Fri; Sat dinner only
CLOSED
Sat lunch, Sun, holidays
HOURS
Lunch noon–2:30 P.M., dinner
6:30–11 P.M.
RESERVATIONS
Advised

Flanking the entrance of the Arcadia are Othello and Pagliachi, two friendly labs who take their role as official greeters very seriously, and as a result endear themselves to everyone who meets them. Once inside, the atmosphere is clubby and life is good for all who eat here. You can sit at a table on the entry level, which is lined with old prints from *Le Petit Journal*. From here you will have a bird's-eye view—along with the twenty-three-year-old blue-and-red parrots, Stanley and Sally, who occupy a corner perch—of the suited businessfolk at lunch and of the coiffed women of a certain age accompanied by men of sympathy who dine in the evening. The downstairs is romantic and certainly more unusual. The small room contains mirror-painted murals by artist Liz Reber, who accomplished the impressive assignment in only twenty-four hours, including the walls in the WC. Great Eaters in London who want just a little more style and atmosphere when dining will appreciate the one-, two-, and three-course set-price menus available for lunch. However, dining at Arcadia at night, when there is only an à la carte menu, is a Big Splurge.

The seasonally selected food has a sophisticated, international cast to it. For winter lunchtime starters, it is hard to chose between mussels in a mild curry and coriander broth or the creamy pumpkin and Parmesan soup. The duck confit served on a bed of cracked wheat is a rib sticker, but not so the light crab cake, with a parsley and lemongrass sauce. For dessert, conservatives will order the strawberry ice cream in a meringue bed, but I think the hazelnut crème brûlée is more interesting. In the evening, the à la carte menu is more expansive. Longtime favorites include the chicken liver and foie gras parfait and the warm smoked duck breast and noodle salad. Main courses aimed at warming you on a cold winter night start with grilled calf's liver on a bed of red lentils accompanied by caramelized onions, and they wind up with a rich, gamey boned quail stuffed with chicken mousse. Contemplating dessert may be hard, but at least share the apple and almond tart with a scoop of calvados ice cream.

NOTE: The entrance to Arcadia is off the footpath leading from 35 Kensington High Street to Kensington Court.

CREDIT CARDS
AE, DC, MC, V

PRICES
À la carte: £22–30; set-price: lunch £9.95 1 course, £13.95 2 courses, £16.95 3 courses

SERVICE
Cover for à la carte £1; 12.5% service charge

CAFÉ FLO (26)
127–129 Kensington Church Street, Notting Hill, W8
Tube: Notting Hill Gate

There are several Café Flo locations, but I like this one because it is more open and relaxing than the others. See page 42 in W1 for a full description of what to expect in these upmarket restaurants.

TELEPHONE: 020 7727 8142
OPEN: Daily
CLOSED: 2 days at Christmas

HOURS: Breakfast: Mon–Fri 9 A.M.–noon; Mon–Sat noon–11:30 P.M., Sun until 10:30 P.M., continuous service

RESERVATIONS: Advised on weekends

CREDIT CARDS: MC, V

PRICES: À la carte: breakfast £5–8, lunch and dinner £12–22; set-price: Mon–Fri noon–5 P.M. £9–11

SERVICE: 12.5% service charge

CAFE PASTA (35)
229–231 Kensington High Street, Kensington, W8
Tube: High Street Kensington

TELEPHONE
020 7937 6314
OPEN
Daily
CLOSED
Christmas Day
HOURS
Mon–Sat 10 A.M.–midnight, Sun until 10:30 P.M., continuous service
RESERVATIONS
Not necessary
CREDIT CARDS
AE, DC, MC, V
PRICES
À la carte £6–15
SERVICE
Discretionary

Cafe Pasta serves reliable Italian food that is perfect for a quick meal with little fanfare in a pleasantly relaxed, child-friendly ambience. While the dishes can hardly be labeled original, they are filling and inexpensive. Best choices include the chicken salad with goat cheese, peppers, and tomatoes on a bed of mixed greens; fusilli with Gorgonzola and nutmeg sauce; penne spiked with spicy sausage and tomato chilies; lemon chicken tossed with egg tagliatelle and garlic; and the ever popular lasagna. Daily specials and seasonal promotions add interest for the locals, as do coffee and light snacks served from 10 A.M. until noon.

There are two other locations in Covent Garden. For details, see pages 134.

COSTAS FISH RESTAURANT (24)
18 Hillgate Street, Notting Hill, W8
Tube: Notting Hill Gate

TELEPHONE
020 7727 4310
OPEN
Tues–Sat
CLOSED
Sun–Mon, holidays
HOURS
Lunch noon–2:30 P.M., dinner 5:30–10:30 P.M.
RESERVATIONS
Not necessary, but advised on Fri
CREDIT CARDS
None
PRICES
À la carte £7–10
SERVICE
Discretionary

Budget-conscious Londoners have been noshing on fish-and-chips for decades. The fish is usually cod, haddock, plaice, or any other whitefish, batter-dipped and deep-fried until golden. It comes to you crunchy on the outside and moist inside. Accompanied by an order of chips (french fries), mushy peas, and a splash or two of vinegar, it makes a satisfying Great Eat in London.

Costas Fish Restaurant is a local fish-and-chips destination owned and managed by Andreas Papadopoulos. It is a spotless fish takeaway in front with a few Naugahyde booths in back. The fish is delivered daily from Grimsby, the batter is made here, and only pure vegetable oil is used to cook the fish. Everything is cooked to order, so prepare to wait during peak meal times. After your fish-and-chips, order one of their apple or banana fritters with strawberry sauce and you will know why the neighbors eat here almost daily. For grilled fish or a Greek meal, try the sister restaurant next door, Costas Grill (see next listing).

COSTAS GRILL (22)
14 Hillgate Street, Notting Hill, W8
Tube: Notting Hill Gate

Costas Grill and its sister restaurant next door, Costas Fish Restaurant (see preceding listing), are in a pretty London neighborhood. From the Notting Hill Gate tube stop, walk along Uxbridge Street toward Hillgate and Campden Hill Road and admire the brightly colored mews houses, many with flower-filled window boxes and tiny street-side gardens. Costas Grill is one of the old neighborhood standbys, exuding a feeling of familiarity and friendliness. London is not a bastion of fine Greek food, but here you can eat plenty of the basics and still spend less than £20. In fact, the owner told me, "You can't spend £20 unless you drink a lot of wine!" Neither the menu, nor the decor, nor George, the all-purpose owner, waiter, and greeter, have ever changed. The food will appeal to carnivores: try the garlic sausages, lamb kidneys cooked in wine, souvlaki (kebabs), or *kefthedes* (meatballs). If you like your fish char-grilled, try their trout, salmon, or sea bass, which all come with rice, potatoes, and vegetables and sell for less than £12 per plate. You can fill up on everything but the desserts, which are on the disappointing side, unless you would be happy with the homemade yogurt and honey or a fruit fritter.

TELEPHONE
020 7229 3794

OPEN
Mon–Sat

CLOSED
Sun, holidays

HOURS
Lunch noon–2:30 P.M., dinner 5–10 P.M.

RESERVATIONS
Advised

CREDIT CARDS
None

PRICES
À la carte £10–15

SERVICE
Discretionary

FFIONA'S (28)
51 Kensington Church Street, Kensington, W8
Tube: High Street Kensington

If you happen to be dining alone, ask to be seated at the long table. I promise you it won't be long before you are talking with your neighbors and making plans to return here often. That is how I met the two people sitting next to me. "How did you find out about Ffiona's?" I asked. They answered, "Oh, friends from Chicago told us about it, and we live across the street. Now we eat here at least two or three times a week." The small restaurant is casual, friendly, comfortable, and above all, fun, and it's run by Ffiona, who does the cooking, and her attractive red-haired sister, Althea, who takes the orders and serves on weekends. Together they make everyone feel welcome and at home. Ffiona's friends say that she's never met a stranger, and I believe it.

TELEPHONE
020 7937 4152

OPEN
Tues–Sun for dinner; Sun lunch

CLOSED
Mon; 4 days at Christmas and Easter

HOURS
Lunch: Sun 1–2:30 P.M.; dinner: Tues–Sat 7–11 P.M., Sun 7–10 P.M.

RESERVATIONS
Advised for Sun lunch

CREDIT CARDS
AE, MC, V

PRICES
À la carte £15–20; set-price Sun lunch £16

The inside is homey: faded fabric-covered walls match the banquette and chair cushions, and sheets of musical scores line the ceiling. There are bleached wood tables, three old clocks, a caricature of Marlene Dietrich, green plants, wine bottles with dripping candles, and soft music in the background. It's a mixed approach to decorating, but it is pure Ffiona, and you wouldn't want to change a thing.

The menu is handwritten in white chalk on a blackboard. I like Ffiona's eggplant fritters, served with a small green salad loaded with red onions, red peppers, and cucumbers. Watch for homemade fish cakes, roast duck, wild salmon, pasta with fresh vegetables, and boiled ham in parsley and white wine. On Sundays, there is always a roast for lunch. For dessert anytime, think lemon tart. It is everyone's favorite.

GEALES FISH RESTAURANT (23)
2 Farmer Street, Notting Hill, W8
Tube: Notting Hill Gate

TELEPHONE
020 7727 7528

FAX
020 7229 8632

OPEN
Mon–Sat; Sun dinner

CLOSED
Sun lunch, 2 weeks at Christmas

HOURS
Lunch noon–3 P.M., dinner 6–11 P.M.

RESERVATIONS
Advised for more than 5

CREDIT CARDS
AE, MC, V

PRICES
À la carte £10–18

SERVICE
12.5% service charge

Geales serves only deep-fried fish in a two-room sea-blue-accented dining room near Kensington Palace. The fish-and-chips are not only relatively inexpensive, but touted by many as the best in London. The selection is basic: cod, haddock, plaice, and salmon are the best sellers. The beef fat used for deep-frying gives the fish a distinct, crusty texture that doesn't overpower it. Side orders of mushy peas, pickles, salad and tartar sauce bump up the price by a pound or so, and the homemade apple crumble or sunken chocolate cake does so by three times that.

PALMS (33)
3–5 Campden Hill Road (off Kensington High Street), Kensington, W8
Tube: High Street Kensington

TELEPHONE
020 7938 1830

OPEN
Daily

CLOSED
2 days at Christmas

HOURS
Coffee and pastries 10 A.M.–noon; continuous service noon–11:30 P.M.

Pasta is still a key buy at Palms, but the menu now includes more starters and meal-size salads, plus meat, fish, and chicken entrées. The appetizers are every bit as interesting as the new main-course meat dishes. All courses have one price, and you can order just one appetizer or splash out for a three-course meal. I like to order several appetizers and share, starting with *bruschetta* (Italian toast rubbed with garlic and mounded with olives and chopped tomatoes), a plate of deep-fried calamari with a citrus vinaigrette, or the *tri-colore* salad (mozzarella, avocado, and sliced tomatoes fanned across the plate and drizzled with basil dressing). For lunch, the chèvre salad or the *salade de Provence*—a warm mix of smoked bacon, mushrooms, potatoes, and spring onions on a bed of mixed greens—will definitely fill you to the brim. You might add an order of hot garlic bread or a freshly baked baguette if you need just a little extra.

The chicken dijonnaise, a grilled breast of chicken with a grain mustard sauce, is as tender as butter, and the olive oil mash that comes with it soaks up the juices wonderfully. The lamb steak marinated in rosemary is another good choice, and so is the omelette with a choice of fillings, served with a salad or potatoes.

Please don't overlook their pastas, made with Palms' own additive- and preservative-free sauces. The choices include a *penne salvatore,* with chicken, spinach, mushrooms, and cream, spinach lasagna, and everyone's favorite, spaghetti carbonara. The two specialty desserts, banana and caramel tart or the tiramisu, will definitely test your willpower.

NOTE: There is another location at Covent Garden (see page 142).

(see page 142).

PHOENICIA ($, 37)
11–13 Abingdon Road, Kensington, W8
Tube: High Street Kensington

Middle Eastern meals do not follow the Western pattern of three courses plus coffee or tea. They start and end with meze: a variety of small dishes of vegetables, salads, meat, and pastries, accompanied by olives and unleavened pita bread to scoop up the food. Lebanese food, in particular, is a delightful collection of flavors from all over the Middle East.

The outstanding attraction at Phoenicia, a Lebanese restaurant, is the all-you-can-eat meze buffet lunch served every day. Other bargains are the two lunch or pre-theater dinners. For the lunch buffet, huge tables are laden with salads, tabbouleh, hummus, pita bread (made here in a clay oven), lamb, chicken fixed numerous ways, vegetables, cheeses, and sweets. If you have never tried Lebanese food, this is the perfect place to start. If you don't get to the lunch buffet or opt for the set-price

RESERVATIONS
Accepted only for more than 8

CREDIT CARDS
MC, V

PRICES
À la carte £5–15

SERVICE
12.5% service charge

TELEPHONE
020 7937 0120

FAX
020 7937 7668

OPEN
Daily

CLOSED
Christmas

HOURS
Noon–midnight, continuous service; meze lunch buffet daily 12:15–3:30 P.M.

RESERVATIONS
Essential for lunch, advised otherwise

CREDIT CARDS
AE, DC, MC, V

PRICES
À la carte: £18–35; meze
buffet: Mon–Sat £14.95, Sun
£16.95, children under 8 half-
price; set-price: Mon–Fri noon–
7:30 P.M. £11 2 courses, £14
3 courses, children's menu £6
SERVICE
£1.50 cover charge, 15%
service charge

lunch or early dinner and decide instead to go for a
regular à la carte meal, there are meze meals for two that
include eight dishes as well as grills, but budgeteers
should be wary of ordering this way, because the bill can
get out of hand if you aren't careful.

NOTE: There is a nonsmoking section. Takeaway and
catering are available.

SCOFF'S EATING HOUSE (38)
267 Kensington High Street, Kensington, W8
Tube: High Street Kensington

TELEPHONE
020 7602 6777
OPEN
Daily
CLOSED
Christmas Day
HOURS
Breakfast: Mon–Sat 7 A.M.–
noon, Sun 9 A.M.–noon; lunch
11:30 A.M.–6 P.M.; dinner
6–11 P.M.
RESERVATIONS
Not necessary
CREDIT CARDS
AE, DC, MC, V
PRICES
À la carte: breakfast £3.30–6,
lunch or dinner £6–12; set-
price: £6 for any pasta or pizza
with a choice of two fillings,
£6.50 for the daily roast, £7 for
2 courses (lunch only)
SERVICE
Discretionary

Everything is out of date at Scoff's Eating House,
especially the prices, which hark back to a time before
most Great Eaters in London were born. The name
doesn't have much pizzazz, and neither does the interior.
The original rustic beams strung with wine bottles compete with a stuffed deer head mounted on a wooden wall.
Career waitresses in red shirts and short black skirts keep
everyone served and happy. Luigi Sbuttoni owns the
restaurant, and he doesn't put on airs. Nor does he stint
on the English and Italian food, which is served in mega
portions. The food scores high for value, just as long as
you arrive before 6 P.M., when you can order all the pasta
and pizza you can eat for less than £7. The roast of the
day with two vegetables and potatoes will be a pound or
so more. The Chicken Sophia Loren costs a mere 5 pence
more than the roast, but look what you get—an eight-
ounce breast of chicken with artichoke hearts covered
with cheese and a light tomato sauce, served with potatoes and a vegetable. If you open the place at 7 A.M., you
can tank up on Luigi's full English breakfast, which
consists of an egg, bacon, sausage, mushrooms, two
pieces of toast, and tea or coffee for less than £4. If you
can find the equivalent in tony Kensington, please send
me the address.

STICK & BOWL (32)
31 Kensington High Street, Kensington, W8
Tube: High Street Kensington

TELEPHONE
020 7937 2778
OPEN
Daily
CLOSED
Christmas Day
HOURS
11:30 A.M.–11 P.M., continuous
service

With only four tables downstairs and as many communal bar tables upstairs, you can see this is not the
place to settle in for the long term. It is, however,
absolutely unbeatable for a fast Chinese meal while shopping along Kensington High Street. One of the most
expensive meals (No. 10) costs around £5.50. For that

you will get one spring roll, one prawn, two spareribs or pieces of sweet-and-sour pork, fried rice, and bean sprouts. There are dozens of other possibilities ranging from soup (sweet corn, wonton, or chicken noodle) to nuts (litchi with ice cream).

NOTE: Takeaway is available.

RESERVATIONS
Not accepted

CREDIT CARDS
None

PRICES
À la carte £5–8; set-price £5.50; minimum charge per person £3

SERVICE
No service charged or expected

WAGAMAMA (31)
26 Kensington High Street, Kensington, W8
Tube: High Street Kensington

Please see page 74 for details on this popular Japanese noodle house. All other information is the same.

TELEPHONE: 020 7376 1717

Pubs

THE SCARSDALE (40)
23A Edwardes Square, Kensington, W8
Tube: High Street Kensington

The Scarsdale is a respectable pub next to Edwardes Square, named in honor of William Edwardes, the first baron of Kensington. The square was designed by a Frenchman as living quarters for French officers in the belief that England would eventually be invaded and occupied by Napoleon. Work began in 1811. A year later the builder went bankrupt and Napoleon began his retreat from Moscow. So much for the invasion of England. Now that you can pass the history quiz, what about the pub?

First of all, it is very pretty. In the past, it has captured the top honors (from a field of 150 entrants) in the Best Floral Display contest for pubs, restaurants, and shops in Kensington and Chelsea. If you go in the spring or summer, you will agree, and best of all, the inside is free from blasting music and clanging pinball machines. There is smoke (this is a pub, after all), but the seating inside around the two fireplaces is comfortable, especially on a cold London day. And finally, the food is above the usual pub grub quality. Go for Sunday lunch, when you have a choice of two roasts served with vegetables, potatoes, and Yorkshire pudding. At other times

TELEPHONE
020 7937 1811

OPEN
Daily

CLOSED
Christmas Day, holidays

HOURS
Mon–Sat noon–11 P.M., Sun noon–10:30 P.M.; lunch noon–3 P.M., Sun until 4 P.M.; dinner 6–10 P.M.

RESERVATIONS
Accepted for more than 6

CREDIT CARDS
MC, V

PRICES
À la carte £7–15

SERVICE
Discretionary

the cook dishes out a varied line that includes chicken Caesar salad, grilled meats, pork and leek sausage with mashed potatoes and onion gravy, and the Scarsdale Platter, heaped with ham, grilled chicken, brie, salad, chutney, and bread.

THE WINDSOR CASTLE (27)
114 Campden Hill Road, Notting Hill, W8
Tube: Notting Hill Gate

TELEPHONE
020 7234 9951
OPEN
Daily
CLOSED
2 days at Christmas
HOURS
Pub: Mon–Sat noon–11 P.M.,
Sun noon–10:30 P.M.; food
service: noon–10 P.M.,
continuous service, except Sun,
when it stops between
4 and 5 P.M.
RESERVATIONS
Not accepted
CREDIT CARDS
AE, MC, V
PRICES
À la carte £6–14
SERVICE
Discretionary

Tucked away between Notting Hill Gate and Kensington High Street is the Windsor Castle, which has the atmosphere of a traditional English country pub. It was built in 1828, during the reign of King George IV, on top of Campden Hill, from where the Royal Windsor Castle could be seen, twenty miles away. Over the years, little has changed. It still has three small bars with the original plank floors and authentic furniture rather than mock Victorian. Conversation flourishes, because pinball machines, jukeboxes, and screaming children have been banished (from the bar area, anyway). Behind the pub lies a leafy, secluded garden with lime, plane, and cherry trees shading the wooden chairs and tables, making it a relaxing place to spend a warm Sunday afternoon. The predictable English pub food is made here and includes sandwiches, ploughman's lunches, salads, and a pasta dish of the day. There are roast lunches on Sunday, and every day the house specialty: oysters or steamed mussels. Desserts are brought in and pass muster, especially if you fancy a fruit crumble or chocolate sponge cake floating in chocolate sauce.

NOTE: There is a nonsmoking section at lunch.

Tearooms, Pâtisseries, and Bakeries

KANDY TEA ROOM (29)
4 Holland Street, Kensington, W8
Tube: High Street Kensington

TELEPHONE
020 7937 3001
OPEN
Tues–Sun
CLOSED
Mon, 2 weeks at Christmas, last
2 weeks in August

Inspired by childhood memories of the tearooms of his native city of Kandy, Sri Lanka, Ananda Wijesiri opened this tearoom, where he graciously serves "nice tea for nice people." His is a proper tea, with scones, clotted cream, jam, and a pot of tea served on Royal

Crown Derby china. Six varieties of tea, along with sandwiches on homemade bread made from organic flour, scones, quiche made with free-range eggs, and salads are also available. The photographs you see around the room are of Queen Elizabeth in her thirties, Sir Noël Coward, and Ananda's three young daughters in their ballerina costumes. The cast-iron teapot over the kitchen door belonged to Wijesiri's family and was used daily between 1933 and 1979; it sat on a wooden fire, filled with water, always ready for a visitor to have a cup of tea.

NOTE: No smoking allowed.

HOURS
Tues–Fri 11 A.M.–5 P.M., Sat–Sun 11 A.M.–6 P.M.; light lunches served 11:30 A.M.–3:30 P.M.

RESERVATIONS
Not necessary

CREDIT CARDS
None

PRICES
À la carte £4.50–8; afternoon tea £6.50–15

SERVICE
Discretionary

THE MUFFIN MAN (36)
12 Wrights Lane, Kensington, W8
Tube: High Street Kensington

The Muffin Man attracts all kinds of people: seniors, mothers and grandmothers with children in tow, friends in for a quick gossip, and power-shoppers looking for a place to regroup before tackling the rest of Kensington High Street. And who can fault their choice, when you see the variety on the menu? The Muffin Man Breakfast, served all day, includes freshly squeezed orange juice, two scrambled eggs, ham, bacon, or sausage, toast and all the trimmings, and tea or coffee. Other breakfast goodies include porridge, toasted tea cakes, warm muffins, and buttery crumpets. Sandwiches are made on brown bread with low-fat butter and can be served in half sizes for children. I love the Original Muffin Man, piled high with chicken, crisp bacon, lettuce, tomato, and cucumber, and rightfully called, "a whole meal in a sandwich." Bridget's Sandwich is a rich mixture of egg salad and tuna flavored with spring onions, capers, and red peppers. Weight watchers will appreciate Diane's Slimming Special salads, with either cottage cheese and prawns or tuna and a hard-boiled egg. Homemade soup, the Muffin Man Rarebit (made with cheese and ale), pasta, and quiches, are also available anytime. In the afternoon, tea is served, along with diet-threatening cakes and pies. Try the lemon cake, the Queen Mother's Cake (with walnuts, dates, and a thin chocolate icing), or the passion cake, the Muffin Man's version of carrot cake.

I have only one complaint about the Muffin Man, and that is the perilous trip to and from the restroom, which requires teetering on steep, narrow stairs to get to it, and

TELEPHONE
020 7937 6652

FAX
020 7937 6649

OPEN
Daily

CLOSED
2 days at Christmas, New Year's

HOURS
8 A.M.–9 P.M., continuous service

RESERVATIONS
Not necessary

CREDIT CARDS
Not accepted

PRICES
£4–10

SERVICE
Discretionary

once there, being wedged into a space half the size of a broom closet. I was told renovations are planned—let's hope so.

NOTE: No smoking allowed.

PÂTISSERIE FRANÇAISE (30)
27 Kensington Church Street, Kensington, W8
Tube: High Street Kensington

See Pâtisserie Française on page 96 for full description. All other information is the same.

TELEPHONE: 020 7937 9574

OPEN: Mon–Sat

CLOSED: Sun, holidays

HOURS: 8 A.M.–6 P.M., table service until 5 P.M.

W11

Notting Hill and Portobello Road

North of Kensington, Notting Hill was once a slum and a haunt of drug dealers and prostitutes. Today, W11 is one of London's most stylish addresses, affordable to anyone able to spend up to five or six million pounds on a place to call home. Those who can are film and media personalities, bankers, and trust-fund yuppies who somehow manage to scrimp by on £200,000 per year. One of the best reasons for visiting the area is the famous Portobello Road Market, one of London's best antique and bric-a-brac hunting grounds, especially early on Saturday mornings. The market dates back to the nineteenth century, when gypsies traded horses here. The street is lined with stalls selling everything from good-quality items to cheap imports. In the neighborhood there is an interesting mix of art galleries, restaurants, and shops. Westbourne Grove, off Portobello Road, is an up-and-coming area of trendy boutiques and restaurants.

Notting Hill is also famous for its annual August carnival, when the streets are filled with a crazy mix of parading costumed participants and pulsating world music.

TOURIST ATTRACTIONS
Portobello Road market

Restaurants

BOOKS FOR COOKS AND RISTORANTE (10)
4 Blenheim Crescent, Notting Hill, W11
Tube: Notting Hill Gate, Ladbroke Grove

TELEPHONE
020 7221 1992

FAX
020 7221 1517 (for ordering books)

EMAIL
info@booksforcooks.com (book orders and inquiries)

INTERNET
www.booksforcooks.com

OPEN
Mon–Sat lunch only; call to check for cooking workshop schedule

CLOSED
Sun, holidays

HOURS
Lunch: Mon–Fri 12:30–1:30 P.M., Sat 2 seatings, noon and 1:45 P.M.; coffee and pastries in the morning and after lunch until around 4 P.M.

RESERVATIONS
Essential

CREDIT CARDS
AE, DC, MC, V

PRICES
À la carte £10–16

SERVICE
Discretionary

With eight thousand books on the shelves, Books for Cooks stocks London's largest inventory of cookbooks—old, new, obscure, well known, ethnic, and gourmet, written in Yiddish, French, German, English, and countless other languages. If it has to do with cooking, Books for Cooks stocks it or knows about it, and they will order it for you and have it shipped if it isn't on the shelf. In addition to the books, cooking workshops take place when the shop is closed. Classes run for three hours, and you receive a printed recipe booklet of what has been prepared, a glass of wine, and of course, a taste of the dishes cooked. It costs £25–30, depending on the course; bring a pen, your undivided attention, and an appetite.

Even if you are not in the market for a cookbook or can't attend one of their classes, you should never consider leaving London without sampling lunch served in the tiny (fifteen-seat) Books for Cooks Ristorante in the back of the shop. The menu changes daily according to the whims of the revolving lineup of chefs, who use recipes from their own cookbooks or those in the series printed by Books for Cooks. Reservations are essential for lunch, which is served only between 12:30 and 1:30 P.M. on weekdays, and for the two seatings on Saturday at noon and 1:45 P.M. To avoid disappointment, I always telephone for my reservation the minute I arrive in London. In the morning and after lunch until around 4 P.M., coffee and pastries are served.

NOTE: Because they are unlicensed, Books for Cooks suggest stopping by Corney and Barrow wine merchants around the corner on Kensington Park Road to purchase a bottle of good wine to have with your lunch (there's no corkage fee).

CALZONE (19)
2a–2b Kensington Park Road, Notting Hill, W11
Tube: Notting Hill Gate

TELEPHONE
020 7243 2003

OPEN
Daily

CLOSED
4 days at Christmas

Calzone takes its name from a way of folding over a pizza so that the toppings are steamed inside. The menu at the sprightly green-and-white eatery is created around dressed-up regular or whole-grain pizzas, a smattering of pastas, and a garden's worth of salads designed to either fill you on their own or complement the rest of your meal. The simple yet tasty range of pizzas all appear at first glance to be too large to finish in one sitting. But the light, thin base makes them easy to consume, because they are not weighed down with a laundry list of gooey toppings. The customers seem to be on the short side of forty, happy in the knowledge that they have found a nifty spot that serves fresh, well-priced food they can afford, whether they are eating it here or ordering it to go.

NOTE: Takeaway is available. There is another Calzone on Fulham Road in South Kensington (see page 208).

see page 208

HOURS
Daily 10 A.M.–noon for coffee and pastry; Sun–Thur noon–11:30 P.M., Fri–Sat until 12:30 A.M., continuous service

RESERVATIONS
Not necessary

CREDIT CARDS
AE, MC, V

PRICES
À la carte £7–14

SERVICE
Discretionary

MR. CHRISTIAN'S (12)
11 Elgin Crescent, Notting Hill, W11
Tube: Ladbroke Grove, Notting Hill Gate

The waitstaff at Mr. Christian's say, "We make people want to come back." Now celebrating more than a quarter of a century in this location, it is clear that they certainly do! After you've spent a Saturday morning braving the crowds at the Portobello Road Market, I urge you to join the queue at Mr. Christian's and sample one of the best sandwiches in London.

During the week this is a delicatessen serving morning croissants and muffins, and midday sandwiches, salads, and hot specials alongside a stunning assortment of salamis, cheeses, pâtés, vintage olive oils, and sixteen varieties of olives. Everything is made on site by a team of five busy cooks. On Saturday, when the Portobello Road Market is in full swing, Mr. Christian's hits its stride with a dazzling sidewalk display of international breads, which are sold whole or sliced up for the sandwiches wolfed down by hungry shoppers. If it is available, be sure to sample the English sourdough bread—a specialty that takes five days to make and lasts up to eight days. I also like the caramelized garlic bread and the Innes loaf, studded either with raisins and walnuts or sun-dried tomatoes. Obviously, I am not the only one who thinks the brownies are devastatingly good . . . more than 120 are sold every day!

NOTE: Mr. Christian's is takeaway only. The Portobello Road Market operates as an antiques and flea market on Friday and Saturday, but it is best on Saturday from 8 A.M. to 1 P.M., when the street stalls are open.

TELEPHONE
020 7229 0501

OPEN
Daily

CLOSED
2 days at Christmas, Notting Hill Carnival weekend (last weekend in Aug)

HOURS
Mon–Fri 6 A.M.–7 P.M., Sat 5:30 A.M.–6 P.M., Sun 7 A.M.–5 P.M., continuous service

RESERVATIONS
Not accepted

CREDIT CARDS
AE, MC, V

PRICES
À la carte £4–8

SERVICE
No service charged or expected

NEW CULTURE REVOLUTION (20)
157–159 Notting Hill Gate, Notting Hill Gate, W11
Tube: Notting Hill Gate

Please see page 92 for details about this Chinese fast-food Great Eat. All other information is the same.

TELEPHONE: 020 7313 9688

192 (15)
192 Kensington Park Road, Notting Hill, W11
Tube: Notting Hill Gate, Ladbroke Grove

TELEPHONE
020 7229 0482

OPEN
Daily

CLOSED
3 days at Christmas and New Year's (varies yearly—call to check)

HOURS
Bar: Mon–Fri 12:30–11 P.M., Sun until 10:30 P.M.; lunch: Mon–Fri 12:30–3 P.M., Sat–Sun until 3:30 P.M.; dinner: Mon–Sat 6:30–11:30 P.M., Sun 7–11 P.M.

RESERVATIONS
Advised

CREDIT CARDS
AE, DC, MC, V

PRICES
À la carte £15–25; set-price: lunch Mon–Fri £12.50 2 courses including coffee, Sun £13.50; dinner Mon–Fri 6:30–7:30 P.M. £14.50 2 courses including coffee

SERVICE
12.5% service charge

With twenty-five wines available by the glass and a wine list with eighty-plus bottles from France, Spain, Italy, Portugal, Australia, and New Zealand, you would think 192 would bill itself as a wine bar. But even though the upstairs is a wine bar at night, the wine is not the true drawing card here—the first-rate food is. The inside, which can seat a hundred diners on spindly metal chairs, features minimal decor, with lavender, yellow, and turquoise walls offsetting the green cotton-velvet banquettes. A touch of glitter is added at night, when the bar is outlined with tiny sparkling fairy lights. The prices and attitude of the staff are refreshingly humble, and the food is consistently varied and well presented.

The set-price menu changes daily, the à la carte weekly. Both offer a range of choices, with portions generous enough to allow grazing through a selection of appetizers and a glass or two of an unknown wine. Consider starting with the 192 Bloody Mary Salad—a gazpacho-style dressing with a vodka kick poured over a poached egg on designer greens—or the French bean, almond, and goat cheese salad. Or, perhaps the steamed mussels or tomato, aubergine, and courgette tart paired with a rocket and Parmesan salad, along with a glass of good wine, will be all you want. The satisfying winter braised lamb shank comes with a pea and mint risotto, and the roast chicken breast is garnished with fresh spinach, Swiss-rosti-style potatoes, and cherry tomatoes for color. Just like the rest of the menu, desserts change with the seasons and are listed with suggested wines, sherries, and ports to accompany them. Always on is a hot pudding, something with chocolate, and assorted cheeses. If the time is right, there will be a pear *tarte tatin* (warm upside-down tart) served with cinnamon ice cream.

ROTISSERIE JULES (21)
133 Notting Hill Gate, Notting Hill, W11
Tube: Notting Hill Gate

It's simple, it's good, it's cheap—it's flame-roasted, free-range chicken sliced onto a sandwich, made into a salad, or at its best, sold by the quarter, half, or whole. To go with your juicy chicken, order a side of creamy potatoes, french fries, corn on the cob, ratatouille, or a salad, with a homemade apple tart or chocolate mousse to top it all off. Everything is made here, nothing is frozen, and preservatives are not in the larder. With an hour and a half's notice they will roast a whole or half leg of lamb, and with two days' notice, they will roast a goose or suckling pig for you. You can eat your feast here or call for free delivery in most parts of London. A dinner for twenty will be delivered piping hot to your door in one hour.

Rotisserie Jules delivers in SW1, SW3, SW5, SW6, SW7, SW10, SW11, W1 (Mayfair), W2, W8, W10, W11, and W14. Delivery is free, except £1 for orders less than £10. For Mayfair and some parts of SW1, SW6, SW11, and W14 there is a £3 delivery charge for orders less than £20. They deliver daily: Monday to Saturday 12:30–3 P.M. and 6–10:30 P.M., and all day on Sunday. Please note they recommend that the roasted meats be eaten immediately, and they do not recommend delivery orders of the french fries, as they get soggy quickly. Get the creamed potatoes instead, and always ask about special salads and vegetables.

NOTE: Other locations are in SW3 (see page 186) and SW7 (see page 205). Only this branch and the one in SW3 are licensed.

TELEPHONE
020 7221 3331 (deliveries only)

OPEN
Daily

CLOSED
Christmas Day

HOURS
Mon–Sat noon–11:30 P.M., Sun until 10:30 P.M., continuous service; delivery hours Mon–Sat 12:30–3 P.M. and 6–10:30 P.M., all day Sun

RESERVATIONS
Not necessary

CREDIT CARDS
AE, MC, V

PRICES
À la carte £5–10; whole chicken with gravy £10 (serves 3–4), whole duck £18 (serves 3–4), whole leg of lamb £25 (one hour notice, serves 4–6)

SERVICE
10% service charge for meals over £15, otherwise discretionary

SAUSAGE AND MASH (6)
268 Portobello Road, Notting Hill, W10
Tube: Ladbroke Grove

If you can't get to the East End to sample this famous English soul-food dish, try your luck at Sausage and Mash at the end of Portobello Road, which is officially in W10, not W11. The location, under a freeway overpass and tube track, is hardly inspiring, but the sausages are first-rate, provided you stick with the traditional combinations and avoid off-the-wall creations such the East Indian with ginger, garlic, and a real chili kick. Vegetarians have three sausage and gravy choices, breakfast is served on Sunday, and there are subs, salads, and dips with tortillas and bread sticks. But the best advice is

TELEPHONE
020 8968 8898

OPEN
Tues–Sun

CLOSED
Mon, one week at Christmas

HOURS
Tues–Sat 11 A.M.–10 P.M., Sun 11 A.M.–8 P.M., continuous service

RESERVATIONS
Not necessary

CREDIT CARDS
MC, V

this: If you aren't prepared to sit around communal tables and tuck into a plate full of real pork sausages with mash and gravy, eat someplace else.

TOM'S (11)
226 Westbourne Grove, Notting Hill, W11
Tube: Notting Hill Gate, or the No. 23 bus, which stops almost at the door

While browsing through the rapidly changing shopping scene along Westbourne Grove, keep Tom's in mind for a reviving cappuccino or a large deli sandwich, or brave the queue that forms daily for breakfast and lunch, which is served in the tiny dining area and garden in the back of the shop. Seating here is at such a premium that you are asked to "be sweet and share your table." Seared salmon teriyaki salad with Chinese cabbage and ginger dressing, or the imaginative roast sweet potato sandwich with rosemary, goat cheese, and baby spinach leaves on focaccia, remind you that this is a trendsetting corner of London. A toasted muffin with black pudding, tomatoes, and bacon with a fried egg on top tells you that London eating habits have not really changed that much. Eggs Benedict with ham, florentine with spinach, or royale with smoked salmon, all covered in rich hollandaise sauce, keep the handsome crowds coming back for Sunday brunch. British farmhouse cheeses, olive oils, wines, a small selection of fruits and vegetables, and even Skippy peanut butter (smooth or crunchy) are available from the deli section.

TOOTSIES (25)
120 Holland Park Avenue, Holland Park, W11
Tube: Holland Park

See Tootsies in W1, page 69, for a full description. At this location, breakfast is served until noon and there is a nonsmoking section. All other information is the same.

TELEPHONE: 020 7229 8567
HOURS: Daily 9 A.M.–11 P.M.

WC1

Bloomsbury

Known as intellectual London, this is a good location with a quiet atmosphere for being so central. It is the former home of the famed Bloomsbury Group of the 1920s and 1930s, which included biographer Lytton Strachey, novelists Virginia Woolf and D. H. Lawrence, and economist John Maynard Keynes. The cornerstones of the area are the British Museum and Russell Square, which is the largest in London after Lincoln's Inn Fields. University of London buildings are scattered throughout the area, as are many fine antiquarian bookshops and print and map specialists.

TOURIST ATTRACTIONS
British Museum, Dickens's House, Percival David Collection of Chinese Art, Coram's Fields, University of London, British Library

RESTAURANTS IN WC1

PUBS

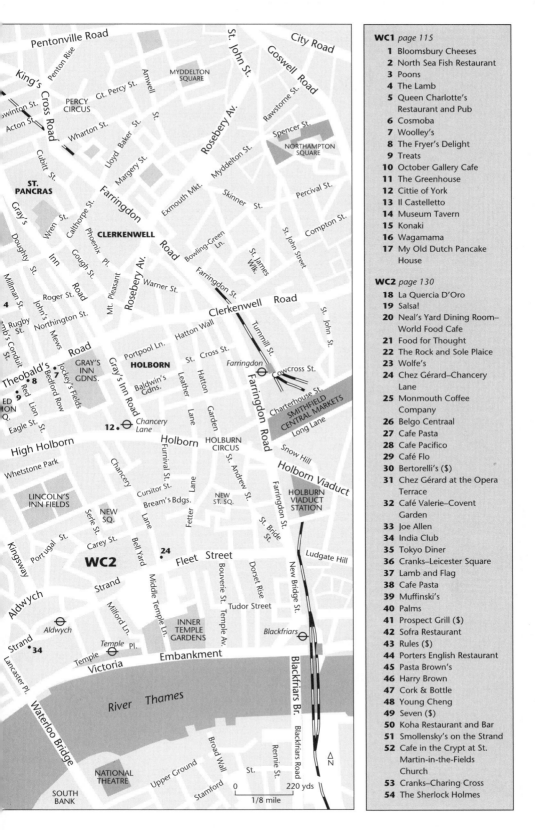

Restaurants

BLOOMSBURY CHEESES (1)
61b Judd Street, Bloomsbury, WC1
Tube: Russell Square, King's Cross

TELEPHONE & FAX
020 7387 7645
OPEN
Mon–Sat
CLOSED
Sun, holidays
HOURS
Mon–Fri 10 A.M.–7 P.M., Sat
until 5:30 P.M.
RESERVATIONS
Not necessary
CREDIT CARDS
MC, V
PRICES
Cheese sold by weight, bread
from £1.50, wines from £5
SERVICE
No service charged or expected

Perfect wine and cheese picnics begin at Bloomsbury Cheeses. The attractive shop, for takeaway only, specializes in unprocessed British farmhouse cheeses, as well as a small selection of international cheeses, also from local farms. To go with your cheese, wines, olives, olive oils, and organic and sourdough breads are sold. I am a fan of their unpasteurized goat's milk cheese from Devon and the Scottish hard cheese from the Isle of Mull. However, the Gloucestershire cow's cheese, rightfully named "Stinking Bishop," won't be on my shopping list anytime soon. Everything is artistically displayed, and the staff is knowledgeable and friendly, which makes Bloomsbury Cheeses a very nice London food-shopping experience.

COSMOBA (6)
9 Cosmo Place (off Southampton Row),
Bloomsbury, WC1
Tube: Russell Square

TELEPHONE
020 7837 0904
OPEN
Mon–Sat
CLOSED
Sun, holidays
HOURS
Lunch 11:30 A.M.–3 P.M.,
dinner 5:30–11 P.M.
RESERVATIONS
Advised on weekends
CREDIT CARDS
MC, V
PRICES
À la carte £10–22
SERVICE
Discretionary

It is reassuring to return to a favorite spot and find it better than it was. That is how I always find Cosmoba, situated on the same side of a pedestrian lane as a trendy wine bar, a ceramics shop, and a haunted pub. Locals recommend Cosmoba as having good value for money. It is a plain, family-run place that has had the same chef for thirty years. The menu is comfort reading for all lovers of Italian food. There is a long list of antipasti, with everything from stuffed zucchini and homemade pâté to a mixed salami plate or melon with Parma ham. Follow that with veal, chicken, steak, or one of the daily specials of venison or pheasant when in season, grilled calf's liver, osso buco (veal shanks) and rice, or lamb steak in a tomato, garlic, and olive sauce. Pasta is well represented, with lasagna, ravioli, spaghetti, tagliatelle, penne, and homemade fusilli, all served with a variety of sauces. When I am feeling virtuous, I order the oranges in caramel sauce for dessert, thinking it is a slightly healthier alternative to the profiteroles (cream puffs) slathered in chocolate or the fat-rich zabaglione (a custardlike dessert made in a copper pot).

THE FRYER'S DELIGHT (8)
19 Theobald's Road, Bloomsbury, WC1
Tube: Holborn

Fast food British-style began with fish-and-chips, and today you can find fish-and-chips shops all over London that vary little in price but are oceans apart in quality. One of the oldest is the Fryer's Delight. When Joan Rivers is in London, this is where she eats her fish-and-chips. So do many *Great Eats London* readers, one of whom wrote to me stating, "The fresh, tender cod was one of the best fish dishes we've ever had anywhere, including meals at expensive fish restaurants." You will know you are close when you pass people in the street munching their cod wrapped in unlined newsprint. You will also recognize it by the cars and taxis double-parked in front, with drivers dashing in to pick up an order.

The cooking is done right in front of you in a tiny room with worn seating and zero decor, other than a wall lined with various write-ups about the place and bottles of vinegar and ketchup and a salt shaker on each table. What counts is the specialty: deep-fried chicken or fish-and-chips served in heaping portions that you will have a hard time finishing. When I asked how much fish-and-chips they sell on a daily basis, I was told, "At least ten to twelve bags of potatoes, each weighing twenty-five kilos, and seven to nine stones of cod." (To do the math, remember that one kilo equals 2.2 pounds and one stone equals 14 pounds.) If you order takeaway, it will be wrapped in plain white paper and handed to you. If you are eating your food here, place your order at the counter, find a seat at one of the five plastic-covered booths with bright orange tabletops, and your heaping plate will be brought to you by the motherly waitress wearing a porch dress and slippers. An order of rock cod and chips with a huge slab of buttered bread will set you back less than £6.

TELEPHONE
020 7405 4114
OPEN
Mon–Sat
CLOSED
Sun, holidays, Aug
HOURS
Restaurant noon–10 P.M., takeaway noon–11 P.M., continuous service
RESERVATIONS
Not accepted
CREDIT CARDS
None
PRICES
À la carte £4.50–6.50
SERVICE
No service charged or expected

THE GREENHOUSE (11)
16 Chenies Street (basement of Drill Arts Center), Bloomsbury, WC1
Tube: Goodge Street

Interest in vegetarian food has increased considerably in London, and there are a number of specialty restaurants that offer excellent vegetarian cuisine at prices most Great Eaters can afford. The Greenhouse, in the basement of the Drill Arts Center (which features feminist, liberal productions), is one of the most popular, despite its laid-back, vaguely hippie air. Seating is

TELEPHONE
020 7637 8038
OPEN
Mon–Sat; Sun lunch only
CLOSED
Sun dinner, holidays

Mon–Fri 10 A.M.–8:30 P.M.,
Sat 10:30 a.m.–8 P.M.,
Sun noon–4 P.M.; coffee and
pastries 10 A.M.–noon, hot food
noon–8:30 P.M., continuous
service

RESERVATIONS
Not accepted

CREDIT CARDS
None

PRICES
À la carte £6–9

SERVICE
No service charged or expected

around shared bare wooden tables in a whitewashed room filled with ads and posters for fringe plays, offbeat art exhibitions, New Age meetings, and yoga classes. I think the best time to go is for lunch, when the selection is at its freshest and best. There is no written menu, but the dishes, which change daily, are listed on a blackboard behind the counter. In addition to the specials of the day, there is usually quiche, a selection of salads, pizza, and one vegan soup. The desserts are special, particularly the carrot walnut cake or the chocolate loaf.

NOTE: No smoking allowed. Students and OAPs (old age persons—i.e., seniors) receive 10% off from 2 p.m. onward. The Greenhouse is unlicensed, but you can BYOB (no corkage fee) or order herbal tea or a dairy or soy smoothie. Please don't confuse this Greenhouse with the Greenhouse in Mayfair, W1—the two are unrelated.

IL CASTELLETTO (13)
17 Bury Place, Bloomsbury, WC1
Tube: Holborn

TELEPHONE
020 7405 2232

OPEN
Mon–Fri; Sat dinner only

CLOSED
Sun, holidays

HOURS
Lunch noon–3 P.M., dinner
5:30–11 P.M.

RESERVATIONS
Advised (ask for a table by the window)

CREDIT CARDS
AE, DC, MC, V

PRICES
À la carte: £15–25; set-price: lunch only £8 pasta of the day and salad, £13 2 courses

SERVICE
£1 cover charge, 12.5% service charge

Some of the most reliable restaurant tips come from owners of family-run bed-and-breakfast hotels that are recommended in *Great Sleeps London*. These are people who have lived in the neighborhood and are always on the lookout for good-value meals, not only for their guests, but for themselves as well. One of the best family-run budget B&Bs near the British Museum is St. Margaret's Hotel (see *Great Sleeps London*). Italian owners Mr. and Mrs. Marazzi have been in this area for decades, and they know what they are talking about when suggesting a good Italian restaurant. They told me about Il Castelletto, run by the Bragoli brothers, headed by the affable Luigi. It is a comfortable sort of place where nothing has changed for years: not the staff, the pink-and-white table linens, the swag curtains, the Windsor armchairs with thin cushions, and certainly not the lusty Italian food.

Regulars know to skip the salads and begin with the hearty Tuscan bean soup or the quickly fried zucchini and aubergines (eggplant). Most of the vegetables served come from one brother's garden, so you know they will be fresh. Pastas are plentiful and filling, with sauces ranging from the plainest garlic, basil, and olive oil rendition on up to those made with fresh seafood. *Crespelle* (crêpes) with spinach and ricotta cheese in a tomato sauce or stuffed with homegrown pumpkin are two other special dishes to consider. Veal dishes are tender; just be sure to order the simple versions, as those drenched in cream sauce tend to get a little heavy. A light finish is the warm zabaglione, which you will have to share, because it is made only for two or more—but let me assure you, you will wish you had the velvety soft custard all to yourself.

KONAKI (15)
5 Coptic Street, Bloomsbury, WC1
Tube: Tottenham Court Road

Konaki is about a two-minute walk from the British Museum. Compared to most Greek restaurants, its interior is serene, with beamed ceilings, comfortable seating, lights on each table in the evening, and live music Thursday to Saturday from 8 p.m. to midnight. The food is filling and generously served, especially the meze (assorted appetizers) for two, at £28. The gargantuan set-price feast is composed of three courses with a choice from ten to fifteen starters, lamb cutlets or chicken or pork souvlaki (kebabs) for the main course, all the fresh pita bread you can eat, and dessert. If you order à la carte, the moussaka is one of their specialties and one of the best I have had in London. Vegetarians are not left out in the cold. There is always a *poly pikilo*—a Greek hot pot, which is a spicy vegetable casserole cooked with wine, or a stew of tender white beans simmered in tomato sauce.

TELEPHONE
020 7580 9730/3712

OPEN
Mon–Fri; Sat dinner only

CLOSED
Sat lunch, Sun, Christmas Day

HOURS
Lunch: noon–3 P.M.; dinner: Mon–Thur 6–11 P.M., Fri–Sat 6 P.M.–midnight

RESERVATIONS
Advised on weekends

CREDIT CARDS
AE, DC, MC, V

PRICES
À la carte: £12–19; set-price: lunch £8 2 courses, dinner £11 3 courses, meze for two £28

SERVICE
12% service charge

MY OLD DUTCH PANCAKE HOUSE (17)
131 High Holborn, Bloomsbury, WC1
Tube: Holborn

True to its name, this restaurant serves 105 varieties of Dutch pancakes, stuffed with everything under the sun and presented on genuine Delft-blue plates to hungry people who love a hearty bargain. In these *pannekoeken,* prepared to order with whole-grain or plain flour, the ingredients are cooked into the crêpelike batter rather than being rolled inside or spooned over the top. When finished, each pancake has a diameter of twelve inches, and you can cut it into 113 square-inch bites. The many fillings include cheese, ham, sausage, bacon, chicken, vegetables, herbs, ice cream, and fresh fruit. Some people actually have room for dessert, and those who do can select from thirty sweet pancake and eight waffle creations, including a summertime treat with fresh strawberries, ice cream, and whipped cream piled on top. There is even a waffle version of the banana

TELEPHONE
020 7242 5200

OPEN
Daily

CLOSED
2 days at Christmas

HOURS
Mon–Sat noon–11:30 P.M., Sun until 10:30 P.M., continuous service

RESERVATIONS
Accepted for more than 5

CREDIT CARDS
MC, V

PRICES
À la carte £8–15

SERVICE
10% service charge for 5 or more and on public holidays, otherwise discretionary

split: a fresh banana waffle with cream, nuts, and chocolate sauce. Whew!

There are two locations, and both boast interiors with a high degree of Dutch kitsch—scrubbed pine tables, blue-and-white-tiled fireplaces, and displays of wooden shoes and antiques throughout. Sometimes there are pannekoeken plates for sale.

NOTE: Each branch (see page 184 for the King's Road location) runs separate promotions at different times of the year. Look for half-priced pancakes and drinks, two-for-one deals, and early-bird and lunch specials.

NORTH SEA FISH RESTAURANT (2)
7–8 Leigh Street, Bloomsbury, WC1
Tube: Russell Square

TELEPHONE
020 7387 5892

OPEN
Mon–Sat

CLOSED
Last Sat before Christmas to the first fresh fish market day after the New Year, Sun, holidays

HOURS
Restaurant: lunch noon–2:30 P.M., dinner 5:30–10:30 P.M.; fish-and-chips takeaway: lunch noon–2:30 P.M., dinner 5–11 P.M.

RESERVATIONS
Advised

CREDIT CARDS
AE, DC, MC, V

PRICES
Restaurant: à la carte £15–22; takeaway: £5–9

SERVICE
Discretionary

For more than two decades, charming Mark Felipe has been running one of the best fish restaurants in this part of London. On one side of the North Sea Fish Restaurant is a fish-and-chips takeaway, on the other a neatly dressed dining room with pink velvet chairs and varnished wooden tables. The only thing on either menu is fresh fish: sixteen varieties deep-fried in pure peanut oil, sautéed, or grilled and served with either homemade tartar sauce, chips, or boiled potatoes. The catch comes in every morning from the Billingsgate fish market. It arrives around 5 a.m., and the North Sea fishmonger spends the next few hours cutting it into serving-size filets. Best sellers in addition to the eighty fish cakes sold each day are the cod, haddock, plaice, and skate, which is a bony fish that is an acquired taste for some. The portions are giant, leaving barely enough room for the slice of homemade truffle, tiramisu, or pineapple fritter for dessert.

NOTE: If you do not want your fish cooked in peanut oil, ask that it be prepared in vegetable oil.

OCTOBER GALLERY CAFE (10)
24 Old Gloucester Street, Bloomsbury, WC1
Tube: Russell Square, Holborn

TELEPHONE
020 7831 1618, 7242 7367

OPEN
Tues–Fri lunch only

CLOSED
Sat–Mon, holidays, Aug

HOURS
Café: 12:30–2:30 P.M.; gallery: 12:30–5:30 P.M.

RESERVATIONS
Not necessary

At the October Gallery Cafe, which is about five minutes from the British Museum, polished wooden tables are set in the back of an art gallery, which displays changing avant-garde art "from around the planet." In warm weather you can sit outside in the plant-filled patio of this Victorian former school building. While the art may appeal to only a distinct few, let me assure you that the vibrant food will please everyone.

Everything is made daily and in small quantities, so there are never any leftovers. For the best selection, arrive when they open (for lunch only), because the locals are on to this one. The choices change daily and can range from a bowl of parsnip soup to spinach pie, Thai chicken, or lamb curry, and dessert finales such as carrot cake or a fruit tart.

NOTE: If you want a glass of wine, you will have to bring it with you, as the café is unlicensed (£1 corkage fee).

CREDIT CARDS
MC, V

PRICES
À la carte £6–9

SERVICE
No service charged or expected

POONS (3)
50 Woburn Place, Russell Square, Bloomsbury, WC1
Tube: Russell Square

Dim Sum is served for lunch on Saturday and Sunday. See Poons in W2, page 93, for full description. Take-away is available.

TELEPHONE: 020 7580 1188
OPEN: Daily
CLOSED: 3 days at Christmas
HOURS: Noon–11 P.M., continuous service
RESERVATIONS: Accepted for 6 or more
CREDIT CARDS: AE, DC, MC, V
PRICES: À la carte £18–28; set-price £11.50–26 per person, 2-person minimum
SERVICE: Discretionary

TREATS (9)
13 Lamb's Conduit Passage, Bloomsbury, WC1
Tube: Holborn

Treats is well named, because eating here is a Great Eat treat for sure. Eli and Yannis Casanova are a dynamic international team. Eli is from Czechoslovakia and Yannis is Greek, and their restaurant's interior evokes a typical Greek café. The narrow, whitewashed space has a blue-tiled counter, framed Greek costumes, hanging green plants, and a painting of Pyrgi, the village on the island of Chios where Yannis was born. Eight small tables are crowded into the back, and on warm days there are a few tables outside.

A full English breakfast costs less than £5, and two slices of toast with peanut butter less than a pound. Sandwiches made to order, jacket potatoes with everything from butter and baked beans to Greek yogurt with herbs, and char-grilled kebabs wrapped in pita bread continue to bring back the regulars. *Taramosalata,* hummus, tzatziki, and *melitzanosalata* (eggplant) are also

TELEPHONE
020 7404 5505

OPEN
Mon–Fri

CLOSED
Sat–Sun, holidays

HOURS
8 A.M.–4 P.M., continuous service

RESERVATIONS
Not accepted

CREDIT CARDS
None

PRICES
À la carte £3.50–7

SERVICE
No service charged or expected

served with pita bread for dipping. Willpower bites the dust when it comes to their cakes, which according to Eli are made especially for them by a Greek granny. All of the breads are made in-house, as are the soups and the falafels, which are served with a green salad. Treats is officially open Monday to Friday from 8 A.M. to 4 P.M., but Eli told me, "If the light's on, we are here."

NOTE: No smoking between noon and 2 P.M. Treats is unlicensed and discourages BYOB.

WAGAMAMA (16)
4 Streatham Street (off Bloomsbury Street), Bloomsbury, WC1
Tube: Tottenham Court Road

This is the original Wagamama in London. See Wagamama in W1, page 74, for a full description. All other information is the same.

TELEPHONE: 020 7323 9223
OPEN: Daily
CLOSED: Several days at Christmas
HOURS: Mon–Thur noon–11 P.M., Fri–Sat until midnight, Sun 12:30–10 P.M., continuous service

WOOLLEY'S (7)
33 Theobald's Road, Bloomsbury, WC1
Tube: Holborn

TELEPHONE
020 7405 3028
FAX
020 7430 2417
EMAIL
woolleycatering@compuserve.com
OPEN
Mon–Fri breakfast and lunch only
CLOSED
Sat–Sun, holidays
HOURS
7 A.M.–3:30 P.M. (but they're usually sold out by 2:30 P.M.), continuous service
RESERVATIONS
Not accepted
CREDIT CARDS
None
PRICES
À la carte £2–6
SERVICE
No service charged or expected

Sandwich shops are a sixpence a dozen in central London. These popular food outlets appeal to office workers on tight schedules and cabbies on the run, and they offer a chance for visitors to rub elbows with the locals, or at least exchange smiles.

On Theobald's Road there are several sandwich shops, but the one to remember is Woolley Brothers. Everything served in this spot, painted bright orange, is made according to the Woolleys' own recipes in the huge kitchen below, which also serves as action-central for their catering business. The ingredients are the best, the food creative, and the results worth many repeat visits. Because there is only one small table in the back courtyard, you should plan on taking your food with you.

Every day there are more than sixteen sandwich choices, plus two specials and ten or more salads that come in small, medium, and huge. Salads range from hazeldorf (hazelnuts, apple, celery, mayonnaise, and raisins), to potato and leek (leeks cooked with herbs and a little oil and mixed with boiled potatoes and lemon mayonnaise dressing), to lively rice (organic white and wild rice tossed with peanuts, parsley, and red peppers with a sweet pickle dressing). Plus, there is a weekly salad special. Vegetarian pies, baked potatoes with hot and cold toppings, breakfast sandwiches, danishes, croissants, cakes, and brownies complete the food picture at this top-drawer Great Eat in London.

NOTE: Takeaway only.

Pubs

CITTIE OF YORK (12)
22–23 High Holborn Street, Holborn, WC1
Tube: Chancery Lane

The Cittie of York, which celebrated its three hundredth birthday in 1995, has more history per square centimeter than almost any pub you will visit in central London. I like it because everything is original. When you first enter, look up at the vats stacked on shelves around the ceiling. Each is capable of holding eleven thousand gallons of beer, and they were in full use until World War II, when they were emptied during the Blitz for fear that bombs would cause them to burst open and flood the pub and the tube station running underneath. The booths along the sides of the main room once had curtains to shield them, but the curtains finally had to be removed because of the indiscreet liaisons that took place when they were closed. The coal fireplace, made from melted-down cannons from the Battle of Waterloo, once stood in the hall of Gray's Inn and has a secret chimney that lies under the floor. If the pub is not too busy, ask to see the brick cellar, where the ale from the Samuel Smith brewery in Yorkshire is stored in wooden casks; it is tapped and vented for twenty-four hours, allowing the beer to settle, before being dispensed at the bar through hundred-foot-long hoses. The pub sells 450 gallons of this ale per week, not to mention just as much stout, lager, and cider.

Next to the pub is the gatehouse to Gray's Inn, where Charles Dickens's David Copperfield lived. Dickens himself worked as a clerk in Gray's Inn and drank at the Cittie of York pub. In addition to following in the footsteps of Dickens, you will join the illustrious past and present company of Dr. Samuel Johnson, Sir Thomas More, Sir Francis Bacon, and Aimee Jane Browning,

TELEPHONE
020 7242 7670

OPEN
Mon–Sat

CLOSED
Sun, holidays

HOURS
Pub: Mon–11:30 A.M.–11 P.M., Sat noon–11 P.M.; hot food served noon–9 P.M.

RESERVATIONS
Not accepted

CREDIT CARDS
AE, MC, V

PRICES
À la carte £5–9

SERVICE
No service charged or expected

whose pictures are displayed around the front bar. Who is Aimee Jane Browning? The young daughter of the present managers and the first child to be born in the Cittie of York. Quite a distinction, I think.

History aside, a pub is for eating and drinking, and you will do both well here. Cooking is taken seriously by Mrs. Browning, and she oversees a revolving preparation of four daily hot dishes—beef and ale pie, chili con carne, pork sausages and mash, chicken with Stilton and broccoli—plus a host of sandwiches, salads, and home-made desserts, the best of which are the treacle sponge pudding, chocolate fudge cake, and lemon pie, all served with custard, cream, or ice cream.

A final note of interest is the manager's hidden window, from which he can clandestinely keep an eye on the pub. The leaded stained-glass windows with the letters S. S. in the main bar provide the vantage point.

THE LAMB (4)
94 Lamb's Conduit Street, Bloomsbury, WC1
Tube: Russell Square

TELEPHONE
020 7405 0713

OPEN
Daily

CLOSED
Christmas Day

HOURS
Pub: Mon–Sat 11 A.M.–11 P.M., Sun noon–4 P.M. and 7–10:30 P.M.; lunch: daily noon–2:30 P.M.; dinner: Mon–Sat 6–9 P.M. (no dinner served on Sun)

RESERVATIONS
Not accepted

CREDIT CARDS
MC, V

PRICES
À la carte £6.50–9.50

SERVICE
No service charged or expected

The Lamb is a magnificent pub in the heart of Bloomsbury. Aside from the beautiful green-tiled exterior, the most striking feature of the pub is the horseshoe bar, with its original etched-glass "snob screens" still in place. These rotating screens were used in Victorian days to shield the pillars of society from view when they were drinking with women of dubious distinction. In the rest of the pub, the wood-paneled walls are decorated with a fascinating display of Hogarth prints and sepia photographs of half-forgotten stars of the Victorian music halls and theaters. On a more current note, there is a large photo of the Queen Mum with a glass of beer in her hand.

The seating throughout is comfortable, and you can always hear what is being said. The Lamb is one of the rare pubs that does not have piped-in music, a blaring jukebox, or banging pinball machines drowning out the gentle hum of conversation. The music you will hear comes from a late-eighteenth-century coin-operated music box, with all the money going to charity. In addition to the usual front sidewalk seating, there is a secluded back patio where on warm days you can drink the afternoon away. Besides the great atmosphere, the Young's beer is good, the lunchtime food is above average and made here, there is a nonsmoking section, and the generally upscale crowd is very friendly.

NOTE: When you leave the pub, turn right on Lamb's Conduit Street and walk to the end and you will come to Coram's Fields, a park dedicated to children where the sign by the entrance reads: "Adults may only enter with a child. If you see an adult who happens to be on their own, please contact a member of the Coram's staff." Ducks, geese, sheep, goats, and a pig live at the park and are happy to receive plenty of petting. The buildings date from 1739, when a foundling hospital occupied the site. It became a playground in 1936 and has recently undergone a huge renovation, making it an even more delightful place to while away an hour or so watching the children delight in their play. Mugs and T-shirts are sold in the office by the entrance, and proceeds go to the park fund.

MUSEUM TAVERN (14)
49 Great Russell Street, Bloomsbury, WC1
Tube: Holborn, Tottenham Court Road

The Museum Tavern is a splendid pub with a long history. It is one of the oldest pubs in Bloomsbury, first opening for business in the early eighteenth century. For more than 265 years it has continued to offer ales, wines, spirits, food, and hospitality to visitors and locals alike. Opposite the British Museum, it was Karl Marx's watering hole during his London days, and it's also rumored to have been one of the gathering places for Virginia Woolf and her Bloomsbury Group, and for Oscar Wilde and his friends. The pub is known for its real ales, which you will find listed and explained on a board as you enter. Because it is such a convenient place for resting tired feet after tramping the corridors of the British Museum, it is wall-to-wall crowded at lunchtime, with most of the hot pub grub gone by 2 P.M. So, for a good selection and a seat, plan to arrive early.

TELEPHONE
020 7242 8987

OPEN
Daily

CLOSED
Christmas Day

HOURS
Mon–Sat 11 A.M.–11 P.M., Sun noon–10:30 P.M.; hot lunch: daily noon–2 P.M. (or until it is gone); dinner 5–11 P.M.

RESERVATIONS
Not accepted

CREDIT CARDS
AE, DC, MC, V

PRICES
À la carte £7–10

SERVICE
No service charged or expected

QUEEN CHARLOTTE'S RESTAURANT AND PUB (5)
1 Queen Square, Bloomsbury, WC1
Tube: Russell Square, Holborn

The history of Queen Charlotte's Larder goes back to 1710, when the first tavern was licensed to operate on this site. When the mentally ill King George III was confined to a hospital on Queen Square across the street, his consort, Queen Charlotte, used the underground cellars at the pub to store delicacies to take to her sick husband. When the alehouse became a full tavern later in King George's reign, it was named the Queen's Larder

TELEPHONE
020 7837 5627

OPEN
Daily, restaurant for dinner only

CLOSED
Christmas Day

HOURS
Pub: Mon–Fri 11 A.M.–11 P.M.,
Sat noon–11 P.M., Sun noon–
10:30 P.M., lunch noon–3 P.M.;
restaurant: dinner daily
6–9:30 P.M.

RESERVATIONS
Advised for restaurant, not
accepted in pub

CREDIT CARDS
MC, V

PRICES
Pub: à la carte £3–10;
restaurant: à la carte £8–12

SERVICE
Discretionary in restaurant, no
service charged or expected
in pub

in honor of Queen Charlotte. The cellars are now used to store beer kegs and are said to be haunted by ghosts. The present-day pub still has its original Georgian facade, with six bricked-up windows recalling the days of the window tax, when property owners boarded up windows rather than pay additional taxes per window. On the last Monday of the month, jazz and blues musicians gather in the pub to talk over old times, and occasionally to play.

History, ghosts, and taxes aside, the best part about this pub today is that it serves hot dinners in its upstairs dining room, highlighting the house specialty, home-made potpies. These meals-in-themselves are filled with vegetables, beef, lamb (the most popular), or chicken, and come garnished with potatoes and vegetables or a salad. Lunch is served in the pub downstairs and consists of above-average bar food, such as chili, steak and kidney pie, sandwiches, ploughman's platters, and fish-and-chips.

NOTE: No smoking allowed in the restaurant.

WC2

Covent Garden, Leicester Square, and the Strand

All distances in London are measured from Charing Cross, the official center of London on the south side of Trafalgar Square. Book lovers won't want to miss a stroll down Charing Cross Road, which is loaded with fascinating secondhand booksellers.

If Charing Cross is London's official center, Trafalgar Square is the sentimental heart of the city. It also has a history as the setting for riots and demonstrations. Once the home of the royal horses, it was made into a square in 1829 to honor Lord Nelson with the 185-foot Nelson's Column. The square is framed by the National Gallery, the National Portrait Gallery, and the St. Martin-in-the-Fields church.

Covent Garden is where the slick and chic meet to eat and drink in an enticing variety of restaurants, which are close to most major West End theaters. By 1974, the Eliza Doolittle flower girls and the famous fruit and vegetable markets had moved to a new location at Nine Elms, outside of London. The market reopened as a collection of boutiques and restaurants with a carnival atmosphere that is one of the liveliest parts of London.

Holborn (pronounced Ho-bun) was the thirteenth-century route for the transport of goods to the city, and it's now the heart and soul of Legal London, where you can walk around the Inns of Court and see the wigged and gowned lawyers heading for court.

Great people-watching is yours anywhere around Leicester Square (pronounced LES-ter). It is perpetually jammed with tourists flocking to one of the many cinemas that ring the square, eating greasy, overpriced junk food, or just standing around checking out the action. There's always a long line at the Half-Price Ticket kiosk in the center of the square, but don't think you will get tickets for any of the top shows for a song, because they are rarely sold here. Tickets here are mainly for lesser-known or fringe shows.

The Strand is a commercial road with incessant traffic and pollution—not much to hold a visitor's interest.

TOURIST ATTRACTIONS
Charing Cross, Trafalgar Square, Nelson's Column, Royal Courts of Justice, St.-Martin-in-the-Fields Church, National Portrait Gallery, Royal Opera House, London Transport Museum, National Gallery, Thames River

($) indicates a Big Splurge

Restaurants

BELGO CENTRAAL (26)
50 Earlham Street, Covent Garden, WC2
Tube: Covent Garden

What a place! If it was not a restaurant, this Belgian brewery hall and eatery would make a good indoor amusement park. Belgo Centraal serves unpretentious food in an—how should I phrase this?—architecturally stimulating environment. The name of the game is excess, and they manage to make some kind of statement at almost every metallic turn. Witness the lighted entry catwalks and zany cargo lift going down to the arched-brick basement, where there's an open kitchen and high-tech loo. Waiters in Trappist-style monk habits wait on diners in the two eating areas. If you arrive without reservations, you will probably sit communal-style at long tables with hard benches in the eating halls. Reservation holders for the restaurant fare only marginally better from a comfort standpoint, if you view sitting on metal chairs with wooden seats as an improvement.

Don't worry—there are good reasons to eat here. They include, of course, the Belgian beers and the mussels, accompanied typically by french fries and mayonnaise. Other good choices are the pork and Chimay beer sausages and mash, *carbonnade flammande*—beef braised in sweet Gueuze beer with apples and plums—and spit-roasted chicken served with apple puree or a creamy wild mushroom sauce. Try desserts of crêpes or *gauffres* (waffles) with either caramelized apples and prunes or mixed forest fruits housed under a blanket of warm Belgian white-chocolate sauce. Whipped cream can be added on request. All the ice cream is homemade.

For Belgo on a budget, the set-price menus are definitely Great Eat deals. Lunch for a fiver (£5), served between noon and 5 P.M., offers four choices: Chimay sausages, Belgian mash, and a soft drink or a beer; a half kilo (one pound) of *moules marinières* (mussels) served with a green salad and a bottle of sparkling water; *tartine de champignons* (toasted rye bread topped with wild mushrooms, cream, and chives, accompanied by a bottle of sparkling water); or pan-fried pork chop with apple puree, salad, fries, and mineral water. "Beat-the-Clock" runs Monday to Friday from 5 to 6:30 P.M. You pay the price at the time shown on your food order for one of the three listed food specials. For example, if you arrive at

TELEPHONE
020 7813 2233

OPEN
Daily

CLOSED
Christmas Day

HOURS
Eating hall: noon–midnight (Sun till 10:30 P.M.), continuous service; restaurant: lunch noon–5 P.M., dinner 5 P.M.–midnight (Sun till 10:30 P.M.)

RESERVATIONS
Advised for restaurant

CREDIT CARDS
AE, DC, MC, V

PRICES
À la carte: £18–28; set-price: lunch £5 1 course and beverage, lunch and dinner £16 2 courses and beverage or ice cream; "Beat-the-Clock": Mon–Fri 5–6:30 P.M.

SERVICE
15% service charge

5:05 P.M., order the *moules marinières,* served with fries and a white beer, and pay only £5.05. Come at 6:29 P.M., and the same dish will cost you £6.29. After 8 P.M., you are looking at more than £12 for the identical meal. Finally, there is the Belgo Complet offered daily for both lunch and dinner. This includes a salad *liégeoise* followed by a kilo pot of *moules marinières* or *provençales* served with fries and mayo and a choice of beer, soft drink, or a dish of homemade vanilla ice cream.

NOTE: If you can't get to Belgo Centraal in London, maybe their newest outpost in New York City will be more convenient for you. It is at 415 Lafayette Street, opposite the Crunch Gym, at the corner of Astor Place and the Joe Papp Public Theater (Tel: 212-253-2828).

NOTE: The shop sells Belgo cookbooks, packs of beer, glasses, and other related gifts; open daily noon–10 P.M.

BERTORELLI'S ($, 30)
44a Floral Street, Covent Garden, WC2
Tube: Leicester Square, Covent Garden

Please see page 41 for a description. All other information is the same.

TELEPHONE: 020 7836 3969
OPEN: Mon–Sat, holidays when the Royal Opera has a performance
CLOSED: Sun, most holidays (call to check)
HOURS: Lunch noon–3 P.M., dinner 5:30–11:30 P.M.

CAFÉ FLO (29)
51 St. Martin's Lane (next to Lumière Cinema), Covent Garden, WC2
Tube: Leicester Square

See Café Flo on page 42 for full description. All other information is the same.

TELEPHONE: 020 7836 8289
OPEN: Mon–Sat; Sun lunch and dinner only
CLOSED: Christmas Day
HOURS: Mon–Sat 9 A.M.–11:30 P.M., Sun 9 A.M.–10:30 P.M., continuous service

CAFE IN THE CRYPT AT ST. MARTIN-IN-THE-FIELDS CHURCH (52)
St. Martin-in-the-Fields Church, Trafalgar Square, WC2
Tube: Charing Cross

St. Martin-in-the-Fields is the parish church for Buckingham Palace. You probably won't run into the Queen taking tea at the Cafe in the Crypt, but you will meet countless others who have come to appreciate this roomy underground restaurant, with its vaulted ceilings, plain wood-slat furniture, and nonsmoking section. The location on Trafalgar Square puts you across from the National Gallery and the National Portrait Gallery and in close walking distance to Piccadilly, Covent Garden, and many West End theaters.

The straightforward home-style cooking is varied, but not always consistent. I have had wonderful dishes on one visit and run into fair sandwiches, a poor cauliflower soup, doughy apple crumble, and tasteless custard the next. Though it's generally good, they don't always bat a thousand in the kitchen. However, the choices change for both lunch and dinner, so you won't strike out for long. In addition to soups and hot mains, there is a cold buffet counter with salads, filled sandwich rolls, and desserts. On Friday and Saturday, the dinner buffet is largely devoted to fish and seafood.

All the profits from the restaurant support the church's charities, especially those that take care of the poor and the homeless. Shoppers may want to devote a few minutes to the bookstore and take a very quick stroll through the Courtyard Craft Market directly behind the church (open daily from 9 A.M. to 6 P.M.). The merchandise is largely T-shirts, cheap Indian clothing, and junk, but now and then there is a stall with something of merit. There is also an art gallery next to the restaurant and the London Brass Rubbing Centre.

Free lunchtime concerts are held in the church at 1 P.M. on Monday, Tuesday, and Friday; choral services are held on Wednesday at 1 and 5 P.M.; and evening concerts are held every night except Wednesday and Sunday starting at 7:30 P.M. Tickets cost between £7 and £18 and are available at the door, in advance from the box office, online at the Web address, or through credit card booking agencies that will charge an additional fee.

NOTE: There is a nonsmoking section.

TELEPHONE
020 7839 4342

INTERNET
www.stmartin-in-the-fields.org

OPEN
Daily

CLOSED
Christmas Day

HOURS
Breakfast: Mon–Sat 10 A.M.–noon; lunch: daily noon–3:15 P.M.; tea: daily 2:30–5:30 P.M.; dinner: Mon–Thur, Sun 6–7:30 P.M., Fri–Sat until 10 P.M.

RESERVATIONS
Not accepted

CREDIT CARDS
MC, V (minimum charge £5)

PRICES
À la carte £5–12

SERVICE
Included

CAFE PACIFICO (28)
5 Langley Street, Covent Garden, WC2
Tube: Covent Garden

TELEPHONE
020 7379 7728
FAX
020 7836 5088
EMAIL
cafepac@aol.com
INTERNET
www.cafepacifico-laperia.com
OPEN
Daily
CLOSED
Christmas Day
HOURS
Mon–Sat noon–11:45 P.M., Sun noon–10:45 P.M., continuous service
RESERVATIONS
Advised for lunch
CREDIT CARDS
AE, MC, V
PRICES
À la carte £15–24
SERVICE
12.5% service charge

Let's face it—if you love Mexican food, going without it can cause deep longing. For years, the Mexican food scene in London ranged from grim to nonexistent. Not any longer. With Cafe Pacifico firmly entrenched on the scene, your Mexican favorites—margaritas, quesadillas, chimichangas, tacos, enchiladas, and fajitas—are all within easy reach in Covent Garden. To really appreciate the place, give it a chance to build some momentum and arrive after 8 P.M. The loud and active crowd will not appeal to the Sun City set, but for people mixing and matching, it's a knockout. If you are in London on Cinco de Mayo (May 5), there will be a live Mexican band to add to the festivities on this Mexican national holiday.

NOTE: Keep an eye on the tab—those margaritas can add up in a hurry.

CAFE PASTA (27)
184 Shaftesbury Avenue, Soho, WC2
Tube: Covent Garden

With mirrors reflecting the tables, each of which is set with a small vase of flowers, and beautiful color photos of Carnival in Venice, this is the prettiest Cafe Pasta in London. Breakfast and snacks are not served here, but the food is just as consistent as it is at the other two locations. See page 100 for details; all other information is the same

TELEPHONE: 020 7379 0198

OPEN: Daily

CLOSED: 2 days at Christmas

HOURS: Mon–Sat 11:30 A.M.–11:30 P.M., Sun until 10:30 P.M., continuous service

SERVICE: 10% service charge

CAFE PASTA (38)
2–4 Garrick Street, Covent Garden, WC2
Tube: Leicester Square

There are no snacks served at this Cafe Pasta. See Cafe Pasta on page 100 for a full description. All other information is the same.

TELEPHONE: 020 7497 2779

OPEN: Daily

HOURS: Mon–Sat noon–11:30 P.M., Sun until 10:30 P.M.

CHEZ GÉRARD (24)
119 Chancery Lane (off Fleet Street), Holborn, WC2
Tube: Chancery Lane

See the Charlotte Street location in W1, page 45, for a complete description. This Chez Gérard stays open longer and serves breakfast and a café menu in its wine bar in addition to its regular lunch and dinner menus. The least expensive breakfast menu is *Le Petit Dejeuner "Express,"* which is a pot of tea or coffee and a choice of pastry. The most expensive is correctly called *Le Grand Carnivore,* and it's a he-man-size breakfast if there ever was one, with steak, lamb cutlet, calf's liver, sausage, bacon, mushrooms, tomatoes, eggs any style, tea, coffee, and orange juice.

TELEPHONE: 020 7405 0290

FAX: 020 7242 2649

OPEN: Mon–Fri

CLOSED: Sat–Sun, holidays

HOURS: Breakfast 8–10:30 A.M., lunch noon–3 P.M., dinner 6–10 P.M., bar 3–11 P.M., wine bar food 3–10 P.M.

PRICES: Set-price: breakfast £3.95–10.95; à la carte: breakfast £4–6, wine bar £8–12

CHEZ GÉRARD AT THE OPERA TERRACE (31)
The Market, the Piazza, Covent Garden, WC2
Tube: Covent Garden

Because it is in the heart of Covent Garden, this Chez Gérard has both a restaurant side, called the Opera Terrace, and a café and bar geared toward lighter fare. The café is *très français,* with plates of cheese and *charcuterie,* baguette sandwiches, assorted salads, and the ever-popular *tarte tatin* (hot upside-down apple tart with ice cream). It serves meals from 11 A.M. to 5 P.M., then becomes a bar serving snacks, *charcuterie,* and cheese plates. I recommend reserving a table with a terrace view, but the table will not be guaranteed. If you can manage to nail a table with a view, you will have a great perch from which to see the beautiful new Royal Opera building and observe the swarm of humanity milling around the piazza below.

At Chez Gérard's Opera Terrace, the same good-value set-price menu found at other branches is available for dinner from Monday to Saturday and for weekend lunches. Please see the Charlotte Street location in W1, page 45, for a full description. Otherwise, the information is the same as in all the Chez Gérard restaurants regarding prices, reservations, credit cards, and service.

TELEPHONE: 020 7379 0666
FAX: 020 7497 9060
OPEN: Daily
CLOSED: Christmas Eve dinner, Christmas Day, Boxing Day
HOURS: Café: lunch daily 11 A.M.–5 P.M.; bar: Mon–Sat 11 A.M.–11:30 P.M., Sun until 10:30 P.M.; restaurant: lunch daily noon–3 P.M., dinner Mon–Sat 5:30–11:30 P.M., Sun until 10:30 P.M.
PRICES: À la carte: café, lunch £8–14; bar snacks £8

CRANKS RESTAURANT–CHARING CROSS (53)
8 Adelaide Street, Charing Cross, WC2
Tube: Charing Cross

This branch of Cranks, next to the tube stop, is mostly a takeaway shop with only a few seats. See the Barrett Street location in W1, page 48, for a full description. All other information is the same.

TELEPHONE & FAX: 020 7836 0660

CRANKS RESTAURANT–LEICESTER SQUARE (36)
17–19 Great Newport Street, Soho, WC2
Tube: Leicester Square

See the Barrett Street location in W1, page 48, for a full description. All other information is the same.

TELEPHONE: 020 7836 5226
FAX: 020 7497 1164

FOOD FOR THOUGHT (21)
31 Neal Street, Covent Garden, WC2
Tube: Covent Garden

TELEPHONE
020 7836 0239
FAX
020 7379 1249
OPEN
Mon–Sat; Sun lunch only
CLOSED
Sun dinner, 10–12 days at Christmas (dates vary)
HOURS
Mon–Sat: breakfast 9:30–11:30 A.M., lunch noon–4 P.M., dinner 4–8 P.M.; Sun: noon–5 P.M., continuous service
RESERVATIONS
Not accepted

On the street level, a small open kitchen vies for space with the cafeteria buffet, one table, and a counter seating three. The whitewashed downstairs dining room is a better place to eat, provided you can manage to find an empty chair, especially during the noon to 1:30 P.M. lunch trade; crowds start lining up outside about fifteen minutes before the door opens. Although the vegetarian food is budget-priced here, it doesn't look or taste as though it's been done on the cheap.

The seasonal menu changes daily and offers balanced contrasts in color, taste, and texture. Each dish is labeled, so you know which is wheat-free, vegan, dairy free, organic, or with nuts. For dessert, taste the fruit scrunch: yogurt, cream, and honey, whipped together and poured over seasonal fruit that is on a bed of crunched, roasted oats. It's better than it sounds. No booze is served, but fresh juices, sparkling water, decaf coffee, herbal teas, barley cup, and soy milk are. Cheers!

NOTE: No smoking. Restaurant is unlicensed; BYOB (no corkage fee). To create Food for Thought dishes in your own home, you can purchase their cookbook, which sells for £9.

CREDIT CARDS
None
PRICES
À la carte £4–9.50, minimum charge at peak times £2.50
SERVICE
No service charged or expected

HARRY BROWN (46)
4 New Row, Covent Garden, WC2
Tube: Leicester Square

Harry Brown is a sandwich bar with a little more zip than most. The neat and tidy interior displays a collection of Edward Hopper–style paintings of chefs, clients, and servers who have worked here. The made-to-order sandwiches, which can be ordered on granary baps (buns), baguettes, focaccia, or ciabatta bread, are huge by any standard. I like the vegetarian sandwich with avocado, mozzarella, sun-dried tomatoes, mushrooms, and eggplant heaped on focaccia or ciabatta. Meat lovers will be happy biting into the steak, melted cheese, lettuce, tomatoes, and sharp mustard creation. The sandwich makers are accommodating and will do anything you want, as long as they have the ingredients. If you are looking for breakfast anytime, try one of theirs. Breakfast here, with its quality ingredients, is a notch above the mundane.

NOTE: Takeaway is available. Please see Pasta Brown's on page 142, which is under the same ownership. The photo on the Harry Brown menu is the grandfather of owner Anthony Brown.

TELEPHONE
020 7240 0230
OPEN
Daily in summer; Mon–Sat in winter
CLOSED
Sun in winter; Christmas Day
HOURS
Mon–Sat 7:30 A.M.–8 P.M., Sun 11 A.M.–7 P.M., continuous service
RESERVATIONS
Not accepted
CREDIT CARDS
None
PRICES
À la carte £5–7
SERVICE
No service charged or expected

INDIA CLUB (34)
143 The Strand, Covent Garden, WC2
Tube: Temple, Aldwych

If you like unadorned Indian food, this is the Great Eats address to remember when you are low on funds. Even though the India Club is on the Strand, it is easy to walk right past it without a second look, as it is hidden up a flight of dark stairs next to a fleabag Indian hotel. The clean but spartan second-floor interior has never changed, probably because there is nothing to it. The largely southern-Indian food is not only cheap but authentic, and the high number of loyal Indian patrons who eat here daily attests to this. For the price of a prefab

TELEPHONE
020 7836 0650
OPEN
Mon–Sat
CLOSED
Sun, holidays
HOURS
Lunch noon–2:30 P.M., dinner 6–10:50 P.M.
RESERVATIONS
Accepted for 6 or more
CREDIT CARDS
None

burger, large fries, and a shake, you can have Mughlay chicken or chicken curry Madras—the house special-ties—along with rice, mango chutney, and Indian tea. A vegetarian meal is equally reasonable, with vegetable or egg curry, dal (lentils), and *chille bhajias* (fritters), all costing less than £3.50 per dish. The eccentric service from long-suffering white-coated waiters is courteous.

NOTE: Restaurant is unlicensed; BYOB (no corkage fee).

JOE ALLEN (33)
13 Exeter Street (corner of Burleigh), Covent Garden, WC2
Tube: Covent Garden

TELEPHONE
020 7836 0651
FAX
020 7497 2148
INTERNET
joeallen.co.uk
OPEN
Daily
CLOSED
2 days at Christmas
HOURS
Mon–Fri noon–1 A.M., Sat–Sun brunch 11:30 A.M.–4 P.M.; regular menu available until midnight, continuous service
RESERVATIONS
Essential at night and on Sun for brunch and evening jazz
CREDIT CARDS
AE, MC, V
PRICES
À la carte: £18–24; set-price lunch: Mon–Sat noon–3 P.M. £15 2 courses, £17 3 courses; pre-theater menu: Mon–Sat 5–6:45 P.M. £15 2 courses, £17 3 courses; Sat–Sun brunch: £16.50 2 courses, £18.50 3 courses, includes Bloody Mary, bucks fizz, or a glass of house champagne
SERVICE
Discretionary

Joe Allen is a fashionable restaurant in a dark alley near Covent Garden. Accessible only to the determined (look for the brass plaque by the door), the popular restaurant is a faithful copy of branches in New York, Miami Beach, and Paris: brick walls lined with photos of film and theater stars, and a jolly waitstaff serving good American food. The big crowd comes in after the theater to order bowls of chili con carne, plates of barbecued ribs with black-eyed peas, wonderful main course salads (try the Caesar), slabs of pecan pie, and oversize chocolate chip or oatmeal cookies and ice cream. At lunch you can have a great eggs Benedict or the popular Joe Allen—half a baked potato with spinach, a poached egg, hollandaise sauce, and a grilled tomato on the side. Insiders order the hamburger with everything; it's not on the menu, so you have to ask for it. On Sunday night from 8 to 11 P.M., Jazz at Joe's is the big drawing card. Even though the late-night diners often seem too chic and the noise levels seem too loud, this is still a great place to grab a late meal and people-watch to your heart's content.

NOTE: If you'd like a souvenir, they have T-shirts and baseball caps for sale.

KOHA RESTAURANT AND BAR (50)
11 St. Martin's Lane, Covent Garden, WC2
Tube: Leicester Square

TELEPHONE
020 7497 0282
OPEN
Mon–Sat
CLOSED
Sun, major holidays

Straddling the line between modern British for the mains and a more international slant for starters and desserts, Koha is a popular destination for pre- and post-theater dining. It's a small restaurant, with a bar in front

PRICES
À la carte £7–12 (minimum charge £4)
SERVICE
Discretionary

and twenty-two covers on bare tables in the back. The mirrors along the banquettes reflect the big clock, so you won't miss your opening, and the wild paintings were created by an Albanian artist. While there are no culinary revelations coming from the kitchen, the food is well prepared, seasonally fresh, and served by a casual, breezy waitstaff. If I am here for lunch, I order the *crescente,* a satisfying appetizer of grilled Mediterranean vegetables under a goat cheese gratin. For a lighter beginning, the plum tomato and red onion salad is good, and for something in between, the creamy herb risotto is a great choice. Toulouse sausages and mash will never lose their appeal, and neither will the rack of lamb or roasted sea bass. Don't worry if you cannot do justice to a big meal, because no one seems to mind if you skip the main course and head for the desserts, which are all made here. The list is not long, but the quality is excellent, especially if you have the tangy lemon tart or slice of dark chocolate truffle mousse cake.

HOURS
Mon–Sat 11 A.M.–11 P.M., continuous service

RESERVATIONS
Advised for dinner

CREDIT CARDS
AE, DC, MC, V

PRICES
À la carte £21–28

SERVICE
50 pence cover per person, service discretionary, 12.5% added for 5 or more

LA QUERCIA D'ORO (18)
16 Endell Street, Covent Garden, WC2
Tube: Covent Garden

Italian food is good in London, even though its popularity has had more ups and downs than the Italian government. New-wave Italian cooking is the hot new thing—but you need a scorecard to keep track of the chefs and restaurants as they jockey to stay abreast of the latest fads.

Enter La Quercia D'Oro, which is as old-world Italian as they come. This Covent Garden trattoria doesn't pay heed to fads, calorie counts, or decorating improvements. It does listen to its portly customers, who are happy with plastic-covered tables and paper napkins, and who come back day after day for mama's *cucina.* Olives and bread and butter start the meal; chocolates, mints, and biscotti end it. In between are big servings of every Italian dish you know and love: steamed mussels in garlic and white wine, minestrone, pastas with tomato, clam, carbonara, or pesto sauces, fresh fish, chicken and veal either sautéed with a few herbs or buried in a decadent cheese and cream sauce. Desserts? Frankly, they are easily forgotten. Wind up instead with a glass of *vin santo* or a bracing espresso.

TELEPHONE
020 7379 5108

OPEN
Mon–Fri; Sat dinner only

CLOSED
Sat lunch, Sun, 2 days at Christmas

HOURS
Lunch noon–3 P.M., dinner 5:45–11:30 P.M.

RESERVATIONS
Not necessary

CREDIT CARDS
AE, DC, MC, V

PRICES
À la carte: £12–22; set-price lunch or dinner: £8.50 2 courses, £11 3 courses

SERVICE
£1 cover charge for bread; 10% service charge for large groups, otherwise discretionary

MONMOUTH COFFEE COMPANY (25)
27 Monmouth Street, Covent Garden, WC2
Tube: Covent Garden

TELEPHONE
020 7836 5272, 7379 4337

FAX
020 7240 8824

OPEN
Mon–Sat

CLOSED
Sun, holidays

HOURS
9 A.M.–6:30 P.M.

RESERVATIONS
Not accepted

CREDIT CARDS
MC, V

PRICES
Cup of coffee £1.50, bag of coffee £6–7.50 per pound

SERVICE
Discretionary

Espresso bars and designer coffeehouses are fast replacing the greasy café for discerning Londoners. Nowhere is this more evident than around Covent Garden, where it seems you can get a cappuccino in a dozen forms, including decaf, flavored, and low-fat. It is hard to recognize the Monmouth Coffee Company as a coffee bar because its four tables, one of which seats only one very small person, are buried in the back behind bags of fresh coffee beans from around the world. All the roasting is done here, and every coffee can be sampled in individually filtered cups before you buy it in bulk. How much bulk coffee do they sell a week? In excess of one ton!

NOTE: No smoking allowed. On Friday and Saturday there's a Monmouth Coffee Company stall at the Borough Market in SE1.

MUFFINSKI'S (39)
5 King Street, Covent Garden, WC2
Tube: Leicester Square, Covent Garden

TELEPHONE
020 7379 1525

INTERNET
www.muffinskis.com

OPEN
Daily

CLOSED
2 days at Christmas

HOURS
Mon–Fri 8 A.M.–7 P.M., Sat 9 A.M.–7 P.M., Sun 10 A.M.–6:30 P.M., continuous service

RESERVATIONS
Not accepted

CREDIT CARDS
None

PRICES
Set breakfast £3–5; à la carte £1.80–5

SERVICE
No service charged or expected

Revolving pans of eighty-plus regular, low-fat, low-sugar, and fat-free muffins; good coffee; an assortment of flavored cappuccinos, lattes, and iced milk smoothies; almost-fat-free frozen yogurt; no smoking; and a friendly staff to serve you or to pack your goodies to go . . . Are we still in London? You bet, and in Muffinski's, where Frances Blunden serves the customers and her husband keeps the oven on full time, turning out his great muffins made only with organic, stone-ground flour and fresh fruits. All the orthodox flavors are here—banana, bran, blueberry, apple-cinnamon—and some further-out choices as well. Try dark chocolate and coconut, strawberry or blueberry studded with white chocolate, or spicy corn and cheese. Bagels, danishes, toast and jam, fries, and chips with dips are here too, but what for? This is strictly the place for all the warm muffins you can eat . . . or take away.

NOTE: No smoking allowed.

NEAL'S YARD DINING ROOM–WORLD FOOD CAFE (20)
14 Neal's Yard (first floor), Covent Garden, WC2
Tube: Covent Garden

TELEPHONE
020 7379 0298

OPEN
Mon–Sat

CLOSED
Sun, holidays (call to check)

HOURS
Lunch: 11:45 A.M.–3:45 P.M.

RESERVATIONS
Not accepted

CREDIT CARDS
MC, V (minimum charge £10)

PRICES
À la carte £7–14; minimum charge during lunch £5

SERVICE
Discretionary

Neal's Yard Dining Room–World Food Cafe is an upstairs haven for Great Eaters searching for healthy dishes at prices that won't take big bites out of their budget. It is above the Neal's Yard Remedies shop and overlooks the Neal's Yard courtyard, ringed with juice and sandwich bars, a New Age walk-in back-rub spot, and the Neal's Yard Bakery, which uses its own stone-ground whole-grain flour in all the breads. The whole atmosphere is a throwback to the hippie movement of the sixties. The open kitchen/dining room serves inter-national vegetarian and vegan dishes to diners who sit at a horseshoe bar facing the cooking and food-prep area, or at small tables positioned around the edge of the room. The wonderful travel photos displayed on the walls are the work of owner Chris Caldicott, who is photographer in residence at the Royal Geographic Society. The *World Food Cafe Cookbook,* which Chris and his wife, Caroline, authored, has recipes from around the world. Each area covered has an introduction to the food of the region, customs, ingredients, and ways the dishes are cooked.

To eat here you must be an adventurous diner willing to try new food combinations and able to tackle oversize portions. The menu features dishes from Mexico, Tur-key, India, Sri Lanka, West Africa, and the Middle East, with the occasional British pudding thrown in for good measure. If you opt for the West African meal, you will have a stew made from sweet potatoes and vegetables cooked in a creamy peanut sauce and served over steamed rice. Accompanying this will be beet salad and a fresh banana on the side. Lighter appetites can be satisfied by filled tortillas, several salad and soup choices, or an assortment of Greek appetizers. The Polish lemon and raisin cheesecake is always tempting if it is available, and so is the flourless French chocolate cake.

NOTE: No smoking allowed. Restaurant is unlicensed; BYOB (95 pence corkage fee).

PALMS (40)
39 King Street, Covent Garden, WC2
Tube: Covent Garden

The Covent Garden Palms follows almost the same basic menu as the Kensington Palms in W8, but prices each dish individually. See Palms, page 102, for a full description. All other information is the same.

TELEPHONE: 020 7240 2939
OPEN: Daily
CLOSED: Christmas Day
HOURS: Noon–midnight, continuous service
RESERVATIONS: Advised for Sat and Sun
PRICES: À la carte £12–18

PASTA BROWN'S (45)
35–36 Bow Street, Covent Garden, WC2
Tube: Covent Garden, Leicester Square

TELEPHONE
020 7379 5775
FAX
020 7379 5872
INTERNET
www.pastabrown.com
OPEN
Daily
CLOSED
3 days at Christmas
HOURS
Daily noon–11 P.M., continuous service
RESERVATIONS
Accepted for more than 5
CREDIT CARDS
AE, MC, V
PRICES
À la carte £14–20
SERVICE
12.5% service charge

Facelifts are great, especially when they turn out well, and Pasta Brown's has had another good one, leaving just enough character intact to keep it interesting. Inspired by the beautifully restored Royal Opera House across the street, the snazzy new look is highlighted by a metal sculpture of the three tenors with spoons and forks as their musical notes. The rest of the space is sparse, with modern versions of captain's chairs surrounding bare tables accented with blue napkins, a blue bottle of mineral water, and one Gerber daisy. Dominating the back space on both levels are the exhibition kitchens. Softening the decor is a photo of the owner's grandmother by the door. (If you have been around the corner to their other restaurant, Harry Brown, page 137, you will remember that the owner's grandfather is pictured on that restaurant's menu.)

Beneath all the new look is still a restaurant with Italian heart and soul. This is evidenced by the almost thirty pastas, ranging from a simple spaghetti Napoli—tomato sauce, garlic, and Parmesan cheese—to *linguine con langoustine,* made with crayfish and dill blended with a béchamel and white wine sauce. The rest of the menu tempts with side orders of salads, garlic bread, homemade soups, assorted chicken dishes, and desserts for which you will extend your caloric boundaries, especially the tiramisu and banoffee (banana and toffee) pie.

PORTERS ENGLISH RESTAURANT (44)
17 Henrietta Street, Covent Garden, WC2
Tube: Covent Garden

Porters is an attractive restaurant decorated with Covent Garden memorabilia. It's great for the family or for visitors in search of something typically English. Sure, it's on the touristy side, but the food and prices are good and no one leaves feeling fleeced. Arrive hungry, forget your diet, and order one of their famous potpies or special monthly dishes and you will not go away disappointed.

The best starters are soups, served with a chunk of crusty white or whole-grain bread. In the winter, try their brown onion, ale, and cheddar cheese soup, or on warmer days, the chilled carrot and orange for a refreshing starter. But make sure to leave plenty of room for the main event, a filling potpie ranging from steak and kidney or Cumberland minced beef and vegetables cooked with ale and herbs, to more offbeat ones such as lamb and apricot, or a fish pie made with cod, salmon, and prawns. Sausage and mash, bubble and squeak, spotted dick . . . no, these are not names from nursery rhymes, but some of the other dishes worth trying at Porters. (These translate as sausage and mashed potatoes; fried mashed potatoes, cabbage, and onions; and sponge cake with raisins and warm custard sauce.) Also on the menu are five grills: steak, chicken breast, lamb's kidneys or lamb steak, and salmon, plus devilled kidneys, fish-and–chips, and fish cakes. They are all good, but frankly, when having a meal at Porters, you should order a potpie and bypass the rest. Whatever you do, don't bypass the desserts, especially the dark chocolate chip pudding, which is steamed chocolate sponge cake with chocolate chips and a chocolate custard. The restaurant warns, "don't ask for it without the chocolate!"

A few doors down street is Porters Bar, serving sandwiches, salads, a handful of main courses, grills, and five desserts. It is a casually comfortable place that is nice for a bite before the theater if you don't want to get into a full meal.

NOTE: They may impose a two-hour time limit at the tables during peak hours.

TELEPHONE
020 7836 6466

FAX
020 7379 4296

INTERNET
www.porters.uk.com;
www.porters-bar.com

OPEN
Daily

CLOSED
Christmas Day

HOURS
Noon–11:30 P.M. (Sun till 10:30 P.M.), continuous service

RESERVATIONS
Advised (essential during peak hours)

CREDIT CARDS
AE, DC, MC, V

PRICES
Restaurant: à la carte £16–22; set-price £18 for any starter or dessert, any pie served with a side dish, a half bottle of house wine, tea, coffee, and the tip included! (2-person minimum); Porters Bar: à la carte £6–10

SERVICE
Discretionary, 10% service charge for 5 or more

PROSPECT GRILL ($, 41)
4–6 Garrick Street, Covent Garden, WC2
Tube: Leicester Square

TELEPHONE
020 7379 0412
FAX
020 7836 3936
OPEN
Mon–Fri
CLOSED
Sun, Dec 24–Jan 2
HOURS
Mon–Fri: lunch noon–3:30 P.M.,
dinner 5:45 P.M.–midnight; Sat
noon–midnight, continuous
service
RESERVATIONS
Advised, especially on
weekends
CREDIT CARDS
AE, MC, V
PRICES
£25–30
SERVICE
Discretionary

Dark, bare tables are set with heavy linen napkins, simple wine glasses, and plain cutlery. A stationary light adds a glow in the evening, when a buzzy, black-clad clientele fills booths and intimate tables for two. At lunch, the tasteful surroundings appeal to the suit-and-tied set from nearby offices. The food is robust, yet modern and satisfying to both hearty eaters and gentle grazers. Old-fashioned cocktails are enjoying a renaissance here, especially the before-dinner dry martini or blueberry gin and tonic, and the after-dinner hits such as the velvet hammer or the grasshopper. The menu puts seasonal ingredients to good use as accompaniments and in the dishes themselves. In the winter, look for baked leek and tarragon tart, French onion soup, or goat cheese salad with oven-dried tomatoes to start. The rosemary roasted chicken with a rich *gratin dauphinois* is a comforting main course. For a new twist on the predictable, look for the seared tuna burger with a sharp green-chili salsa or the Prospet hamburger with caramelized onions, both garnished with fried potatoes. Ever present dessert temptations force a choice between a chocolate brownie topped with vanilla ice cream and slathered in fudge sauce and the delicious poached spiced pear with a scoop of cinnamon ice cream melting over it.

THE ROCK AND SOLE PLAICE (22)
47 Endell Street, Covent Garden, WC2
Tube: Covent Garden

TELEPHONE
020 7836 3785
EMAIL
ahmetziyaeddin@hotmail.com
INTERNET
www.rockandsoleplaice.com,
www.rockandsoleplaice.co.uk
OPEN
Daily
CLOSED
Christmas Day
HOURS
Mon–Sat, 11:30 A.M.–
10:30 P.M., Sun noon–10 P.M.
continuous service
RESERVATIONS
Not accepted
CREDIT CARDS
None

Regulars come from the neighborhood and around the globe to eat at Ismet Ziyaeddin's excellent fish-and-chips restaurant, which opened in 1871, making it one of London's oldest. I have met people from northern Cyprus and New Jersey, and others living only two blocks away, when I have eaten here. My mail indicates that many Great Eaters in London continue to count themselves among the faithful. There are other things on the menu: steak and kidney pie, hamburgers, sausages, and some unadventurous desserts. Ignore these and pay attention only to the halibut, cod, salmon, plaice, skate, or Dover sole—or any other daily fish that is offered. Whether you enjoy eating your fish-and-chips (with a side of mushy peas to be really authentic) at one of the seven indoor tables next to the kitchen, sitting at a picnic table on the sidewalk, or as you walk down the street, you can always be assured of fresh deep-fried fish that is so good that you, too, will be back many times.

RULES ($, 43)
35 Maiden Lane, Covent Garden, WC2
Tube: Covent Garden

In 1798, the year Napoleon opened his campaign in Egypt, Thomas Rule opened his oyster bar in Covent Garden. In all its years, spanning the reigns of nine monarchs, Rules has been owned by only three families, and it still flourishes as the oldest restaurant in London and is certainly one of the most well known and loved. Throughout its long history, Rules has been the haunt of artists, lawyers, journalists, actors, and great literary talents. Charles Dickens brought playbills to Rules for performances he produced and performed in, and King Edward VII entertained his lover, Lillie Langtry, in a first-floor room with a private entrance. The past lives on in the hundreds of drawings, paintings, and cartoons displayed on the walls. The late Sir John Betjeman, then poet laureate, described the ground-floor interior as "unique and irreplaceable, and part of the literary and theatrical history of London." The restaurant seats more than two hundred people on its three floors, employs a staff of one hundred, and serves an average of five hundred people a day.

Rules has always made quality and value its priorities, and it continues to maintain its reputation for solid, dependable food with service that is not just excellent but friendly. The kitchen specializes in classic game cookery. Rules owns an estate in the High Pennines, known as England's last wilderness, which supplies the game for the restaurant and where it is able to exercise its own quality controls and determine how the game is treated. The other meat and poultry served comes from lean, healthy, free-range animals, and the fresh fish includes both wild salmon and sea trout.

I am saving the best for last: their incredibly priced afternoon and pre-theater suppers, where you can choose any two courses from the menu, including their special dishes prepared for two, which are prime rib, rack of lamb, whole roast pheasant, and grilled Dover sole. All main courses are garnished with potatoes and a vegetable. Considering where you are and the quality of the

PRICES
À la carte £12–16

SERVICE
Discretionary

TELEPHONE
020 7836 5314

FAX
020 7497 1081

EMAIL
info@rules.co.uk

INTERNET
www.rules.co.uk

OPEN
Daily

CLOSED
A few days at Christmas (dates vary)

HOURS
Noon–midnight, continuous service

RESERVATIONS
Essential

CREDIT CARDS
AE, DC, MC, V

PRICES
À la carte £40–48; set-price Mon–Fri 3–5 P.M. (except in Dec) £22.95 any 2 courses

SERVICE
Discretionary; 12.5% service charge for 6 or more

food, the service, and the magnificent surroundings, this has to qualify as one of London's better gourmet Great Eats. This set-price meal is available Monday to Friday from 3 to 5 P.M. throughout the year, with the exception of December.

SALSA! (19)
96 Charing Cross Road, Soho, WC2
Tube: Tottenham Court Road

TELEPHONE
020 7379 3277
OPEN
Mon–Sat dinner only
CLOSED
Sun, holidays
HOURS
5:30 P.M.–2 A.M.; meals served Mon–Thur 5:30 P.M.–12:30 A.M., Fri–Sat until 1:30 A.M.
RESERVATIONS
Essential for 6 or more, strongly advised otherwise
CREDIT CARDS
MC, V
PRICES
À la carte £15–25; set-price £16–22 per person (4-person minimum), selection of tapas
SERVICE
10% service charge; no cover charge before 7 P.M., after 8 P.M. £2–8 cover charge per person (depends on time you arrive)

Salsa! is one hot ticket—a South America–themed restaurant that draws the young, the bold, and the beautiful. These stylish patrons sample tapas, sip exotic cocktails, and dance the night away. There are live bands six nights a week, a six-foot-by-six-foot video screen and satellite TV, and a DJ with a sixteen-channel sound mixer. For those who need to brush up their rusty sambas, lambadas, bossa novas, or merengues, there are dance lessons between 6:30 and 9 P.M. every night. If it's rhythmic and sexy, they dance to it here, and believe me, after a pitcher or two of margaritas or a few San Miguel beers, the place is alive, moving, and uninhibited. The live music starts at 9 P.M., and there may be queues. However, if you are here before 7 P.M., there are no lines, no cover charges, and you can partake of the 40-percent-off Happy Hour drinks (5:30 to 8:30 P.M. Monday to Friday), with a dance lesson thrown in. For the best effect, go with a group and spend the evening munching on chips, dips, mini tortillas, potato skins, grilled chorizo, fried calamari, Cuban spiced fish cakes, barbecued riblets, and tiny fajitas. During busy times there is a minimum charge of £10 per person seated at a table and a limit of two hours at the table. When your time is up, just head for the bar and dance till you drop.

If you are in the neighborhood during the day, drop by the Salsa Café, open 8 A.M.–6 P.M. Monday to Saturday for coffee, sandwiches, pastries, fruit juices, and milk shakes.

SEVEN ($, 49)
1 Leicester Square, WC2
Tube: Leicester Square

TELEPHONE
020 7909 1177
FAX
020 7909 1178
INTERNET
www.homecorp.com
OPEN
Mon–Sat

Seven is on the seventh floor of this corner building right on Leicester Square. Getting to the restaurant is formidable: unless you have a reservation, you won't get beyond the secret-service-type door guard, who confirms your reservation by phone, then admits you to the bank of elevators, which whisk you to the restaurant. Once there, the view is sheer seventh heaven, especially at night or on a clear, warm London day, when you can sit ringside on the terrace and have a bird's-eye view of everything from Westminster Abbey to the Houses of Parliament, St. Martin-in-the-Fields, St. Paul's, and the London Eye. If you can't brave the elements, try for a window seat inside. No promises are made concerning table location, but I found that going when they open is the best way to nab a prime spot.

So the view and the surroundings are stunning . . . what about the food? While not Michelin star material, it is definitely good, straightforward, and worth a second trip. The set-price menus offer imaginative dishes that do not taste, look, or make you feel *budget* in any way. Consider a choice between crab bisque or a butternut risotto with roasted tomatoes and basil oil to begin. Follow with a duck confit, garnished with grilled chicory and sautéed potatoes, and for the finale, either a slice of ginger and vanilla cake or *fondant au chocolat* with ice cream, all for less than the price of a front-row seat to the latest London must-see theater production. Ordering à la carte will naturally bump the bill into the Big Splurge category, but I think grilled sea scallops on a bed of herbed risotto, stuffed saddle of lamb, or Dover sole with artichokes and cèpes are definitely worth the added investment.

SMOLLENSKY'S ON THE STRAND (51)
105 The Strand, Covent Garden, WC2
Tube: Charing Cross

Looking for a great place to take your family for a treat? The American-owned and -inspired Smollensky's is the ticket. Providing a taste of home for all ages, it will surely offer something for every member of your party. Starting with the small fry, the children's menu is highlighted by its own cocktail list, main courses, desserts, and milk shakes. On weekends from noon to 3 P.M., entertainers and special events keep the kids busy; at 2:30 on Saturday, all the little ones are invited for a Punch and Judy show, and on Sunday to a magic show. There is also a clown who paints willing faces, free helium balloons, and a variety of T-shirts for sale. If that isn't enough, there is also a play area for tots under seven and Nintendo games for the older ones.

For the grown-ups, there are two sets of live jazz on Sunday evenings starting at 8:15 P.M., with a £5 cover

CLOSED
Sat lunch, Sun, holidays

HOURS
Mon–Fri lunch noon–2:45 P.M.; Mon–Sat dinner 6–11:45 P.M.

RESERVATIONS
Absolutely essential

CREDIT CARDS
AE, MC, V (a credit card guarantee is taken for parties of 5 or more)

PRICES
À la carte: £30–38; set-price lunch, pre-theater dinner (6–7 P.M.): £17 2 courses, £20 3 courses

SERVICE
12.5% service charge

TELEPHONE
020 7497 2101

FAX
020 7836 3720

INTERNET
www.smollenskys.co.uk

OPEN
Daily

CLOSED
2 or 3 days at Christmas

HOURS
Mon–Wed noon–midnight, Thur–Sat noon–12:30 A.M., Sun noon–5:30 P.M. and 6:30–10:30 P.M.; special children's events Sat–Sun noon–3 P.M.

RESERVATIONS
Advised, especially on weekends for children's events; essential on Sun nights for jazz if you want to see the stage

charge. From Monday to Saturday nights at 7 P.M. there is a piano player (no cover charge), and on Thursday, Friday, and Saturday nights, DJ dancing starts at 10 P.M., again with no cover charge.

Mom and Dad can relax Monday through Saturday from 5:30 to 8 P.M. during the half-price Happy Hour, then slip into a comfortable banquette and enjoy one of the main draws on the menu: perfectly grilled steak served with one of eight sauces and golden-fried potatoes. Dieters must beware of the dazzling dessert lineup, starring a large bowl of Erna's chocolate mousse. If you finish your first helping, there is no charge for the second.

Don't forget Smollensky's when looking for a place to celebrate Valentine's Day, Halloween, and Thanksgiving, when special three-course menus are offered.

NOTE: There is a nonsmoking policy on Saturday and Sunday from noon to 3 P.M., during the children's activities.

CREDIT CARDS
AE, DC, MC, V
PRICES
À la carte £20–26, children £8–10
SERVICE
£5 cover charge on Sun evening whether eating, drinking, or listening to the jazz; service discretionary

SOFRA–TAVISTOCK STREET (42)
36 Tavistock Street, Covent Garden, WC2
Tube: Covent Garden

See Sofra–Mayfair in W1, page 65, for a full description. All other information is the same.

TELEPHONE: 020 7240 3773/3972

TOKYO DINER (35)
2 Newport Place, Chinatown, WC2
Tube: Leicester Square

The Tokyo Diner is a reliable outpost of Japanese food in London. The concept is carried out in a simple bi-level interior, where the speedy turnover allows diners to enjoy affordable, satisfying food that is freshly prepared to order. They have a no-tips policy and are open 365 days a year from noon until midnight.

The menu is explicit, with each dish and its history explained. *Donburi* are one-course meals starring Japanese rice with a variety of toppings, including soft-cooked eggs. *Bento* meals are featured—these are box lunches served in sectioned dishes filled with noodles, rice, sashimi, pickles, and perhaps one or two other tidbits. Curries, sushi, seasonal dishes, and soba and udon noodles with countless toppings can be washed down with Kirin beer, sake, or Japanese tea. Slurping is encouraged, at least when it comes to eating the noodles.

NOTE: There is a nonsmoking section.

TELEPHONE
020 7287 8777
OPEN
Daily
CLOSED
Never
HOURS
Noon–midnight, continuous service
RESERVATIONS
Not accepted
CREDIT CARDS
MC, V
PRICES
À la carte £7–11
SERVICE
No service charged or expected

WOLFE'S (23)
30 Great Queen Street, Covent Garden, WC2
Tube: Covent Garden

Wolfe's is just around the corner from the New London Theater on Drury Lane, where the musical *Cats* has been performed for years. It is a very smart, clubby sort of place, with dark paneling, upholstered banquette seating, little table lights, a mirrored ceiling, and a long bar at which the singles seem to greet, drink, and eat, hoping to meet someone interesting. Most of the staff, headed by friendly Nick, have been serving the loyal patrons for more than twenty years.

Long recognized as the salvation of many a famished diner, Wolfe's is best enjoyed for what it is: a great place for a cooked-to-order designer hamburger, a large salad, or a guilt-inspiring dessert. If you wander too far from these choices, prices increase significantly. The big draw has always been the Wolfeburger, which is removed from the fast-food ghetto thanks to the quality of the naturally fed Scottish beef and the charbroiling cooking process. You can have yours bare (without its toasted sesame seed bun), but with a generous helping of cottage cheese and a salad instead. Or, step up to the Continental Wolfeburger, accessorized with fresh vegetable puree and your choice of potato garnish—creamed, baked, fried, or croquettes. The chef recommends ordering the hamburgers to be cooked "medium" and reminds you that they are not in the fast-food business; therefore, please allow them more time to prepare your food properly. For the under-twelve set, Wolfe's has a children's menu with a small Wolfeburger or fried eggs with french fries and a salad. For everyone, there is a page devoted to desserts, with a dozen or more ice-cream creations, along with cakes, pies, tarts, and the unbelievably good specialty, a Waffle-Wolfe: two scoops of vanilla ice cream sandwiched between warm waffles and smothered in hot chocolate and whipped cream.

TELEPHONE
020 7831 4442

INTERNET
www.wolfes-grill.com

OPEN
Daily

CLOSED
2 days at Christmas

HOURS
Mon–Sat noon–midnight, Sun 1–8 P.M., continuous service

RESERVATIONS
Advised

CREDIT CARDS
AE, DC, MC, V

PRICES
À la carte: £15–20; set-price: £12 lunch, dinner £13 any 2 courses

SERVICE
No service charge for bills under £40, 12.5% service charge for bills over £40

YOUNG CHENG (48)
22 Lisle Street, Leicester Square, WC2
Tube: Leicester Square

This is the dressier version of the Young Cheng Shaftesbury Avenue location (see page 76). It has polished floors and comfortable seats, the waitstaff are dressed in black pants, white shirts, and maroon vests, and you will pay slightly higher prices. The window is lined with dripping ducks, and you can see the cooking

TELEPHONE
020 7287 3045

OPEN
Daily

CLOSED
Christmas Day

HOURS
Noon–midnight, continuous service

RESERVATIONS
Not necessary
CREDIT CARDS
AE, MC, V
PRICES
À la carte £7–10; set-price
£9–15
SERVICE
Discretionary

and chopping going on in front of you. The food is just as good as on Shaftesbury Avenue: try the crab, lobster, or crispy duck served with Mandarin pancakes and hoisin sauce, or for a much cheaper eat, the rice with pork spareribs, or beef, all for less than £9. While here, check out the Chinese herbalist and dental clinic two doors away—things haven't changed in this shop for centuries.

Pubs

LAMB AND FLAG (37)
33 Rose Street (off Garrick Street), Covent Garden, WC2
Tube: Covent Garden

TELEPHONE
020 7497 9504
OPEN
Daily
CLOSED
Christmas Day
HOURS
Pub: Mon–Thurs 11 A.M.–
11 P.M., Fri–Sat until 10:45 P.M.,
Sun noon–10:30 P.M.; food
service: daily noon–3 P.M.
RESERVATIONS
Not necessary
CREDIT CARDS
None
PRICES
Sandwiches from £4, daily
specials and roasts from £7.50
SERVICE
No service charged or expected

The Lamb and Flag is a pub that has remained largely unchanged since it opened in 1772 and was called the Coopers Arm. Later it became the Bucket of Blood, after the poet John Dryden was attacked out in front. Today it is quiet, and just hidden enough to escape the Covent Garden hordes. Its charm lies in its old wooden floors and wainscoted walls. Hot pub food is served for lunch daily, the fare consisting of toasties and doorstops (each is a type of pub sandwich), a ploughman's plate, and a roast. No food is served at night, but on Sunday evenings, live Dixieland jazz keeps the place hopping.

THE SHERLOCK HOLMES (54)
10 Northumberland Street, Charing Cross, WC2
Tube: Charing Cross, Embankment

TELEPHONE
020 7930 2644
FAX
020 7839 5864
EMAIL
sherlock@popmail.dircon.co.uk
INTERNET
www.sherlock.dircon.co.uk
OPEN
Daily
CLOSED
Christmas Day

No self-respecting Sherlock Holmes devotee will be able to resist this pub, a shrine to the great detective and his creator, Sir Arthur Conan Doyle. Inside are countless mementos that will thrill any fan, including photos of famous actors who have played the role of the sleuth on stage and screen. The first-floor restaurant has a perfect replica of Holmes and Watson's cluttered 221B Baker Street study, with its book-lined walls, Holmes's deerstalker hat and cloak hanging on a hook, handcuffs, a syringe, a sofa covered with the detective's papers, and a model of the man himself. Why is a pub so devoted to

Sherlock Holmes so far from Baker Street? As all real Holmes buffs will tell you, this was the site of the Northumberland Hotel, which is mentioned in the novel *The Hound of the Baskervilles.* Naturally, there are Holmes T-shirts and memorabilia for sale.

One must be reminded that this is a pub, and food and drink are served. Downstairs is primarily for basic pub food, sandwiches, and serious drinking. The upstairs serves proper meals in a more formal setting. The mainly English-based dishes are named after characters and places in the stories and reflect slightly better cooking than you will find in most pubs. In the summer, tables and umbrellas are set up outside.

HOURS
Bar: Mon–Sat 11 A.M.–11 P.M., Sun noon–10:30 P.M.; pub food: Mon–Sat noon–10 P.M., Sun noon–2:30 P.M. and 6–10 P.M.; restaurant: Mon–Thur noon–3 P.M. and 5:30–10 P.M., Fri–Sun continuous service noon–10 P.M.

RESERVATIONS
Advised for restaurant only

CREDIT CARDS
MC, V

PRICES
Pub: à la carte £7–9; restaurant: £12–20, minimum charge £8

SERVICE
Discretionary in restaurant, no service charged or expected in pub

Tearooms, Pâtisseries, and Bakeries

CAFÉ VALERIE–COVENT GARDEN (32)
8 Russell Street, Covent Garden, WC2
Tube: Covent Garden

See Pâtisserie Valerie in W1, page 79, for a full description. Café Valerie faces the Piazza at Covent Garden. It began as a bookstore and tearoom in 1725 and was a meeting place for London's literati, including the diarist Mr. James Boswell, who met the famous Dr. Samuel Johnson here for tea in 1763.

TELEPHONE: 020 7240 0064
OPEN: Daily
CLOSED: Christmas Day
HOURS: Mon–Sat 7:30 A.M.–11 P.M., Sun 9 A.M.–6 P.M., continuous service

Wine Bars

CORK AND BOTTLE (47)
44–46 Cranbourn Street (off Leicester Square), Soho, WC2
Tube: Leicester Square

New Zealander Don Hewitson was one of the first to introduce Londoners to the wine bar, and his has become a legend, attracting connoisseurs who appreciate reasonably priced and consistently good food and wine in pleasant surroundings. Please do not let the location,

TELEPHONE
020 7734 7807

FAX
020 7636 1110

EMAIL
Don_Shiraz@hotmail.co.uk

INTERNET
www.donhewitsonlondon winebars.com

OPEN
Daily
CLOSED
Christmas Day, New Year's
Day
HOURS
Mon–Sat 11 A.M.–midnight, Sun
noon–10:30 P.M., continuous
service
RESERVATIONS
Accepted only before 12:45 P.M.
for lunch and before 6:30 P.M.
for dinner
CREDIT CARDS
AE, DC, MC, V
PRICES
À la carte £10–15; set-price
lunch £11 2 courses, £13 3
courses
SERVICE
Discretionary

between a greasy spoon and a sex shop, deter you. Once down the stairs and in the basement, with its poster- and print-covered walls, you will rub elbows with an attractive crowd that always returns to this oasis of style just off Leicester Square.

One of the most popular dishes is a simple one: a layered ham and cheese pie, similar to a quiche, but don't tell Don I told you this—he has a fit when it is referred to as a quiche. He calls it "our renowned raised ham and cheese pie." The Cork and Bottle homemade burger with salsa, chips, and a salad; a half dozen oysters; hot spicy sausages; hot and cold specials; or Don's spicy chicken and apple salad satisfy the lunch and dinner crowd, and wines from all over the world keep the drinkers happy. On Sunday, turn up for the brunch, which offers bucks fizz, smoked salmon, scrambled eggs, green salad, and a selection of cheeses. Don even does dessert. I haven't been able to stray from the chocolate fudge pie, but the vanilla ice cream with honeycomb butterscotch sauce is always tempting.

If you like the Cork and Bottle, you will also like Don's Hanover Square Wine Bar and Grill, near Oxford and New Bond Streets in W1 (see page 84).

SW1

Belgravia, Knightsbridge, Pimlico, and Victoria

The Duke of Westminster owns two prime portions of London: Mayfair and Belgravia, both of which are vying for "most expensive real estate" status. Belgravia, which is between Sloane Street and Buckingham Palace Gardens, was originally an area that housed servants of Buckingham Palace. Today it's a quiet, dignified neighborhood with ten acres of private gardens in its center. The houses and flats are painted in the same cream and white colors and were built by Thomas Cubitt in the 1820s. Warning: Belgrave Road leading away from Victoria Station is not a good stretch of road. It is full of sleazy B&Bs that, with a few exceptions (see *Great Sleeps London*), should be avoided, no matter how slim your budget is.

The Mall is the beautiful processional leading up to the gates of Buckingham Palace, where tourists gather faithfully each day hoping to catch sight of one of the royals or to watch the changing of the guard. You will know if the queen is in residence if you see the royal standard flying. Nearby is St. James's Place, which was built by King Henry VIII and is the place where the death of the former sovereign and the accession of the new one is announced. It is also the London home of Prince Charles. All foreign ambassadors are accredited to "the Court of St. James's," but the palace is not open to the public. St. James's Park has all anyone could wish for in a royal park, including pelicans descended from a pair given to Charles II.

Pimlico is far from tourist central, but it does have its admirers, especially those looking for a quiet area close to the River Thames and the Tate Britain, as well as antiques buffs who enjoy the shops along Pimlico Road where it meets Lower Sloane Street.

In the forecourt of Victoria Station is London's largest tourist information center. The area around the station is not known for its sights, fine restaurants, or entertainment value, but there are many good, inexpensive B&Bs around Victoria Station, notably on Ebury Street (see *Great Sleeps London*).

Westminster is the small section of London containing the Houses of Parliament, Big Ben, and Westminster

SW1

1 Stockpot–Panton Street
2 Café Flo
3 Getti
4 The West End Kitchen
5 Red Lion
6 Wagamama
7 YO! Sushi
8 Osteria d'Isola ($)
9 The Grenadier
10 Zafferano ($)
11 Star Tavern
12 Mövenpick Marché
13 The Albert
14 The Footstool at St. John's Church
15 Jenny Lo's Tea House
16 The Green Cafe
17 Olivo ($)
18 Oliveto
19 Ebury Wine Bar
20 Seafresh
21 UNo 1
22 Capri Sandwich Bar
23 Grumbles
24 Chimes
25 Peter's Restaurant
26 Caraffini Restaurant ($)
27 The Orange Brewery
28 Roussillon ($)

HYDE PARK

MAYFAIR

The Serpentine

Serpentine Road

Rotten Row

Hyde Park Corner

HYDE PARK CORNER

Knightsbridge

LOWNDES SQUARE

BELGRAVE SQUARE

Brompton

HANS PL.

CADOGAN SQUARE

Sloane Street

EATON SQUARE

BELGRAVE

EBURY PL.

SLOANE SQUARE

DUKE OF YORK'S HEADQUARTERS

King's Road

Pimlico

RANELAGH GARDENS

Royal Hospital Road

Chelsea Bridge Road

0   220 yds
1/8 mile

Abbey. Whitehall is bureaucratic, governmental London. The prime minister lives at 10 Downing Street, and the chancellor of the exchequer at No. 11. New Scotland Yard, is here and so are the Cabinet War Rooms, from which Winston Churchill and his chiefs of staff directed the British efforts in World War II.

($) indicates a Big Splurge

Restaurants

CAFÉ FLO (2)
11 Haymarket, Piccadilly, SW1
Tube: Piccadilly Circus

For details on this branch of Café Flo, please see page 42. All other information is the same.

TELEPHONE: 020 7976 1313

CAPRI SANDWICH BAR (22)
16 Belgrave Road, Victoria, SW1
Tube: Victoria

Escape the food sleaze in and around Victoria Station and walk down Belgrave Road, where you will find the Capri Sandwich Bar, where the same family members have been working behind the counter since 1949. It doesn't look like much, with its four round tables, steamy windows, and assembly-line sandwich counter. A sandwich is a sandwich, you may say, but at the Capri, you will bite into upmarket exceptions. I like the toasted mozzarella and ham with sun-dried tomatoes, artichokes, and a dash of Dijon mustard, or the mozzarella-cheese number layered with tomatoes, olives, and fresh basil. Weekly sandwiches get top billing, and so do the Capri's homemade soups: smoky bacon and mushroom, potato and leek, and spinach and nutmeg. Peanut-butter fans can have their sandwich four ways: plain, or with honey, dates, or bananas. All the meats are roasted here, and the spreads are made here as well. If you don't want a sandwich, you can design your own filling for a jacket potato, order a salad or an onion and cheddar cheese omelette, or eat a jelly doughnut. The usual coffees are served, as are fruit juices.

NOTE: There is a nonsmoking section. Takeaway is available.

TELEPHONE
020 7834 1989
OPEN
Mon–Fri lunch only
CLOSED
Sat–Sun, holidays
HOURS
7 A.M.–3:30 P.M., continuous service
RESERVATIONS
Not accepted
CREDIT CARDS
None
PRICES
À la carte £2.50–7, minimum charge £3 during peak times
SERVICE
No service charged or expected

CARAFFINI RESTAURANT ($, 26)
61–63 Lower Sloane Street (corner of Holbein Mews), Sloane Square, SW1
Tube: Sloane Square

If you are not pinching your pence too hard, Caraffini, a short stroll from Sloane Square, offers contemporary Italian cuisine prepared with imagination and a knowing hand. Despite the bare floors and crowded dinner atmosphere, the restaurant looks, feels, and is elegant, thanks to the tables, which are beautifully set with crisp linens, heavy cutlery, sparkling crystal, and fresh flowers.

TELEPHONE
020 7259 0235
OPEN
Mon–Sat
CLOSED
Sun, holidays
HOURS
Lunch 12:15–2:30 P.M., dinner 6:30–11:30 P.M.

RESERVATIONS
Essential
CREDIT CARDS
AE, MC, V
PRICES
À la carte £26–35
SERVICE
£1.25 cover charge, service
discretionary

The service, by a waitstaff wearing black pants and blue shirts, is professional yet friendly, and is appreciated by the smartly dressed Chelsea patrons.

The menu offers tantalizing choices, such as tiger prawns in hot chili and olive oil, mixed wild mushrooms with polenta, and a beef carpaccio with spinach and fresh Parmesan for starters. Seasonally, the choices reflect the best of the market. In the spring, I love the fresh artichoke with garlic mayonnaise and the tuna with *borlotto* (kidney) beans and raw onions as out-of-the-ordinary starters. The grilled baby chicken with fresh rosemary and the fresh salmon with ginger, spring onion, and soy sauce are both top sellers. So is the simply grilled calf's liver with sage and the rack of lamb with a crust of fresh herbs. There are plenty of pastas to try, and a trio of risottos. If you like truffles, Caraffini's will make you want to return often just for this dish. Don't overlook the desserts, which are all made here and are perfectly balanced to end this special meal on a sweet note.

CHIMES (24)
26 Churton Street, Pimlico, SW1
Tube: Pimlico

TELEPHONE
020 7821 7456
OPEN
Daily
CLOSED
2 to 3 days at Christmas, New Year's Day
HOURS
Lunch noon–2:30 P.M., dinner 6–10:15 P.M.
RESERVATIONS
Suggested for dinner and for Sunday lunch
CREDIT CARDS
AE, MC, V
PRICES
À la carte: £10–22; set-price: dinner £13.95 2 courses, Sunday-roast lunch £11
SERVICE
Discretionary, 10% service charge for 6 or more

Over the years, English food has had a bad rap, and no wonder. Overdone meats swimming in gluey gravy, served with mushy peas, soggy chips, limp carrots—it was a cuisine that seemed as cold and gray as the London fog. But after one meal at Chimes, where you will mix with locals eager to dip into a memorable, delicious bite of their heritage, your faith will be rapidly restored, and your opinions are guaranteed to change.

The long menu makes for some interesting reading, mostly for its variety of individual meat pies. There is the West Country, which is cidered cod and haddock with tomatoes, mushrooms, and parsley; the chicken pie, with celery and almonds in a sherry and cream sauce, with a puff pastry lid; the fidget pie, made with ham, potato, onion, and apple; or the Gloucestershire lamb pie, with fresh rosemary and apples served with a short-crust top. These, plus a host of monthly specials based on old English recipes and a traditional Sunday-roast lunch, have made Chimes a smart destination for those looking for the real thing in English food. Chimes also stocks a variety of draft ciders from major independent producers and many fruit wines, including elderflower, damson, plum, and raspberry. For dessert, the puddings are a must, especially the orange treacle tart, served with dairy cream or hot custard.

A nice thing to remember about Chimes is that you can come here either for a full meal in the upstairs dining room or have only a glass or two of their unusual wines or ciders and eat a light meal at the wine bar in front.

NOTE: No beer is served. There is a downstairs dining room, which is usually used for private parties.

THE FOOTSTOOL AT ST. JOHN'S CHURCH (14)
Smith Square, Westminster, SW1
Tube: Westminster, St. James's Park

St. John's Church on Smith Square is considered one of the masterpieces of English Baroque architecture. Since its completion in the early 1700s, it has survived fires, lightning, bombs, and plans to tear it down. Now, thanks to the efforts of the Friends of St. John's, the church has been beautifully restored and is at the forefront of London's cultural and musical life. The church is the setting for a heavily subscribed concert series with afternoon and evening performances by noted artists.

The Footstool restaurant is in the crypt of the church. Lunch caters to two sorts of pocketbook. You have the choice of going through a self-service buffet line and selecting from hot and cold dishes, salads, baked potatoes with assorted fillings, and a range of tempting desserts. Or you can sit at one of the formally set tables and order from the menu, which changes monthly. On concert evenings only, a preordered, prepaid set-price meal will be laid out for you at a table complete with flowers and candles. What better way to relax from the rigors of the day than to dine in one of the most beautiful churches in London, enjoy a nice meal with a glass of wine, and then listen to a beautiful concert?

TELEPHONE
020 7222 2779

OPEN
Mon–Fri lunch only; dinner on concert evenings only

CLOSED
Sat–Sun, holidays unless there is a concert, week between Christmas and New Year's

HOURS
Lunch 11:30 A.M.–2:45 P.M., dinner 6–10 P.M. on concert evenings only

RESERVATIONS
Advised for the à la carte restaurant lunch, essential by noon for concert evenings (by noon Fri for weekend concerts)

CREDIT CARDS
AE, MC, V

PRICES
À la carte: lunch only restaurant £18–24, buffet £7–12; set-price: concert dinners only £14 2 courses, £16 3 courses, both including coffee

SERVICE
Discretionary, 12.5% service charge for 6 or more

GETTI (3)
16–17 Jermyn Street, Piccadilly, SW1
Tube: Piccadilly Circus

Please see page 53 for details. All other information is the same.

TELEPHONE: 020 7734 7924
FAX: 020 7734 7924
OPEN: Daily, including holidays
CLOSED: 2 days at Christmas
HOURS: Lunch noon–3 P.M., dinner 6–10:30 P.M.

THE GREEN CAFE (16)
16 Eccleston Street, Belgravia, SW1
Tube: Victoria

TELEPHONE
020 7730 5304
OPEN
Mon–Fri; Sat breakfast only
CLOSED
Sat afternoon and evening, Sun, holidays
HOURS
Mon–Fri 6 A.M.–6:30 P.M., Sat 6:30 A.M.–noon, continuous service
RESERVATIONS
Not accepted
CREDIT CARDS
None
PRICES
À la carte £3.50–7
SERVICE
No service charged or expected

A London cabbie told me he has been eating at the Green Cafe for almost forty years. That was all I needed to know to make it a top Great Eating priority for the day. Nostalgia buffs will be glad I did. The Fioris family has been opening the door to this little hole-in-the-wall since 1955, treating everyone not just as paying customers, but as members of their extended family. Brother Andrew has now retired, but John is still here, running the upstairs operation while his cousin holds the fort in the kitchen downstairs.

Only seven tables are set in the green room, which is usually filled with beefy working-class regulars diving into a multitude of sandwiches, heartburn-inducing hot specials, and that holy grail of grease: the full English breakfast. If you order with wild abandon, you will probably have a hard time spending more than £6 or £7. Avoid any soup other than the homemade minestrone, as the rest are straight from Heinz. Do consider the house specialty, spaghetti Bolognese, or any of the sandwiches, which are made on bread baked by the family. The puddings may not be worth an extra half hour on the treadmill, but I love their jam roll with custard or their rhubarb crumble.

NOTE: Takeaway is available, but alcohol is not.

GRUMBLES (23)
35 Churton Street (off Belgrave Road), Pimlico, SW1
Tube: Pimlico

TELEPHONE
020 7834 0149
FAX
020 7834 0298
OPEN
Daily
CLOSED
3 days at Christmas, New Year's Day, Good Friday
HOURS
Lunch: Mon–Sat noon–2:30 P.M., Sun noon–3 P.M.; dinner: Mon–Sat 6–11 P.M., Sun 6–10:30 P.M.
RESERVATIONS
Advised for dinner
CREDIT CARDS
AE, DC, MC, V

Smart Great Eaters pack the tables every lunch and dinner at Grumbles, which serves good food and wine at noninflationary prices. The pine-paneled walls and closely packed bare wood tables and chairs create an informal look that is softened in the evening by fresh flowers and candles on each table, even those in the almost-airless basement. The best part about eating in the basement is viewing the display of old photos of Grumbles employees on the stairway wall going down.

The food leans toward French provincial, with the odd English dish and Sunday-roast lunch. Starters range from a simple soup of the day or a watercress, bacon, and avocado salad to snails in garlic or duck-liver parfait flavored with port wine. Meat lovers have loads of choices, ranging from steak to chicken to and lamb.

Vegetarians will have few worries with the spinach and Parmesan cheese pancakes with tomato sauce and cheese topping. Grumbles' fish cakes and fresh fish catches are constant favorites, and so are the desserts, which are all made here and loaded with guilty calories. Weekly wines are always featured.

PRICES
À la carte: £18–22; set-price (lunch only): Mon–Sat £11 2 courses, £14 3 courses; Sun £13 2 courses, £15 3 courses

SERVICE
£1 cover charge, 10% service charge

JENNY LO'S TEA HOUSE (15)
14 Eccleston Street, Belgravia, SW1
Tube: Victoria

Noodle houses are currently high on the list for healthy eating in London. The daughter of the late Ken Lo has set up shop on her own, around the corner from what was once her father's famous restaurant. The action at Jenny's takes place in a bright room with red-and-purple-lacquered walls, black tables, and simple chairs, all offset by a tank of live fish. The placemat-menu is a simple listing of what they offer: either rice, noodle soup, or wok-fried noodles topped with combinations of duck, pork, chicken, vegetables, seafood, beef, curry, herbs, and seasonings. No MSG is used in the kitchen. There are fourteen side dishes—including spring rolls, pickled vegetables, and crisp seaweed—and three desserts. To drink, you have a choice of chrysanthemum and mint herbal teas, or a cleansing tea, which has been blended by a qualified Chinese herbalist for strengthening the liver and kidneys.

TELEPHONE
020 7259 0399

OPEN
Mon–Sat

CLOSED
Sun, holidays

HOURS
Lunch: Mon–Fri 11:30 A.M.–3 P.M., Sat noon–3 P.M.; dinner: Mon–Sat 6–10 P.M.

RESERVATIONS
Not accepted

CREDIT CARDS
None

PRICES
À la carte £7–14, minimum charge £5 per person

SERVICE
Discretionary

MÖVENPICK MARCHÉ (12)
Portland House, Bressenden Place, Victoria Station, SW1
Tube: Victoria

The Mövenpick Marché is housed in a modern glass structure known as the Portland House. You enter at the street level and go downstairs to what looks like a big, open food market with fresh fruit and produce displayed throughout. Each stand is a food-serving area. There is no set-price menu and no set time to eat. Just come as you please and have whatever turns on your taste buds. Once you have decided what to eat, your meal is cooked for you while you wait. You select your food from a huge variety of cheeses and cold meats, antipasti, salads, pastas and *rösti*, stir-frys, grilled meat and fish, raclette (dinner only), pastries to die for, and the creamiest ice creams you can imagine. Guests record their food selections on a personal checkout ticket that becomes their bill.

TELEPHONE
020 7630 1733

OPEN
Daily

CLOSED
Christmas Day, some holidays (call to check)

HOURS
Market: Mon–Sat 11 A.M.–11 P.M., Sun 11 A.M.–9 P.M., continuous service; coffee shop: Mon–Sat 7:30 A.M.–11 P.M.

RESERVATIONS
Accepted for large parties only

CREDIT CARDS
AE, DC, MC, V

PRICES
À la carte £7–17

SERVICE
No service charged or expected

A stylish bar designed as a sailing ship offers a Happy Hour from 5 to 7 P.M. nightly. Live music entertains patrons from 7 to 10 P.M. Thursday through Saturday evenings. There is also a coffee shop by the entrance, but I think the draw at Mövenpick is the market.

Even if you do not eat at this Mövenpick, you positively must stop by and use the ladies' or men's toilets. I know this sounds odd, but I promise you they win the sweepstakes for the most fantasy-filled, amusing, and imaginative public loos in Great Britain. I will say no more, other than don't miss these WCs, please.

NOTE: There is a nonsmoking section. Fresh produce and gourmet goodies are for sale.

OLIVETO (18)
49 Elizabeth Street, Belgravia, SW1
Tube: Victoria

TELEPHONE
020 7730 0074
OPEN
Daily
CLOSED
Christmas Day
HOURS
Mon–Fri lunch noon–3 P.M.,
Sat–Sun until 4 P.M., dinner
daily 7–11:30 P.M.
RESERVATIONS
Advised
CREDIT CARDS
AE, MC, V
PRICES
À la carte £18–24
SERVICE
Discretionary

At Oliveto—the pizza and pasta spin-off of Olivo (see next listing)—the food is amazing for the price, especially considering the high-rent area. It is served in an uncomplicated yet chic room where only paper napkins, salt and pepper shakers, and a cruet of garlic or hot-pepper-infused olive oil grace the bare tables. The locals flock here, and during prime feeding hours, the two harried waiters covering the twenty-five tables need track shoes and stamina to withstand the high-density crunch. The all-Italian menu confines itself to a few well-chosen starters, a half dozen pastas, twice as many pizzas, and desserts guaranteed to keep cholesterol levels raised to the max.

OLIVO ($, 17)
21 Eccleston Street, Belgravia, SW1
Tube: Victoria

TELEPHONE
020 7730 2505
OPEN
Mon–Fri; Sat–Sun dinner only
CLOSED
Sat–Sun lunch, holidays
HOURS
Lunch noon–2:30 P.M., dinner
7–11 P.M.
RESERVATIONS
Essential for both lunch and
dinner
CREDIT CARDS
AE, MC, V

Olivo is a modern Italian restaurant that has been a success since the day it opened, thanks to its delicious, constantly changing menu. For the effort and ingredients put into every dish, it is an excellent value (especially at lunch), and you have to take your hat off to the imagination and ambition of the chef. The strikingly simple interior has bright royal blue and gold walls with a marigold-stenciled strip dividing the middle. Heavy cutlery and a small vase of fresh flowers rest atop paper-covered tables.

The lunch caters to office workers, offering a set-price menu geared toward fast, good meals for those with time and budget limits. But lunch can also be a madhouse, with hungry patrons standing about and the frenzied staff trying to oblige. The pace is more leisurely at night, when only an à la carte menu is available. As the evening wears on, however, a crescendo builds, and by 10 P.M., every table is taken and the restaurant is in full swing again.

The food has a Sardinian influence, making it appealing to those who like zing in their flavorings. Two good beginnings are the air-dried tuna tossed with green beans and sun-dried tomatoes or the dish of colorful char-grilled vegetables with olive oil, chili, and basil. Pasta portions are flexible; you can either order them as main courses or dine daintily on them as starters. In April and May, watch for *tagliatelle alle cozze e asparagi* (fresh tagliatelle with mussels and asparagus) or *linguine al granchio* (linguine with fresh crab, garlic, and chili). In the late fall and winter you will find pheasant ravioli, a lusty oxtail casserole cooked in red wine and served with polenta, and a flavorful marinated lamb steak. To finish in style, Italian style that is, order *sebada,* a traditional Sardinian pastry filled with sweet cheese and dressed with honey.

PRICES
À la carte: £25–35; set-price (lunch only): £17 2 courses, £19 3 courses

SERVICE
£1.50 cover charge, service discretionary

OSTERIA D'ISOLA ($, 8)
145 Knightsbridge, Knightsbridge, SW1
Tube: Knightsbridge

Oliver Peyton's Isola opened to rave reviews and quickly became the fashionable dining destination in Knightsbridge. The upper floor is a high-ticket restaurant, but in the downstairs *osteria,* an industrial-size, leather and chrome-mirrored space, the sufficiently sleek clientele pays half the price and has twice the fun. When you arrive, turn your attention to the vast wine list, which offers more than sixty-four Italian wines by the glass. You can also order a "wine flight," which is five tasting-size glasses of wine grouped into types, such as Chardonnay, Aromatic White, Powerful Reds, and Super Tuscans.

The food, fortunately, does not take a backseat to the excellent wines. For a trendy, light weekday lunch, order the *antipasti deliziosi,* a selection of eight daily changing appetizers, and on the weekends the *fine settimana,* a three-course brunch (children under ten are free). Wonderful pastas are served in three sizes: starter, main, or to share. They and the fresh fish, tender lamb shanks with

TELEPHONE
020 7838 1044

OPEN
Daily

CLOSED
2 days at Christmas

HOURS
Mon–Sat noon–11 P.M., Sun until 10:30 P.M., Sun brunch noon–3 P.M., continuous service

RESERVATIONS
Advised for Thur–Sat, Sun brunch

CREDIT CARDS
AE, DC, MC, V

PRICES
À la carte £28–35; set-price: lunch Mon–Fri *antipasti deliziosi* £11–16, brunch Sat–Sun, £22 (children under ten are free)

SERVICE
12.5% service charge

beans and a celery pesto, and desserts to die for make the Osteria d'Isola a stellar choice for Great Eats in Knightsbridge.

PETER'S RESTAURANT (25)
59 Pimlico Road, Belgravia, Sloane Square, SW1
Tube: Sloane Square

TELEPHONE
020 7730 5991
OPEN
Daily
CLOSED
Holidays
HOURS
Mon–Sat 6 A.M.–10 P.M.,
Sun 8 A.M.–4 P.M., continuous service
RESERVATIONS
Not accepted
CREDIT CARDS
None
PRICES
À la carte £4–8
SERVICE
Included

"Hey lady, anyone eating at Peter's should go into training, 'cause this ain't no sissy food!" barked the tattooed cabbie sharing my breakfast table the first time I ate here. He must have seen the look on my face as the waitress brought his breakfast platter, overflowing with sausage, bacon, beans, fried eggs, fried bread, grilled tomatoes, and mushrooms, accompanied by several cups of strong coffee and plenty of sugar. Lordy! Peter's has been feeding London cabbies for years and has become almost hallowed ground for the many regulars who risk their health to eat here. Salt, sugar, and caffeine are the holy trinity at this typical blue-collar café, where the artery-clogging grub is served in mountainous portions. You can order less than the burly regulars do, but beware: This is not the home of tea, toast, and crumpets. Nor is it a bastion of service with a smile. Some of the staff need definite attitude adjustments, and the sooner the better.

If you miss the breakfast grease-out, there is always lunch or dinner, when you can roll up your sleeves and dig into one of the daily Italian specials, one of Peter's popular chicken dishes, which come with potatoes and three vegetables, or the shepherd's pie, served in a casserole that would serve eight easily. Orders are placed at the counter, and when they are ready, the waiter or waitress shouts over everyone, "Who gets the fried liver?" You'll want to leave your mother-in-law home for this one, but if you are hungry and have no cholesterol or waistline worries, but a few in the cash department, Peter's is an experience you should not miss.

If you are interested in interior decorating and antiques, this stretch of Pimlico, leading into Sloane Square, is fertile hunting ground, with many noted shops, including Lord Linley's, which is across the street and down a few doors from Peter's. For those not up on the family tree of the current royals, Lord Linley is Princess Margaret's son.

NOTE: Restaurant is unlicensed; BYOB (no corkage fee).

ROUSSILLON ($, 28)
16 St. Barnabas Street, Pimlico, SW1
Tube: Sloane Square

Eating at Roussillon, in a quiet residential location not far from Sloane Square, is a very special treat. Inside, there is a casually elegant feel of a lovely French country home, with soft pastel shades and contemporary paintings. The rustic, high-quality French menu changes every two weeks and includes a garden menu (for dinner only) that will please any vegetarian gourmet. On a cold December evening, I like to start with either a watercress and sorrel soup or the caramelized carrots with Parmesan cheese, followed by poached organic duck eggs with thistle cream or the rich pumpkin risotto. Meat eaters and seafood lovers will love the grilled scallops on a bed of red chard, the roasted sea bass with braised chicory, capers, and olives, or the roasted fillet of Scottish venison with a black truffle and celery puree. Meat eaters, fish fanciers, and vegetarians alike will be united on their choices for a grand finale: either the delicately flavored pear soufflé or the velvety chocolate one. Wines are served by the glass or bottle, and the staff is very helpful in helping you to select the wine that best fits both your meal and your budget.

TELEPHONE
020 7730 5550

FAX
020 7824 8617

INTERNET
www.roussillon.co.uk

OPEN
Mon–Sat

CLOSED
Sat lunch, Sun, holidays

HOURS
Lunch Mon–Fri noon–2:30 P.M., dinner Mon–Sat 6:30–10:30 P.M.

RESERVATIONS
Essential

CREDIT CARDS
AE, DC, MC, V

PRICES
Set-price lunch: £16 2 courses, £20 3 courses; dinner: £31 2 courses, £37 3 courses, £44 4 courses; garden menu (dinner only): 3 courses £37

SERVICE
12.5% service charge

SEAFRESH (20)
80–81 Wilton Road at Warwick Road, Victoria, SW1
Tube: Victoria

Marios Leonidou is the second-generation family member at the helm of this popular fish-and-chips shop near Victoria Station. The fish is all fresh, the portions enormous, and the prices very much in the budget realm of Great Eats in London. Preparations of the usual standards are reliable and competent and can be ordered fried in a light ground-nut oil or grilled, accompanied by either chips or boiled potatoes. One of the house specialties, the seafood plate, consists of cod, haddock, plaice, skate, Scotch salmon, king prawns, shrimp scampi, and calamari. It is served all on one plate and all for one person. The homemade fresh-fish soup, made with chunks of whitefish, the prawns, the mussels, the Dover sole, and the deep-fried scampi are other specialties I can heartily recommend.

Spam fritters, pork sausage, southern-fried chicken, and jacket potatoes slathered with beans are also on the menu, but for goodness sakes, not here! Fish should definitely be your order at the Seafresh. If it is possible

TELEPHONE
020 7828 0747

OPEN
Mon–Sat

CLOSED
Sun, 2 weeks at Christmas and New Year's, holidays

HOURS
Noon–10:30 P.M., continuous service

RESERVATIONS
Not necessary

CREDIT CARDS
AE, MC, V

PRICES
À la carte £15–28

SERVICE
10% service charge

that you have room for dessert, any of the three house desserts—apple pie, chocolate cake, or sherry trifle, all swimming in cream—will ensure you probably won't be hungry for the next twenty-four hours.

STOCKPOT–PANTON STREET (1)
38 Panton Street, Piccadilly Circus, SW1
Tube: Piccadilly Circus

See Stockpot–Soho in W1, page 68, for a full description.

TELEPHONE: 020 7839 5142

TUBE: Piccadilly Circus

OPEN: Daily

CLOSED: Christmas Day

HOURS: Breakfast 7–11 A.M., lunch 11:30 A.M.–4:45 P.M., dinner 4:45–11:30 P.M.

RESERVATIONS: Not accepted

CREDIT CARDS: None

PRICES: À la carte: £6–10; set-price: English breakfast daily £5, lunch Mon–Fri £4 2 courses, Sat–Sun £7 3 courses, dinner daily £7 3 courses, minimum charge at peak times £2.50

SERVICE: Discretionary

UNo 1 (21)
Corner of Denbigh Street and Warwick Way, Pimlico, SW1
Tube: Victoria

TELEPHONE
020 7834 1001

OPEN
Mon–Sat

CLOSED
Sun, holidays

HOURS
Lunch noon–3 P.M., dinner 6:30–11:30 P.M.

RESERVATIONS
Advised after 8 P.M.

CREDIT CARDS
AE, MC, V

PRICES
À la carte £10–15; set-price: Mon–Fri lunch £14–16 3 courses including coffee

SERVICE
12.5% service charge for 5 or more, otherwise discretionary

While hardly destination dining, UNo 1 is a useful address to have if you are staying in one of the B&Bs along Warwick Way. It is also a friendly establishment, where singles don't feel out of place. I think it is especially nice in the summer, when you can sit outside on the shaded, protected sidewalk terrace that wraps around the corner site. At lunch it is filled with a business crowd of cute young things and their bosses. In the evening, tourists from the nearby hotels and B&Bs fill the first seating, with the locals arriving after 8 P.M. Popular antipasti are the *duetto di bruschette pugliese*—a duo of toasted ciabatta breads, one spread with tomato, olive oil, basil, and oregano and the other with sun-dried tomato, olive oil, and lots of garlic—and the *pane e companatico,* this time ciabatta bread served with a whole roasted garlic and four different dips. Variety of choice is the only problem with the dozen or more pastas, any of which can be customized to your own liking. The same goes for the pizzas. Also on board are the usual grilled meats and handful of fresh fish. The best thing I have to say about the desserts is, thank goodness the chef isn't responsible for the forgettable retinue.

WAGAMAMA (6)
Lower ground floor, Harvey Nichols, 109–125 Knightsbridge, SW1
Tube: Knightsbridge

Japanese food is well represented at Harvey Nicks, with YO! Sushi on the fifth floor and Wagamama in the basement. Wagamama wins my vote as the vastly better choice. For details, please see page 74.

TELEPHONE: 020 7201 8000
HOURS: Mon–Sat noon–11 P.M., Sun 12:30–10 P.M.

THE WEST END KITCHEN (4)
5 Panton Street, Piccadilly Circus, SW1
Tube: Piccadilly Circus

Every budget-minded diner in London soon learns about the Stockpot restaurants. The West End Kitchen, on the same block as a Stockpot, was opened by the original owner of the Stockpot chain after he had sold those restaurants and retired. Obviously, retirement did not suit him, and a new restaurant was the solution. The West End Kitchen follows the same penny-pinching formula as the Stockpots, with a twice-daily changing menu. The almost austere surroundings consist of pine booths with plastic seats (shared at crowded times) and white walls. A collection of the owner's *Spy* prints from 1911 and 1912 softens the antiseptic look to a degree. The no-surprise, basic menu includes a two- or three-course set-price lunch and dinner, both for less than £5. There are at least three choices for each course—say, soup of the day, smoked mackerel, or garlic bread to start; fish pie, grilled liver (check to see what animal it comes from), or vegetarian lasagna to follow; and rhubarb and apple pie with custard, Jell-O, or sponge pudding for dessert. Two cholesterol-loaded English breakfasts are available, both offering the usual high-calorie fry-up of eggs, sausage, bacon, beans, fried tomato, mushrooms, toast, and coffee. If the kitchen is known for any dish, it is the Lancashire Hotpot, a boyhood favorite cooked by the owner's mother. What is it? Basically, a mutton stew with root vegetables and potatoes; it's served only once a week.

TELEPHONE
020 7839 4241

OPEN
Daily

CLOSED
Christmas Day

HOURS
Breakfast 7–11:30 A.M., lunch 11:30–4:45 P.M., dinner 4:45–11:45 P.M.

RESERVATIONS
Not accepted

CREDIT CARDS
None

PRICES
À la carte £5–9; set-price: Mon–Fri lunch £4 2 courses, £5 3 courses, Sat–Sun lunch and nightly dinner £6

SERVICE
Discretionary

Considering the portion size and variety of food, the prices are terrifically cheap, but don't expect to eat for gourmet pleasure, but rather for sustenance.

YO! SUSHI (7)
Fifth Floor of Harvey Nichols, 109–125
Knightsbridge, SW1
Tube: Knightsbridge

This YO! Sushi is on the fifth floor of Harvey Nichols, the famous Knightsbridge luxury store. YO!—what a joke. On my last visit, all the sushi chefs were British, and everything was on view in the exhibition kitchen, including the dishwasher and food trash. Nevertheless, the place was packed. YO!—go figure.

See page 75 for a full description. All other information is the same.

TELEPHONE: 020-7201 8641

HOURS: Mon–Sat noon–11 P.M., Sun noon–6 P.M.

ZAFFERANO ($, 10)
15 Lowndes Street, Belgravia, SW1
Tube: Knightsbridge

TELEPHONE
020 7235 5800

OPEN
Mon–Sat

CLOSED
Sun, holidays

HOURS
Lunch noon–2:30 P.M., dinner
7–11 P.M.

RESERVATIONS
Essential as far in advance as
possible

CREDIT CARDS
AE, DC, MC, V

PRICES
Set-price lunch: £20.50
2 courses, £23.50 3 courses;
dinner: £32.50 2 courses,
£37.50 3 courses, £42.50
4 courses

SERVICE
Discretionary

I am often asked to name my favorite restaurant in a particular city. Here is my answer for London: Zafferano, which has been awarded a Michelin star. If I had only one meal to eat in London, it would be here. In fact, writing about it now makes me wish I could pick up the phone and reserve my table. Because reservations are in such high demand, I always book my table at Zafferano at the same time I book my next flight to London.

Everyone who eats at Zafferano agrees that it serves some of the best food he or she will have in London, in addition to offering top value for the dining pound. Owner-chef Giorgio Locatelli worked in Paris at the Michelin two-star Laurent, and it is this French influence that lifts his cooking far above the ordinary Italian fare. The set-price two- and three-course lunches and dinners, which change to reflect seasonal products, are bargains to behold, especially when you consider the high-caliber ingredients and preparation that go into each dish.

The stylish restaurant is beautifully decorated with massive, color-coordinated floral displays. Crisp linens, lovely table arrangements, nice paintings, and attentive service set the formal tone for the wonderful food to come. Just reading the menu is a pleasure. Depending on the season and your main course, you might begin with a salad of French beans with Jerusalem artichokes and Parmesan cheese, the unique sweet-and-sour skate salad, a beautiful baked aubergine topped with mozzarella especially flown in three times a week from Naples, or another one of my favorites, a deep-fried envelope of Swiss chard with fontina cheese. Bold pastas include pheasant ravioli with rosemary, chestnut tagliatelle with wild mushrooms, or the unusual combination of buckwheat pasta ribbons tossed with savoy cabbage, leeks, and sage.

Meat-based entrées favor simplicity over complexity and star several char-grilled dishes. If you are feeling slightly adventurous, try the roast rabbit cooked with Parma ham and served with polenta. Less daring but delicious in their own right are the char-grilled chicken breast with spinach and the steamed hake with a garlic, parsley, and vinegar sauce. When it comes time for dessert, do not even consider leaving without tasting something, even if you have room only to share with your dining companion. The hot chocolate tart with licorice ice cream is one you might be willing to share, but frankly, the walnut cannoli filled with mascarpone and truffle honey, or the tiramisu served in its own biscuit cup surrounded by a heavenly sea of espresso sauce, are two creations you will want all to yourself.

Pubs

THE ALBERT (13)
52 Victoria Street, Westminster, SW1
Tube: St. James's Park

The Albert is a handsome pub positively bursting with atmosphere. Here you have it all: polished wood, original gas lamps, engraved glass windows that were removed and hidden during World War II, and a "division bell," which calls members of Parliament back to the House of Commons in time to vote. A set of old Victorian prints depicts the evils of drinking, and portraits of past and present prime ministers glare down at diners on the Victorian stairwell leading to the restaurant. This is one of the few pubs where reservations in the upstairs restaurant are necessary if you hope to get a table during busy lunch hours.

TELEPHONE
020 7222 5577/7606

OPEN
Daily

CLOSED
2 days at Christmas

HOURS
Pub: Mon–Sat 11 A.M.–10:30 P.M., Sun noon–10 P.M.; restaurant: daily noon–9:30 P.M.; continuous service

RESERVATIONS
Advised for restaurant

CREDIT CARDS
AE, DC, MC, V

PRICES
À la carte: pub £6–8, restaurant, £10–18; set-price: restaurant £17 3 courses, coffee and service included

SERVICE
No service charged or expected in the pub, discretionary in the restaurant

If you eat downstairs, you'll enjoy pub food while standing or sitting very close to your neighbor, who will probably be part of one of the endless tour groups that stream through. If you are more serious about your meal, reserve a table upstairs, where you are served an appetizer and can select your main-course roast at the carving table or order salmon, chicken Kiev, lemon sole, or vegetable lasagna. All plates are garnished with potatoes and vegetables or a salad. Desserts are brought to your table on a three-tier trolley loaded with cakes, fresh fruits, and a tray of English cheese and crackers. Freshly brewed coffee completes the substantial repast.

THE GRENADIER (9)
18 Wilton Row (corner of Old Barrack Yard), Belgrave Square, SW1
Tube: Knightsbridge

TELEPHONE
020 7235 3074

OPEN
Daily

CLOSED
2 days at Christmas, New Year's

HOURS
Bar: Mon–Sat noon 11 P.M., Sun until 10:30 P.M.; lunch Mon–Sat noon–1:30 P.M., Sun noon–3 P.M.; dinner Mon–Sat 6–9:30 P.M., Sun until 9 P.M.

RESERVATIONS
Advised for restaurant

CREDIT CARDS
MC, V

PRICES
Pub: £6–8; restaurant: à la carte £22–26, Sun roast £14

SERVICE
Discretionary in restaurant, not expected in pub

Packed with history, tall tales, and the ghost of a former guard who was caught cheating at cards and supposedly murdered outside the pub, the Grenadier retains its title as one of the better-known pubs in London. In the beginning, it was the Duke of Wellington's Officers' Mess. Later it became the Guardsman, an inn frequented by King George IV. Since becoming the Grenadier, it has been host to both the famous and the infamous, and it has been a popular film location, including an appearance in *Around the World in Eighty Days*. The money you see on the ceiling has been sent by customers from around the world to pay back the money that the guard stole while he was cheating at cards.

In addition to the front bar, serving sandwiches and ploughman's lunches, there are two small, formally set dining rooms where typically British fare is served for lunch and dinner. One of the best times to go to the Grenadier is on Sunday, when Tom, the bartender here for forty years, dispenses the best Bloody Marys in London. Just how popular are they? During his three-hour shift, he serves between 80 and 150 of the drinks to tourists and locals alike, who usually stay on for plates of roast beef and Yorkshire pudding or honey-roast ham, which are served all day.

THE ORANGE BREWERY (27)
37 Pimlico Road, Pimlico, SW1
Tube: Sloane Square

Orange Square was developed in the nineteenth century and served as a pleasure haunt. Today's remaining link to its rural past is the Orange Brewery, where six thousand pints of homemade brews are made and consumed weekly. The microbrewery is popular thanks to these specialty beers, which are geared toward party animals. The most famous and award-winning beers, are the SW1, named after the brewery's postal code, a classic bitter with a hoppy aroma and fruity, malty finish, and the SW2, a darker and more powerful bitter that has full flavor and an intense finish. The patrons are a mixed bag of Sloanies, Pimlico types, the odd batch of workers during the day, and those with fun on their mind and youth on their side after sundown. This is a place for serious drinkers looking to have a good time.

The blackboard menu displays a short list of the usual pub grub: beef and ale pies, sausage and mash, beef lasagna and garlic bread, and a spicy bean burger and chips, all geared toward sticking to the ribs of drinkers, thus allowing for the consumption of a few more pints.

NOTE: Brewery tours can be arranged in advance.

TELEPHONE
020 7730 5984

OPEN
Daily

CLOSED
Christmas Day

HOURS
Mon–Sat 11 A.M.–11 P.M., Sun noon–10:30 P.M.; food service daily noon–9 P.M.

RESERVATIONS
Not accepted

CREDIT CARDS
AE, MC, V

PRICES
À la carte £6–9

SERVICE
No service charged or expected

RED LION (5)
2 Duke of York Street, St. James's, SW1
Tube: Piccadilly Circus, Green Park

The tiny Red Lion pub, just off Jermyn Street near Piccadilly Circus, is a true jewel. It began as a gin palace. In the 1800s, beer was taxed, but not gin, making gin the "beer of that day." It has been said that this tax resulted in gin's killing more people at this time than all the wars fought in Ireland in that era. Today, much of the original pub remains intact. Look for the hand-etched, silver-leafed mirrors with each panel depicting a different English flower, the wraparound mahogany bar, which is a single piece of wood unjointed in the middle, and the gas rose ceiling lights. Outside by the entrance is a brass plaque with a polite notice: "Customers wearing dirty work clothes will not be served." This is a dignified and quiet pub, with no music or pinball machines to break the concentration and conversation of the sophisticated customers who stop by daily at their regular time. Sandwiches are

TELEPHONE
020 7321 0782

OPEN
Mon–Sat

CLOSED
Sun, holidays

HOURS
11:30 A.M.–11 P.M.

RESERVATIONS
Not accepted

CREDIT CARDS
None

PRICES
À la carte £8–9.50

SERVICE
No service charged or expected

served every day, and on Friday and Saturday, fresh fish-and-chips (cod or haddock in a special beer batter); when the spirit moves the chef, hot meat pies are served too.

STAR TAVERN (11)
6 Belgrave Mews West, Belgravia, SW1
Tube: Knightsbridge

It takes some searching to locate the Star Tavern because it is off the beaten track for most casual visitors. There is no actual pub sign, just a large star suspended from a metal bracket above the entrance and prize-winning flowering baskets hanging outside from May to September. The pub is a friendly place that welcomes new faces. The main ground-floor room is similar to a gentlemen's club. There are tables, chairs, a carpeted floor, globe lights, and revolving fans suspended from the ceiling. A real fire adds a welcoming touch on cool days. The cozy upstairs lounge has an open fireplace, a small bar in one corner, and large windows overlooking the cobbled mews below. Every day the pub offers all the basic fare pub-goers know and love, from doorstop sandwiches filled with ribeye steak or ham and cheese to cod in parsley sauce.

TELEPHONE
020 7235 3019

OPEN
Daily

CLOSED
2 days at Christmas

HOURS
Pub: Mon–Fri 11:30 A.M.–11 P.M., Sat 11:30 A.M.–3 P.M. and 6:30–10:30 P.M., Sun 11:30 A.M.–3 P.M. and 7–10:30 P.M.; food service: lunch daily noon–2:30 P.M., dinner Mon–Sat 6:30–9 P.M., Sun 7–9 P.M.

RESERVATIONS
Not accepted

CREDIT CARDS
MC, V

PRICES
À la carte lunch £6–10, dinner £9–12

SERVICE
No service charged or expected

Wine Bars

EBURY WINE BAR (19)
139 Ebury Street, Belgravia, SW1
Tube: Victoria

The Ebury Wine Bar has a well-deserved reputation as one of London's premier wine bars, serving consistently good food and excellent wines. The professionally dressed patrons are sophisticated and should be, considering that the neighborhood boasts some of the most expensive real estate in London. It is the sort of place to which these locals bring family, friends, and business colleagues from abroad so they will forget that old chestnut about the Brits being a stuffy lot who don't know how to mix, relax, and have fun. The narrow interior combines the look and feel of a Paris bistro, with metal-base tables, wooden chairs, and bare floors. The menu changes often, displaying international and British cooking. Appetizers might include spicy fish cakes with

TELEPHONE
020 7730 5447

FAX
020 7823 6053

EMAIL
ebury@eburywinebars.co.uk

OPEN
Daily

CLOSED
2 days at Christmas

HOURS
Bar: 11 A.M.–11 P.M., continuous service and bar food; restaurant: Mon–Sat lunch noon–3 P.M., dinner 5:30–10:30 P.M., Sun noon–9:30 P.M.

RESERVATIONS
Advised

peanuts and a sweet chili cucumber on the side, roasted mushrooms with smoked anchovies, or a Caesar salad served as a starter or main course, either plain or with roast chicken or smoked salmon. The main-course special, Cumberland sausages with mashed potatoes, fried onions, and gravy, is always present, and so is old-fashioned meat loaf with bubble and squeak and a duet of steak options with either pepper or béarnaise sauce. Bar snacks are always available for those popping in for a special featured wine and a munchie or two, and on Sunday, the neighbors arrive for brunch and order French toast or pancakes with bacon and maple syrup, grilled calf's liver with black pudding, bacon and mash, or the ever pleasing scrambled eggs and ham. No matter when you go to the Ebury Wine Bar, the service is efficiently friendly and knowledgeable.

CREDIT CARDS
AE, DC, MC, V

PRICES
À la carte: bar £4–8, restaurant £20–26

SERVICE
12.5% service charge

SW3

Brompton and Chelsea

TOURIST ATTRACTIONS
Chelsea Old Church, Thames
River, Chelsea Royal Hospital,
King's Road

Brompton Road starts at the Knightsbridge tube stop by Harrods and cuts through this tony section of London. The area is chiefly composed of expensive townhouses occupied by yuppies talking on their cell phones while driving their Range Rovers and nannies pushing prams carrying expensively dressed, adorable babies.

Chelsea is also the haunt of London yuppies, known as Sloane Rangers and Hooray Henries. The main thoroughfare is King's Road, a private road until the nineteenth century, extending from Sloane Square. Hipsters, punks, and fashion weirdos still ply King's Road hoping to soak up some of its past, when it was the center of all things wild and strange in London. Today the street is filled with boutiques (both far out and far in), trendy cafés, restaurants, and pubs. Tucked along quiet side streets are colorful three- and four-story mews houses with tiny front gardens, and usually larger ones in back, out of view. A point of interest about "the mews": They were originally the stables and carriage houses for the wealthy, who lived in grand houses. The word *mews* comes from the cages used to hold hawks when they were molting. In the middle ages, these hawks were kept in the stables area, so the horses' quarters became known as "the mews," taken from the French verb *muer,* to molt. The tube stop is Sloane Square, and it's a very long walk to most destinations, unless you jump on buses 11 or 22, which go up and down King's Road. Along the Thames is a short street called Cheyne Walk (pronounced CHAIN-y). Over the years it has been home to George Eliot (No. 4), Dante Gabriel Rossetti (No. 16), and Mick Jagger (No. 48). Other noteworthy neighbors have been J. M. W. Turner, Sir Thomas More, Thomas Carlyle (whose house is at 24 Cheyne Row), James Whistler (who painted his mother at No. 19), and Johnny Rotten and the Sex Pistols.

One of my favorite places in London is the Chelsea Physic Garden. The walls around the garden make it almost tropical, and flowers bloom year-round. The garden was established in 1673 by the Society of Apothecaries and was used for studying the medicinal properties of herbs and other plants.

Sir Christopher Wren's Chelsea Royal Hospital is still the home of the Chelsea Pensioners, retired servicemen who wear their uniforms—a dark blue overcoat in winter, a bright red one in summer—as they walk along King's Road, when not performing good deeds such as visiting the sick, marching in parades, and serving as Chelsea's official greeters. The Pensioners do these deeds with goodwill and a smile in exchange for room, board, clothing, and a daily portion of beer and tobacco. In May, the hospital grounds play host to the world famous Chelsea Flower Show.

RESTAURANTS IN SW3

PUBS

TEAROOMS, PÂTISSERIES, AND BAKERIES

WINE BARS

($) indicates a Big Splurge

SW3

HYDE PARK

Kensington Road

Kensington Gore

ROYAL ALBERT HALL

KNIGHTSBRIDGE

MONTPELIER SQ.

TREVOR SQ.

2.

Prince Consort Road

Prince's

Ennismore

Gardens

Cheval Pl.

Brompton Road

Hans Rd.

Queen's Gate Ter.

Imperial College Road

Exhibition

Ennismore

Gardens

Garden

Mews

Beaufort Gdns.

Beauchamp Pl.

.5

.4

Queen's Gate

SCIENCE MUSEUM

Road

VICTORIA AND ALBERT MUSEUM

OVINGTON SQ.

Yeoman's Row

6.

Elvaston Place

7.

E. Gdn. Mews

.8

Egerton Terrace

9.

Street

Queen's Gate Pl.

NATURAL HISTORY MUSEUM

Egerton Gdns.

10.

Ovington St.

Lennox Gdns.

Cromwell Road

THURLOE SQUARE

Brompton Road

Walton

Hasker St.

First St.

11

Milne

Gloucester Road

Gardens

Stanhope

Queen's

Thurloe St.

South Ter.

.13

12.

Mossop St.

Denyer St.

Rawlings St.

Harrington Road

South Kensington

Pelham Street

Draycott

14

Cadogan

SOUTH KENSINGTON

Gloucester Rd.

Queen's Gate

Road

Summer

Cranley Pl.

ONSLOW SQUARE

Pelham Cr.

Road

Lucan

Sloane Avenue

Avenue

15

Rosary Gdns.

Old

Brompton

Onslow Gdns.

Place

Fulham

Pond Place

Sydney

Ixworth Place

Elystan St.

SW3

Elystan Place

Cranley Gdns.

Foulis Ter.

17

Cale Street

Godfrey St.

Jubilee Pl.

MARKHAM SQ.

Drayton

Roland Gardens

Neville Ter.

South Parade

CHELSEA SQ.

Dovehouse Street

Street

St. Luke's St.

Britten

King's Road

Radnor Walk

Priory Wk.

Evelyn Gardens

18.

Elm Park

Old Church St.

Manresa Rd.

19

CHELSEA

.20

Shawfield St.

Flood

Gilston Road

Gardens

Elm Park Rd.

.21

Chelsea Manor

Redcliffe Rd.

Fulham Road

Mulberry Walk

CARLYLE SQ.

22

Glebe Pl.

Margaretta Ter.

Oakley

26

Redburn St.

Seymour Walk

Park Walk

Limerston St.

Beaufort St.

24.

23.

King's Road

25

Old Church St.

Upper Cheyne Row

Phene St.

Street

27.

PAULTONS SQUARE

Cheyne Walk

Edith Grove

Gertrude St.

Lamont Rd.

King's Road

Beaufort St.

Danvers St.

28.

Cheyne Walk

Albert Bridge

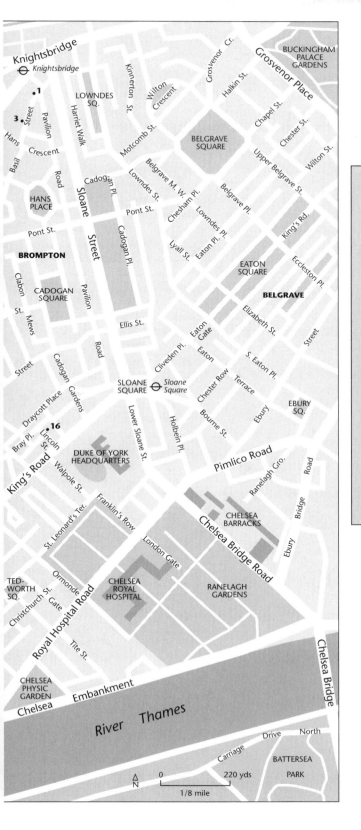

SW3

1 Stockpot–Knightsbridge
2 Richoux–Knightsbridge
3 Le Metro
4 Pâtisserie Valerie
5 S & P Patara
6 Monza ($)
7 Brasserie St. Quentin ($)
8 Beverly Hills Bakery
9 Baker and Spice
10 The Enterprise
11 The House ($)
12 Admiral Codrington
13 Itsu
14 Beccofino
15 Elistano
16 The English Garden ($)
17 S & P Patara
18 Riccardo's
19 Dan's ($)
20 The Coopers Arms
21 Stockpot–King's Road
22 My Old Dutch Pancake House
23 Big Easy
24 Rotisserie Jules
25 New Culture Revolution
26 Phene Arms
27 Ed's Easy Diner
28 Kings Head and Eight Bells

Restaurants

BECCOFINO (14)
100 Draycott Avenue, Chelsea, SW3
Tube: South Kensington

TELEPHONE
020 7584 3600, 7581 3387

OPEN
Mon–Sat

CLOSED
Sun, holidays

HOURS
Lunch 12:30–2:30 P.M., dinner 7–11:30 P.M.

RESERVATIONS
Advised for dinner

CREDIT CARDS
AE, MC, V

PRICES
À la carte £18–24; set-price (lunch only) £12 3 courses

SERVICE
£1.30 cover charge, service discretionary

Warm sienna colors, velvet banquettes, walls crowded with oil paintings, and an Italian staff (including Louis and Pio from the former Au Bon Acceuil) create the mood of this restaurant in Chelsea. Tables set with heavy silver and starched linens underscore the formal tone. It all sounds expensive, but the food and atmosphere add up to an unbeatable dining combination that guarantees many repeat visits. Yes, there are more modern, trendier, not to mention more expensive Italian restaurants in London, but the Chelsea locals and I are in total agreement: trendy doesn't always equal good food, let alone good value, but Beccofino has both, and it is our favorite neighborhood choice when we're in the mood for Italian.

Trying to decide what to order is a problem, but a nice one. If you are here for lunch, you can have the Great Eat set-price menu, which might include the soup of the day or grilled sardines, *saltimbocca di pollo* (chicken cooked with ham and sage in a wine sauce), *trota alla Doria* (fresh trout with a light cucumber, lemon, and butter sauce) and your choice of dessert. Otherwise, you might want to start with the Beccofino salad, made with spinach, mozzarella, avocado, and warm bacon; the fat asparagus, served warm with a butter sauce or cold with a vinaigrette; or perhaps the grilled mushrooms with garlic and radicchio. The homemade pastas and sauces are some of the best in London. And the risotto, bursting with seafood, garlic, and chili peppers in a light tomato sauce, is, in a word, delicious. The veal *picatta* in lemon sauce, the roast lamb, or the roast chicken make good alternatives to pasta, and so do any of the daily specials. It is hard to save room for dessert, but the temptation is strong when you see them displayed so seductively in the center of the room. The selections change every day, but the cloudlike custard is a must if it is there, and so are the fat spring strawberries or sliced mangoes. Lingering over an espresso is the perfect ending to your excellent meal. When reserving for dinner, please bear in mind that the best time to arrive is around 9 P.M.; otherwise, you could be dining alone.

BIG EASY (23)
332–334 King's Road, Chelsea, SW3
Tube: Sloane Square, then bus 11, 19, or 22

Arrive starved and be prepared to party the night away at the Big Easy on King's Road, where the signs posted around the big room laughingly tell you what to expect: "Down home cookin' and uptown hoofin'," or "Emily Post fainted here," and "Duncan Hines never ate here . . . Betty Crocker wishes she hadn't." Heel-kicking live music every night, a buffed-bod staff, and wild drinks with names such as Kickass Lemonade, Miami Whammy, and Tropical Itch keep the masses jazzed and pulsating. It all happens in a big, rough-hewn, barnlike building that serves a taste of American and almost-Cajun cooking. That's not all. The Big Easy is the home of the ultimate Scottish prime beef steaks, which range from ten to twenty-four ounces and come smothered with béarnaise or peppercorn sauce and are accompanied by either crisp onion rings or Caesar salad. Classic American burgers with whatever toppings you want on them; crab, shrimp, and lobster platters; barbecued chicken or ribs; three-way fajitas; huge sandwiches; and soups, salads, and pasta are just a few of the other belt-busting meals offered every day of the week. There is a two-for-one Happy Hour all night on Monday and Tuesday and from 4 to 7:30 P.M. Wednesday through Friday. Children always eat free if the adults order an entrée. And as the sign says, "If you are in a hurry, we'll mail your lunch"—fast service is not a virtue here, but the mammoth portions are.

NOTE: There's a two-hour table limit at peak hours. The Big Easy is available for hoedowns, hootenannies, hullabaloos, and other private parties. A nonsmoking section is available, as is takeaway, and Big Easy T-shirts and teddy bears are for sale.

TELEPHONE
020 7352 4071

FAX
020 7352 0844

OPEN
Daily

CLOSED
Christmas Day

HOURS
Noon–midnight (Fri–Sat till 12:30 A.M.), continuous service

RESERVATIONS
Advised on weekends

CREDIT CARDS
AE, MC, V

PRICES
À la carte: £10–20; set-price: Mon–Fri noon–5 P.M. £5.95 2 courses; kids eat free when adults order a main course

SERVICE
12.5% service charge

BRASSERIE ST. QUENTIN ($, 7)
243 Brompton Road, Knightsbridge, SW3
Tube: Knightsbridge

Expect a French brasserie atmosphere, French-accented waiters clad in black, and a dinner bill around £30 when you are dining à la carte at St. Quentin. If you go for lunch or early in the evening, it will be half that. Consistent with the restaurant's French background, you can also expect your food, wine, and service to be taken seriously. The stylish and urbane crowd reflects this part of London, and to feel a part of it all, you will

TELEPHONE
020 7589 8005

FAX
020 7584 6064

INTERNET
www.sante-gcg.com

OPEN
Daily

CLOSED
Christmas Day

HOURS
Lunch: Mon–Sat noon–3 P.M.,
Sun and holidays until 3:30 P.M.;
dinner: daily 6:30–10:30 P.M.

RESERVATIONS
Advised

CREDIT CARDS
AE, DC, MC, V

PRICES
À la carte: £25–32; set-price
(lunch daily, dinner 6:30–
7:30 P.M.): £15.50 2 courses,
£17.50 3 courses, £12 2-course
vegetarian option 2 courses

SERVICE
12.5% service charge

want to dress for success and be sure to make a dinner reservation. The excellent-value set-price lunch and dinner menus change weekly, and in keeping with the times, they include vegetarian dishes for first and second courses. If I am not ordering the set-price menu, I like to start with the *salade St. Quentin,* which is made with baby hearts of romaine lettuce and sprinkled with grilled baby sweet corn, asparagus, sun-dried tomato, and Parmesan cheese in a basil dressing. I thought the risotto and truffles looked small, but the dish was so rich and filling that I had trouble finishing it all. The lamb shank served with parsley-potato puree is delicious, and so is the roast duck with turnips and the grilled whole Dover sole served with lemon and parsley butter. Dessert is a deliberate attempt to destroy discipline, especially the lemon tart, served with a dollop of crème fraîche and a sprinkling of candied lemon peel. Coffee is served with a piece of chocolate.

DAN'S ($, 19)
119 Sydney Street, Chelsea, SW3
Tube: Sloane Square, then bus 11, 19, or 22

TELEPHONE
020 7352 2718

OPEN
Mon–Sat

CLOSED
Sun, holidays, Dec 24–Jan 2,
a few days at Easter

HOURS
Lunch noon–2:15 P.M., dinner
7:15–10:30 P.M.

RESERVATIONS
Advised for the garden area,
especially in summer

CREDIT CARDS
AE, MC, V

PRICES
Set-price lunch: £14 2 courses,
extra course £4; set-price
dinner: £24, extra course £5.50

SERVICE
12.5% service charge

If I am in the mood for a lovely meal after browsing through the shops at the lower end of King's Road, I walk down Sydney Street just past the Chelsea Market and enter the green door at Dan's. The airy interior is formally dressed in crisp linens, sparkling crystal, signature china, and a great collection of primitive animal prints, on loan from a friend of the owner who deals in them. The select tables are in the garden and conservatory, where the ceiling can be rolled open on pretty days. The clientele is aloof and rich, and the owners, who hold court behind the bar or at a table by the entrance, know them all.

The set-price-only menu for both lunch and dinner offers two or three courses with several well-prepared, seasonally appropriate choices for each dish. At lunch the choices change three times a week and the final tab is not a Big Splurge. Go for dinner and you will have a Big Splurge total. Lighter dishes are featured midday, perhaps starting with a zucchini and celery cream soup, with salmon teriyaki and stir-fried vegetables for the main course and passion fruit crème brûlée as the ending. Whenever you are at Dan's for dinner, in addition to the seasonal preparations, you can count on the warm goat cheese and roasted eggplant salad, honey- and ginger-roasted duck with sesame noodles, and fresh fish and a lusty chocolate truffle cake with coffee-bean sauce, which always makes a dramatic sweet finale.

ED'S EASY DINER (27)
362 King's Road, Chelsea, SW3
Tube: Sloane Square, then bus 11, 19, or 22

See Ed's Easy Diner in W1, page 50, for a full description. All other information is the same.

TELEPHONE: 020 7352 1956

OPEN: Daily

CLOSED: Christmas Day

HOURS: Mon–Thur 11:30 A.M.–11:30 P.M., Fri 11:30 A.M.–midnight, Sat 9 A.M.–1 A.M., Sun 9 A.M.–11:30 P.M., continuous service; deliveries 6–11 P.M.

ELISTANO (15)
25–27 Elystan Street, Chelsea, SW3
Tube: South Kensington

Elistano doesn't look that special, but the Sloane Ranger crowd that packs it daily tells you differently. Thanks to word of mouth, not the glitzy firestorm of publicity that many London restaurants seem to need to fill their tables, this is a popular Italian restaurant in a hidden corner of Chelsea.

The two inside rooms are done in austere good taste with cocoa-brown walls, bare tables on stone slab floors, and a palm tree in an imported pot. In front there is a little outdoor terrace. Because it is always filled to capacity, it does get noisy, especially in the evening, when diners can linger over another bottle of good red wine. Service can get rather erratic because there are usually only two or three waiters (wearing jeans, speaking with heavy Italian accents), who seem to enjoy working at their own slow pace.

The seasonal menu takes an Italian point of view, playing it safe and sound with starters of grilled vegetables, deep-fried mozzarella, beef carpaccio, and a crisp spinach salad. Not all pastas are brilliant. The *fusilli alla Siciliana,* loaded with eggplant, mozzarella, and tomato sauce, had zip, but the *linguine alle vongole,* with fresh clams, garlic, and olive oil received the A+ of the evening. The dunce cap was placed on the *orecchiette con broccoli,* ear-shaped pasta with a weak, watery sauce of what tasted like frozen broccoli without a hint of other seasoning. Veal, chicken, and fish dominate the *secondi piatti,* and most come nicely garnished. Practice has made

TELEPHONE
020 7584 5248

FAX
020 7584 8965

OPEN
Daily

CLOSED
Dec 24–Jan 4

HOURS
Lunch 12:30–2:45 P.M., dinner 7–10:30 P.M.

RESERVATIONS
Essential, at least two days ahead for Fri–Sat

CREDIT CARDS
AE, DC, MC, V

PRICES
À la carte £18–25

SERVICE
Discretionary

perfect with two of their desserts: tiramisu and *torta della nonna*. If there are two of you, order both and share.

THE ENGLISH GARDEN ($, 16)
10 Lincoln Street, Chelsea, SW3
Tube: Sloane Square

TELEPHONE
020 7584 7272

FAX
020 7584 1961

OPEN
Tues–Sun

CLOSED
Mon, 2 days at Christmas

HOURS
Lunch Tues–Sun 12:30–2:30 P.M., dinner Tues–Sat 6–11 P.M., Sun until 10:30 P.M.

RESERVATIONS
Essential

CREDIT CARDS
AE, DC, MC, V

PRICES
À la carte: £30–35; set-price lunch: £21.50 3 courses (Sun £25 3 courses)

SERVICE
12.5% service charge

For a meal with someone special or simply to taste how fine British cooking really can be, reserve a table at the English Garden, a converted Chelsea townhouse with food to match its stylish setting and clientele. Inside, the English Garden resembles a minimalist country home, with soft, beige, suede-covered high-back chairs positioned around tables holding a vase of one or two flowers. Dining at one of these tables or on a cushioned banquette in the skylighted conservatory in back is a delightful experience.

The menu changes daily and is always interesting and unusual, with dishes presented in just the right portions. The à la carte meals can quickly become expensive, so going at midday and ordering from the set-price lunch menu is a wiser option for many. Depending on the time of year you might start lunch with a gratin of artichokes with wild mushrooms and Parmesan cheese or a soft-boiled egg with black pudding, brioche, and bacon—a wonderful twist on this English breakfast staple. Your main course could be Norfolk pigeon with figs, cèpes, melted foie gras, and red chard or rabbit with celeriac cream, grain mustard, and roast garlic. Desserts are works of art, not only in taste but in looks. Perhaps you will have the tiramisu garnished with vanilla-coated figs; a cannelloni of banana, dates, saffron, and vanilla and ginger ice cream; or the unusual lemon tart with crème fraîche and basil syrup. Yes, it will cost more than most meals, but it is worth the Big Splurge for the memories that will last long after you have left London.

THE ENTERPRISE (10)
35 Walton Street, Chelsea, SW3
Tube: South Kensington

TELEPHONE
020 7584 3148

OPEN
Daily

CLOSED
2 days at Christmas, some holidays (call to check)

The Enterprise began life as a gloomy pub serving dreary food, and it basically stayed that way until it was rescued by Kit and Tim Kemp, the savvy owners of two of London's most recognized boutique hotels (see the Dorset Square Hotel and the Pelham Hotel in *Great Sleeps London*). Drawing on their interior-design talents, which epitomize good taste and style, they transformed the pub into a thirty-six-seat restaurant that is one of the area's most sought-after casual dining destinations. For proof, witness the wait during Sunday lunch, or try to get a dinner table after 9 or 9:30 P.M., when (inexplicably) no reservations are taken.

The substantial appetizers and salads can be ordered as starters or mains. If you are sharing, the quesadillas with salsa and guacamole or the new-potato skins topped with caviar and sour cream are succulent choices. Follow these with a light-handed entrée such as the signature smoked-haddock fish cakes, a vegetarian pasta of the day, or the featured sausages (ostrich when I was there). How will you get through dessert? Very well if you the order the banoffee (banana and toffee) pie or the lemon tart.

HOURS
Lunch: Mon–Fri 12:30–2:30 P.M., Sat–Sun 12:30–3:30 P.M.; dinner: Mon–Sat 7– 11 P.M., Sun until 10:30 P.M.

RESERVATIONS
Accepted for lunch Mon–Fri only

CREDIT CARDS
MC, V

PRICES
À la carte £20–28

SERVICE
£1 cover charge, 12.5% service charge

THE HOUSE ($, 11)
3 Milner Street, Chelsea, SW3
Tube: Sloane Square

At the House, the charm of dining in intimate rooms filled with chintz and impressive decorative furniture is pleasant, despite the proximity of your well-dressed neighbor. As is true with most fine dining in London, the best time to eat at the House is at lunch, when there is a three-course meal for significantly less than you will pay for almost the same food served for dinner. The talented chef has created a modern British menu with a seasonal focus that blends tried-and true-dishes with a newer, leaner look that appeals on all levels. Consider the smoked quail with a corn cake and grape butter to start. I know it sounds odd, but it does work. So does the pork- and pepper-stuffed squid with saffron rice and chorizo cream, and the more familiar butternut squash and Parmesan cheese risotto. Vegetarians will love the casserole of autumn vegetables, loaded with wild mushrooms and chestnuts. Roast duck with braised beets and bacon or roast veal with a sage gnocchi are just two other main-course choices. My favorite fall dessert is the paper-thin apple tart topped with cinnamon ice cream, but my dining companion voted for the chocolate espresso custard with crispy, sugary churros.

TELEPHONE
020 7584 3002

FAX
020 7581 2848

OPEN
Daily

CLOSED
Sat lunch, Sun, 2 days at Christmas, New Year's Day

HOURS
Lunch Mon–Fri, noon–2:30 P.M., dinner Mon–Sat 6–11 P.M.

RESERVATIONS
Essential

CREDIT CARDS
AE, DC, MC, V

PRICES
Set-price lunch £20 3 courses, dinner £29 3 courses

SERVICE
12.5% service charge

ITSU (13)
118 Draycot Avenue, Chelsea, SW3
Tube: South Kensington

This was the first Itsu to open in London, and it has maintained its integrity and popularity. For the second location in Soho, see page 56. All other details are the same.

TELEPHONE: 020 7584 5522 (restaurant), 020 7644 6666 (deliveries)
FAX: 020 7581 8716

MONZA ($, 6)
6 Yeoman's Row, SW3
Tube: Knightsbridge

TELEPHONE
020 7591 0210
EMAIL
monzarestaurant@msn.com
OPEN
Mon–Sat
CLOSED
Sun, Mon lunch, holidays, 2 weeks in Aug (dates vary)
HOURS
Lunch Tues–Fri noon–2:30 P.M., dinner Mon–Sat 7–11 P.M.
RESERVATIONS
Advised for lunch, essential for dinner
CREDIT CARDS
AE, DC, MC, V
PRICES
À la carte £30–35
SERVICE
£1.70 cover charge, service discretionary

Tucked away on a mews street a minute or two from Harrods and Harvey Nichols is Monza, where one look inside tells you the owner is a Formula One race-car enthusiast. The colorful setting, with a pretty, protected outside terrace, is coolly casual, and the service from waiters wearing checkered-flag aprons tied over black pants is excellent. In the kitchen, attention to the smallest detail is evident in every wonderful dish that is served. In addition to the regular bill of fare, the restaurant is known for its own bufala mozzarella, freshly baked breads, dessert soufflés, homemade ice creams, and creative daily specials. When ordering, you could almost close your eyes and put your finger on anything on the intelligently constructed, Italian-based menu and come up with a winner. I think the best starter is one of the most simple: grilled eggplant and slices of Parma ham with melting mozzarella and oregano-infused olive oil. If the lobster pasta is available, you won't be sorry you selected it, but it is very rich, so pace yourself. The whole-wheat spaghetti with fresh vegetables is a lighter alternative. Lamb cutlets sautéed with grappa and fresh mint leaves offers a new twist on this familiar dish, while the calf's liver with balsamic vinegar and shallots stays true to tradition. Dessert can be summed up in just two words: chocolate soufflé.

MY OLD DUTCH PANCAKE HOUSE (22)
221 King's Road, Chelsea, SW3
Tube: Sloane Square, then bus 11, 19, or 22

See My Old Dutch Pancake House in WC1, page 121, for a full description. All other information is the same.

NOTE: It's a long walk from the Sloane Square tube stop, but since King's Road is great for shopping and browsing, the walk might turn out to be a good way to work up an appetite or to work off your meal afterward. If you go between 11:30 A.M. and 12:30 P.M. for Sunday breakfast, you will have basically the same menu, but the prices will be around 15 percent less.

TELEPHONE: 020 7376 5650

OPEN: Daily
CLOSED: Christmas Day
HOURS: Mon–Thur noon–11 P.M., Fri–Sat noon–midnight, Sun 11:30 A.M.–10:30 P.M.

NEW CULTURE REVOLUTION (25)
305 King's Road, Chelsea, SW3
Tube: Sloane Square, then a long walk or take bus 11, 19, or 22

See New Culture Revolution in W2, page 92, for a full description. All other information is the same, including the sparse surroundings.
TELEPHONE: 020 7352 9281

RICCARDO'S (18)
126 Fulham Road, Chelsea, SW3
Tube: South Kensington

Calling all grazers who like to nosh on a variety of small dishes and not have a week's worth of food dumped in front of you: Riccardo's on Fulham Road, where every course is appetizer size, is for you. Seating is inside a basic room brightened by fresh flowers on the tables, or on the covered, heated terrace in front. Of course, you have to like Italian-inspired food to even think of Riccardo's, where the menu is long and most of the diners are regulars, many of them Italian.

Successful eating here means you should home in on the dishes everyone in your party would like to share, or at least taste. For your midday or evening repast, get going with a bowl of raw vegetables dipped in an anchovy-garlic sauce; the antipasti *Toscani,* featuring prosciutto, salami, crostini, and frittata; and an order of *caprese pomodori secchi*—fresh avocado, bufala mozzarella, and sun-dried tomatoes. Vegetarians have a multitude of options: grilled vegetables and Gorgonzola, pizza topped with fresh tomato and mozzarella (capers optional), ravioli filled with spinach or aubergine and ricotta and tossed in butter and sage, and grilled polenta with wild mushrooms. Classic Florentine risotto made with squid ink, fresh Scottish salmon, and pesto; baby calamari stewed with chili; or grilled sardines with garlic, parsley, oregano, and lemon should keep the fish eaters happy. Italian sausage and lentils, skewered quail wound with peppers and zucchini, carpaccio, and Tuscan meatballs will please carnivores. Desserts don't strike high notes, and you will probably be too full, but the tiramisu

TELEPHONE
020 7370 6656
OPEN
Daily
CLOSED
Major holidays, last 2 weeks of Aug (how Italian!)
HOURS
Lunch noon–3 P.M., dinner 6:30 P.M.–midnight
RESERVATIONS
Advised after 7:30 P.M.
CREDIT CARDS
AE, DC, MC, V
PRICES
À la carte £10–20
SERVICE
12.5% service charge

is authentic, as is the *cantucci con vin santo*—a plate of crisp Italian nut cookies served with a glass of sweet wine for dipping.

ROTISSERIE JULES (24)
338 King's Road, Chelsea, SW3
Tube: Sloane Square, then bus 11, 19, or 22

See Rotisserie Jules in W11, page 113, for a full description. This branch and the one in W11 are licensed. All other information is the same.

TELEPHONE: 020 7351 0041 (restaurant), 020 7221 3331 (delivery)

OPEN: Tues–Sun

CLOSED: Mon, major holidays (call to check)

HOURS: Tues–Fri 5–11 P.M., Sat–Sun noon–11 P.M., continuous service

S & P PATARA (5)
9 Beauchamp Place, Knightsbridge, SW3
Tube: Knightsbridge

TELEPHONE
020 7581 8820

FAX
020 7581 2155

OPEN
Daily

CLOSED
Never

HOURS
Lunch noon–3 P.M., dinner 6:30–11 P.M.

RESERVATIONS
Advised

CREDIT CARDS
AE, DC, MC, V

PRICES
À la carte: £20–26; set-price lunches: £11.95–14.95 2 courses, £14.95 and £ 17.95 3 courses

SERVICE
12.5% service charge

The S & P story began on October 14, 1973, when five brothers and sisters opened a small ice cream store on the corner of Soi Prasanmitr in Bangkok. They called it S & P Ice Cream Corner. From that humble beginning, the shop grew into a chain of restaurants called S & P Patara, with branches in Bangkok, Geneva, Taipei, Singapore, and London. Both London locations are bright and clean with adequate lighting and subtle Thai decorating touches. Service is polite and shyly accommodating.

The set-price lunches and any of the stir-fried rice and noodle dishes offer excellent value. The level of spices can be turned up or down in the coconut chicken, beef, or prawn curries and in several stir-frys starring duck, pork, or beef sirloin. The sweets will probably not become addictive, but they are interesting to try, especially the steamed coconut custard in pumpkin or the baked banana with vanilla ice cream and toasted almonds.

S & P PATARA (17)
181 Fulham Road (corner of Sydney Street), South Kensington, SW3
Tube: South Kensington

See S & P Patara above for a full description. There is a nonsmoking section in the basement at this branch. All other information is the same.

TELEPHONE & FAX: 020 7351 5692

STOCKPOT–KING'S ROAD (21)
273 King's Road, Chelsea, SW3
Tube: Sloane Square, then bus 11, 19, or 22

See Stockpot–Soho in W1, page 68, for a full description. All other information is the same.

TELEPHONE: 020 7823 3175
OPEN: Daily
CLOSED: 2 days at Christmas, New Year's Day
HOURS: Mon–Sat 7:45 A.M.–11:30 P.M., Sun 11:30 A.M.–11 P.M., continuous service
RESERVATIONS: Not accepted
CREDIT CARDS: None
PRICES: À la carte: £6–12, minimum charge at peak hours £2.50; set-price: breakfast £4–5, lunch and dinner £6
SERVICE: 10% service charge

STOCKPOT–KNIGHTSBRIDGE (1)
6 Basil Street, Knightsbridge, SW3
Tube: Knightsbridge

See the Stockpot–Soho in W1, page 68, for a full description. All other information is the same.

TELEPHONE: 020 7589 8627
CLOSED: 2–3 days at Christmas and Easter
HOURS: Mon–Sat 7:30 A.M.–11:30 P.M., Sun noon–10:30 P.M. (no breakfast served on Sun), continuous service
SERVICE: 10% service charge

Pubs

ADMIRAL CODRINGTON (12)
17 Mossop Street, Brompton, SW3
Tube: South Kensington

The Admiral Cod, as it is called, has a reputation as one of the better-known gastropubs in this section of Chelsea. During the seventies and eighties it was a happening place, frequented by Lady Diana, Prince Andrew, and Fergie. In the past decade it suffered at the hands of a series of managers, which unfortunately led to its decline, especially in the food department. Now, however, it is back and in full, fashionable glory. Well-known London decorator Nina Campbell has reworked the pub by converting the dining room into a chic space with a retractable glass roof that opens on warm days. The wood-paneled front part of the pub was left almost

TELEPHONE
020 7581 0005
FAX
020 7589 2452
EMAIL
longshot@dial.pipex.com
INTERNET
www.thecod.co.uk
OPEN
Daily
CLOSED
2 days at Christmas

HOURS
Pub: Mon–Sat 11:30 A.M.–
11 P.M., Sun noon–10:30 P.M.;
lunch: pub and restaurant
Mon–Fri noon–2:30 P.M., Sun
until 3:30 P.M.; dinner:
restaurant only, nightly
7–10:30 P.M.

RESERVATIONS
Essential for the restaurant

CREDIT CARDS
AE, MC, V

PRICES
À la carte: pub £7–10,
restaurant £24–28

SERVICE
No service charged or expected
in the pub; 12.5% service
charge in the restaurant; 50
pence cover charge for dinner in
restaurant

intact and still has a staff of friendly bartenders kibitzing with the knots of regulars who drop in to swap lies and war stories.

A new chef has revamped the restaurant menu by tossing out the standard, worn-out pub dishes and replacing them with sophisticated dishes with well-defined flavors at very affordable prices. Diners testify to the restaurant's popularity by filling the hotly contested tables for both lunch and dinner, which means reservations are vital, unless you are prepared to wait and participate in the scrimmage for a table. The chef's well-justified success is evident in his daily renderings of fresh fish, as well as in other dishes such as a foie gras and chicken-liver parfait; a Caesar salad with a soft poached egg and roasted prosciuto; a rigatoni of lobster, shrimp, and ricotta cheese; caramelized breast of chicken served with a sweet potato *rösti,* mixed peppers, red onions, and garlic; or braised pheasant and celeriac pie. Desserts provide a good supporting cast, with *tarte tatin* of pear, lavender crème brûlée, and homemade ice cream. There is a less complicated lunch menu served at the bar every day, and on Sunday, regulars know to turn up for the roast beef and Yorkshire pudding.

THE COOPERS ARMS (20)
87 Flood Street, Chelsea, SW3
Tube: Sloane Square

TELEPHONE
020 7376 3120

OPEN
Daily

CLOSED
Never

HOURS
Mon–Sat 11 A.M.–11 P.M.,
Sun noon–10:30 P.M.; lunch
12:30–3 P.M.

RESERVATIONS
Advised for Sun lunch

CREDIT CARDS
AE, MC, V

PRICES
À la carte £10–20

SERVICE
Discretionary for table service,
otherwise no service charged or
expected

The high cost of dining reduces many unknowing London visitors to pub grub consisting of greasy sausages, microwaved casseroles, or bowls of gassy chili con carne. You will have none of this unpleasant fare at the Coopers Arms, a pub that not only serves decent food, but has a history of interesting patrons, both human and otherwise. Neighborhood regulars have included Vanessa Redgrave's mother, who lunched here daily, and a ninety-six-year-old man who stopped by every day for his beer and to tend to the plants. Both are gone now, and so are the green plants that were so lovingly cared for. Presiding over the activities at the present time is a stuffed bear in one corner, a hat-wearing moose who watches patrons from his position above the bar, and a massive mounted wahoo fish, caught by one of the regular patrons off the Kona Coast in 1998.

The yellowed walls are proof that pubs are one of the last refuges of tobacco addicts, but Coopers is big enough to absorb everyone and their smoke. The fireplace warms on a damp day, newspapers invite dallying, and eyeballing the Chelsea crowd sipping beer and recounting memories is a great pastime. If you go for Sunday lunch, get there early: by early afternoon, there is no place to stand or to sit.

The daily chalkboard menu (for lunch only) can be ordered at the bar or at a table for the same price. If you are meat-and-potatoes eater, you will have three or four selections revolving around pork and lamb and a beef or chicken dish with an Oriental slant. Vegetarians need not panic; there is always a dish for them. For dessert, order a fresh fruit crumble unashamedly covered with cream, soft custard, or ice cream. In addition to the usual number of beers, wines from around the world are strongly featured.

KINGS HEAD AND EIGHT BELLS (28)
50 Cheyne Walk, Chelsea, SW3
Tube: Sloane Square

The Kings Head and Eight Bells, originally two separate inns, is a historic Chelsea pub dating from the late sixteenth century. Between 1524 and 1534 the inns were part of the estate of Sir Thomas More, chancellor of England, who lived around the corner on Beaufort Street. In 1580 the two separate inns, the Kings Head and the Eight Bells, were merged into one. It is said that Henry VIII called here on his way up the Thames to Hampton Court, when the gentry would patronize the Kings Head and their entourage would use the Eight Bells. Located in the fashionable Cheyne Walk facing the River Thames, it has always been a favorite stop for the famous writers and artists who have lived in the neighborhood (see the SW3 introduction). The comfortable pub is worth the hike from the Sloane Square tube stop. If you use a good map and the Michelin Green Guide as you go along, you will find all sorts of interesting tidbits about this part of London that will add to your visit. The pub's kitchen offers the standard soups, chili, homemade meat pies, grills, fish-and-chips, sausages and mash, sandwiches, and Sunday-roast lunch. The bathrooms are notably nice.

TELEPHONE
020 7352 1820

OPEN
Daily

CLOSED
Never

HOURS
Mon–Sat 11 A.M.–11 P.M., Sun noon–10:30 P.M.; food service Mon–Sat noon–10 P.M., Sun 12:30–4 P.M. and 7–10 P.M.

RESERVATIONS
Not necessary

CREDIT CARDS
MC, V

PRICES
À la carte £7–12

SERVICE
No service charged or expected

PHENE ARMS (26)
9 Phene Street (corner Margaretta Terrace), SW3
Tube: Sloane Square, South Kensington, long walk

For a hundred years, the Phene Arms had only four owners. The fifth, Carmen and Wesley Davis, were customers for six years before they decided they liked the

TELEPHONE
020 7352 3294

FAX
020 7352 7026

OPEN
Daily
CLOSED
Christmas Day
HOURS
Mon–Sat 11 A.M.–11:30 P.M.,
Sun noon–10:30 P.M.
RESERVATIONS
Not necessary
CREDIT CARDS
AE, DC, MC, V
PRICES
À la carte £5–18
SERVICE
No service charged or expected

pub so much they would buy it. For ten years now, they both have been holding court as the friendly hosts. It is a likable spot for many reasons. First, it has a history. It was named after John Samuel Phene, a world traveler and noted Chelsea character who built the "Gingerbread Castle" on the corner of Oakley Street in 1905 and introduced trees to the urban areas of London. He was offered a knighthood for his work, but refused it. Second, it has a fabulous outdoor seating area that is shaded in the summer and warmed with heaters on cooler days. Upstairs there is a bright, sunny room for private parties. Third, the food and the wine at the Phene Arms are head and shoulders above the competition. Everything is cooked to order, so nothing has that mass-produced look or taste that is prevalent in so many pubs. The Davises are serious about their wines and offer either a French chardonnay or sancerre as the house variety. Finally, given the cast of characters who count this pub as their own, the visit is rarely dull.

Tearooms, Pâtisseries, and Bakeries

BAKER AND SPICE (9)
46 Walton Street, SW3
Tube: Knightsbridge

TELEPHONE
020 7589 4734
FAX
020 7823 9148
OPEN
Daily
CLOSED
1 week to 10 days at Christmas
and Easter, holidays
HOURS
Mon–Sat 7 A.M.–7 P.M.,
Sun 8:30 A.M.–2 P.M.
RESERVATIONS
Not necessary
CREDIT CARDS
MC, V
PRICES
Bakery goods £1.80 and up,
deli £2 and up
SERVICE
No service charged or expected

For fabulous breads, divine muffins, great cookies, decadent brownies, a super deli, and homemade soups and sandwiches to behold, it simply doesn't get any better than the Baker and Spice. The little shop is only a few minutes away from Harrods, and in my opinion, it outstrips the famed department store, especially in the bakery department. There are only two spindly tables outside, so unless you are lucky, and the weather cooperative, plan to take your food with you.

BEVERLY HILLS BAKERY (8)
3 Egerton Terrace, Knightsbridge, SW3
Tube: Knightsbridge

Oh, I can almost smell the muffins now . . .

The Beverly Hills Bakery was often my early-morning London treat as I walked from my flat to buy the morning papers. What delicious decisions I had as the hot-from-the-oven, preservative-free muffins were brought out. Should I have two minimuffins or one large dark chocolate, carrot, lemon, blueberry, or honey bran raisin muffin to go with my pot of brewed tea or hot chocolate? If I felt especially virtuous, I could still indulge in one of the fat-free muffins.

Muffins aren't the only treats. Look for the home-made quiches, soups (from noon on), salads, and ready-made sandwiches piled on assorted breads and rolls. May I tempt you further with the cookies, carrot cake made with pineapple, cheesecakes, and almost illegally rich chocolate cake or brownies?

"Remember us and your friends will remember you"—this is the motto for the bakery's gift baskets (starting at £26), which they can prepare and send anywhere in the U.K. and deliver free in London. Each basket has an assortment of minimuffins, cookies, brownies, and Beverly Hills jam (which is marvelous, by the way). They will cater a kids' party and throw in the balloons, send a corporate basket, send a basket with a gingham bear to a new mom, guarantee true love with their Valentine basket, fill a festive Christmas basket, or pack your order in a tin for you to deliver yourself.

NOTE: There's no public rest room. No smoking allowed.

TELEPHONE
020 7584 4401

INTERNET
www.beverlyhillsbakery.com

OPEN
Daily

CLOSED
2 days at Christmas, New Year's Day, major holidays (call to check)

HOURS
Mon–Sat 7:30 A.M.–6:30 P.M., Sun 8 A.M.–5 P.M.

RESERVATIONS
Not accepted

CREDIT CARDS
AE, MC, V

PRICES
À la carte bakery £3–8, gift baskets from £26

SERVICE
No service charged or expected

PÂTISSERIE VALERIE (4)
215 Brompton Road, Knightsbridge, SW3
Tube: Knightsbridge

Please see Pâtisserie Valerie in W1, page 79, for a full description. The Knightsbridge location, on Brompton Road just down the street from Harrods, is more relaxed and spacious. It has the added advantage of an expanded menu and a changing display of French art posters, all of which are for sale. All other information is the same.

TELEPHONE: 020 7823 9971
OPEN: Daily
CLOSED: Holidays

HOURS: Mon–Fri 7 A.M.–7 P.M., Sat 7:30 A.M.–7 P.M., Sun 8 A.M.–6 P.M.

RESERVATIONS: Not necessary

CREDIT CARDS: AE, MC, V

PRICES: À la carte £5–18, minimum charge at peak times £7.50

SERVICE: Discretionary, 10% service charge for 5 or more

RICHOUX–KNIGHTSBRIDGE (2)
86 Brompton Road, Knightsbridge, SW3
Tube: Knightsbridge

See Richoux–Mayfair in W1, page 81, for a full description. All other information is the same.

TELEPHONE: 020 7584 8300

OPEN: Daily

CLOSED: Christmas Day

HOURS: 8 A.M.–9 P.M., breakfast served all day

PRICES: À la carte £7–18; set-price (served all day): £11 2 courses; £15 3 courses; minimum charge £10 Mon–Fri noon–3 P.M., all day Sat–Sun, holidays

SERVICE: Discretionary, 10% service charge for 6 or more

Wine Bars

LE METRO (3)
28 Basil Street, Knightsbridge, SW3
Tube: Knightsbridge

TELEPHONE
020 7589 6286

OPEN
Mon–Sat

CLOSED
Sun, holidays

HOURS
7:30 A.M.–10:30 P.M., continuous service

RESERVATIONS
Not necessary

CREDIT CARDS
AE, MC, V

PRICES
À la carte £8–20

SERVICE
10% service charge

Le Metro wine bar is around the corner from Harrods, a handy location if you and your shopping companion or tagalong need sustenance or a drop to drink while combing the shops in Knightsbridge. Le Metro tries to be all things to all people and generally succeeds, though it rarely excels in any one area. You can start your day with croissants and a glass of fresh orange juice or a cup of cappuccino. Later on, stop by for one of the daily specials or a salad. In the afternoon they serve light teas, and in the evening the menu is structured so that you can order a bowl of soup and another appetizer or go for every course. Because it *is* a wine bar, at any time there are a baker's dozen of both white and red wines available by the glass, allowing you to sample not only French and California wines, but also those from Chile, New Zealand, Australia, Italy, and South Africa.

SW5

Earl's Court

Earl's Court is often called "Kangaroo Court" because it serves as the unofficial headquarters of London's large Australian community. It is also a backpacker's haven and hangout, thanks to the many low-priced (and very low quality, in most cases) hostels and B&Bs. Around the tube stop is a fertile ground for druggies and their hangers-on, which makes this area a bit dicey at night. However, the SW5 Great Eats listings are absolutely safe anytime. There is a saving grace, and that is the huge convention and exhibition center, but unless you are doing business there, this is not a top-choice location for most tourists, unless economy is your sole and primary issue.

TOURIST ATTRACTIONS
Earl's Court Exhibition Centre

RESTAURANTS IN SW5

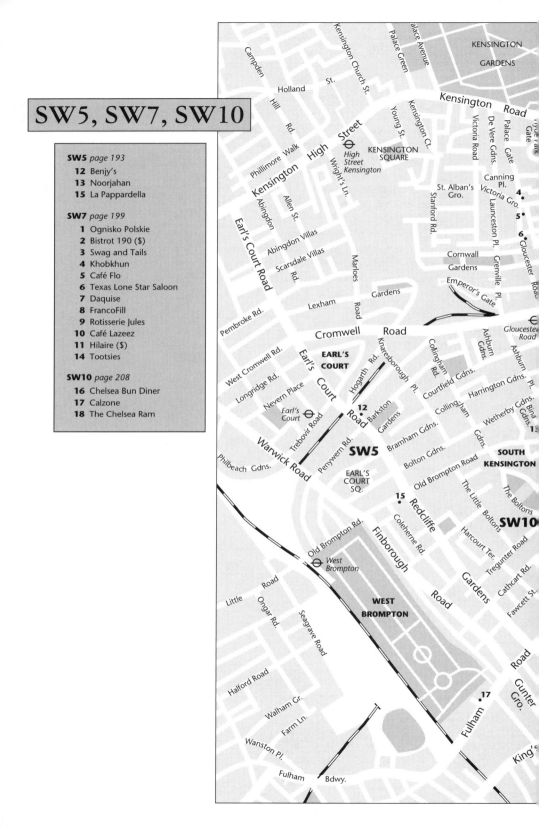

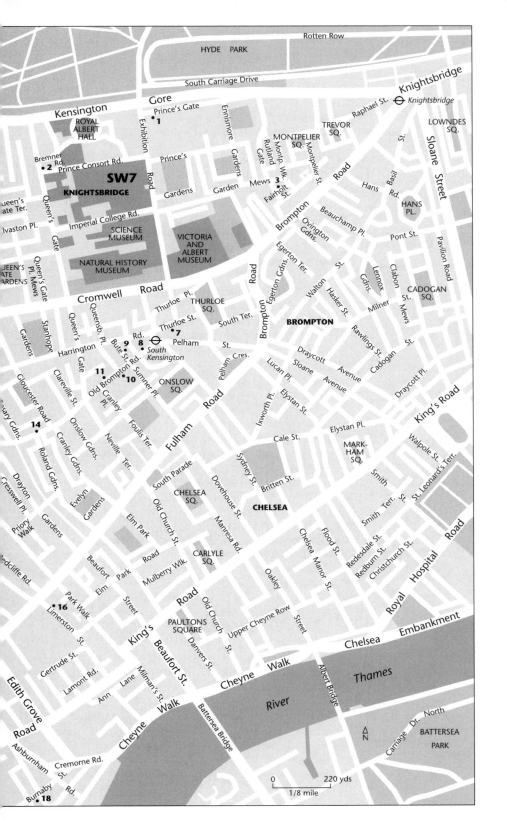

Restaurants

BENJY'S (12)
157 Earl's Court Road, Earl's Court, SW5
Tube: Earl's Court

TELEPHONE
020 7373 0245

OPEN
Daily

CLOSED
Holidays

HOURS
Mon–Sat 6:30 A.M.–9:30 P.M.,
Sun 7A.M.–9:30 P.M., breakfast
served daily until 4:30 P.M.,
continuous service

RESERVATIONS
Not accepted

CREDIT CARDS
None

PRICES
À la carte £5–9, minimum
charge £3.50

SERVICE
Discretionary

Benjy's claim to fame is breakfast, served until late afternoon in a utilitarian coffee shop with plastic ketchup and A.1. sauce dispensers gracing its tables, around which sit a colorful clientele of poor and cash-strapped international cheap eaters. If you want to send your cholesterol level into overdrive and max out your fat-gram allowance for the next two months, eat one of Benjy's breakfasts. More specifically, gorge on the Builder Breakfast. For about £4, you will be served a platter overflowing with bacon, two sausages, eggs, baked beans, toast, and all the coffee or tea you can consume. For the same price, you can dive into a sirloin steak, eggs, beans, peas, chips, and again, all the coffee or tea you want. Lesser mortals can order smaller versions or à la carte. The menu also lists sandwiches, specials, and other dishes cooked according to the chicken-fried-steak school of culinary excellence. But remember, the best meal at Benjy's is breakfast. The statements on the menu say it all in terms of the management's attitude and service: "This is not the Ritz, so be prepared to share a table, you might make a friend," and "When there is a queue at the door, vacate your table promptly," and "The only thing served small is the bill."

NOTE: No alcohol allowed; restaurant is unlicensed.

LA PAPPARDELLA (15)
253 Old Brompton Road, Earl's Court, SW5
Tube: Earl's Court

TELEPHONE
020 7373 7777, 7259 2933

OPEN
Daily

CLOSED
Holidays

HOURS
Noon–midnight, continuous
service

RESERVATIONS
Advised for dinner

CREDIT CARDS
AE, DC, MC, V

PRICES
À la carte £15–20

SERVICE
Discretionary

Readers continue to write to me about La Pappardella. If other restaurants knew about these rave notices, they would dispatch spies to La Pappardella to take serious notes. One woman admitted that she ate here every night during her London stay and had the Pappardella Surprise three times! Others have loved minestrone with fresh Parmesan and the *gamberoni all'aglio*—butterflied prawns with butter, wine, and garlic sauce, served on a bed of rice—saying it was one dish they never wanted to end.

These readers and I definitely agree that La Pappardella is one of London's best roll-up-your-sleeves Italian restaurants. Many nights, there's a line by 9 P.M.

waiting to get into this noisy trattoria along Old Brompton Road, where seating is sardine-style on red seats squeezed around little marble-topped tables. In the summer, the best tables are outside in the back garden, where there is more space and the noise from the banter between the diners and the young waitstaff is less strident. Actually, this bright and colorful repartee only adds to the enjoyment of the inexpensive food, which is good from the first bite to the last, and all of it is made here—from the bread to the pasta to the sauces that cover it.

It is important to go easy on the appetizers and not fill up on the homemade pizza bread before anything else arrives. Begin with a light choice: the grilled mixed veggies with a splash of fresh lemon and olive oil or the carpaccio—raw, thinly sliced beef fillet served with rocket salad and Parmesan shavings. All the familiar pastas are here, along with gnocchi, cannelloni, and lasagna. Pizza lovers have eighteen choices, and the more than fifteen preparations of veal, beef, and chicken will appeal to meat eaters. Portions are all oversize to begin with, but if you are feeling Herculean, larger helpings are always available. By the time you get to dessert, a scoop of ice cream or sorbet may be all you will be able to fit in.

NOORJAHAN (13)
2A Bina Gardens (off Old Brompton Road), South Kensington, SW5
Tube: Gloucester Road, South Kensington (both long walks)

Where to go for some reliable Indian food? One choice is Noorjahan, the local favorite in an area of South Kensington that has several restaurants serving food from the subcontinent. Tandoori chicken and lamb, plus a wide variety of curries, headline the menu. If you are a beginner with Indian food, order the chicken *tikka masala,* one of the chef's most popular specialties. Tandoori, or tikka, is a staple of northern Indian cooking. The meat, usually lamb or chicken, has been marinated in herbs and cooked in a tandoor—an Indian clay oven—which cooks the meat quickly, sealing in the juices and leaving the outside crisp. Noorjahan's version is cooked with ground almonds and cashews, fresh cream, yogurt, and mild spices. Add a vegetable, rice, and naan—the puffy, chewy Indian bread also cooked in the tandoor—and you will be all set. Old Indian-food hands

TELEPHONE
020 7373 6522

OPEN
Daily

CLOSED
2 days at Christmas

HOURS
Lunch noon–2:30 P.M., dinner 6–11:45 P.M.

RESERVATIONS
Advised

CREDIT CARDS
AE, DC, MC, V

PRICES
À la carte £20–25; set-price lunch or dinner £19.50 3 courses with tea or coffee

SERVICE
10% service charge

will want to try a fish or meat curry, or one of the prawn dishes, ranging from sweet-and-sour to spicy and hot. For dessert, I suggest *kulfi,* the Indian ice cream flavored with cardamom and pistachios.

The service is always polite and helpful at explaining each dish, the food is dependable time after time, the kitchen is up to cleanliness standards (which is not the case at most Indian restaurants in London), and the simple dining room with fresh flowers on each table is attractive. It all adds up to a nice Indian meal.

NOTE: Special dishes can be prepared if requested in advance. Takeaway is available.

SW7

South Kensington and Knightsbridge

Knightsbridge is an upmarket shopping paradise, anchored by Harvey Nichols and Harrods, where extravagance is the top commodity. The side streets around Harrods are choked with chauffeured limousines ferrying Middle Eastern potentates and taxies stacked three deep waiting for tourists. Smart designer boutiques line Sloane Street, and very expensive shops make window-shopping along Beauchamp (pronounced BEE-chum) Place about all most of us can afford.

South Kensington is an appealing residential area with many nice hotels and restaurants. It is also known for its "Museum District"—the Victoria and Albert (decorative arts), Natural History (dinosaurs), and Science and Technology Museums (with interactive exhibits) are all here. The gold Albert Memorial (built to commemorate the beloved husband of Queen Victoria) and the Royal Albert Concert Hall are also in the neighborhood.

TOURIST ATTRACTIONS
Albert Memorial, Royal Albert Hall, Kensington Gardens, Hyde Park, Natural History Museum, Science Museum, Victoria and Albert Museum

RESTAURANTS IN SW7 (see map page 194)

Bistrot 190 ($)	200
Café Flo	200
Café Lazeez	201
Daquise	201
FrancoFill	202
Hilaire ($)	202
Khobkhun	203
Ognisko Polskie	204
Rotisserie Jules	205
Texas Lone Star Saloon	205
Tootsies	206

PUBS

Swag and Tails	206

($) indicates a Big Splurge

Restaurants

BISTROT 190 ($, 2)
190 Queen's Gate, Kensington, SW7
Tube: Gloucester Road

TELEPHONE
020 7581 5666

FAX
020 7581 8172

OPEN
Daily

CLOSED
Christmas Day

HOURS
Lunch noon–2:30 P.M., dinner
7–10:30 P.M.

RESERVATIONS
Advised

CREDIT CARDS
AE, DC, MC, V

PRICES
À la carte £25–32

SERVICE
12.5% service charge

Bistrot 190 is the upstairs neighbor of the more expensive Queensgate 190, in the basement of the Gore Hotel next door (see *Great Sleeps London* for a description of this fabulous hotel). At Bistrot 190, bare floors dotted with tables scattered in a room bedecked with great prints and paintings, old mirrors, and garlands set the stage for this bustling, ever-popular spot overflowing with a classy crowd. When you are seated, try to avoid the central tables on the main path of the waitstaff, who are forced into a slow jog when the restaurant operates at peak capacity.

The seasonally conceived identical lunch and dinner menu displays a fondness for combinations that truly work. For a wintry appetizer, I love the game and asparagus terrine with a sprinkling of wild berries. If I am famished, I order the poached egg and Parma ham with potato *rösti,* spinach, and tomato hollandaise, which is so rich and filling it could serve as a meal in itself. For a different vegetarian main course, look for the parcel of spiced vegetables served with bok choy, wild rice, and a mild curry sauce. Pheasant braised in port wine; slow-cooked lamb shank that was so tender it fell off the bone, served with a duo of risottos (tomato and saffron); and pan-fried, honey-glazed red snapper were all voted winners at my table. If you have had either the chocolate and pear crumble under a warm custard sauce or the orange and raspberry crème brûlée once, you will want them to be on the menu every time you eat here, which, if you are in London for any length of time, you will do more than once.

NOTE: Management's policy: "Smokers and users of mobile phones are asked to be considerate of others."

CAFÉ FLO (5)
25–35 Gloucester Road, Kensington, SW7
Tube: Gloucester Road

For details, see page 42. All other information is the same.

TELEPHONE: 020 7589 1383

CAFÉ LAZEEZ (10)
93–95 Old Brompton Road, South Kensington, SW7
Tube: South Kensington

When booking at Café Lazeez on Old Brompton Road, be specific and request a table in the café downstairs for a more casual meal, or in the room upstairs for a more formal dinner. The South Kensington branch has al fresco tables and live jazz in the café-bar.

NOTE: The other two Lazeez restaurants are in Soho (W1), page 43, and Clerkenwell (EC1), page 224.

TELEPHONE: 020 7581 9993
FAX: 020 7581 8200
EMAIL: cafelazeez@compuserve.com
OPEN: Daily
CLOSED: Never
HOURS: 11 A.M.–1 A.M., continuous service
RESERVATIONS: Advised
CREDIT CARDS: AE, DC, MC, V
PRICES: À la carte £15–32
SERVICE: £1 cover charge, 12.5% service charge

DAQUISE (7)
20 Thurloe Street, South Kensington, SW7
Tube: South Kensington

If you have been to Eastern Europe, you will recognize Daquise. During the morning and at teatime, this popular Polish gathering place operates as a café and attracts a cross section of families with small children, toothless pensioners, and dignified Polish émigrés sharing memories over plates of their native food and glasses of steaming tea. If you arrive for lunch or dinner, chances are you will be seated downstairs, where the more appealing atmosphere resembles a Polish country cottage with bright table coverings and painted handicrafts scattered around the room. Order a shot or two of one-hundred-proof vodka or a Polish beer while waiting for the robust specialties of beet soup, salted herring, fried pork or buckwheat sausages, pork knuckle, pierogi (pasta shells stuffed with cheese, meat, or cabbage and mushrooms), beef or vegetable stroganoff, or the house specialty: crispy potato pancakes served with sour cream and applesauce. For dessert, save room for pancakes slathered in ice cream, orange caramel sauce, and almond flakes or rolled with cream cheese and raisins. If that is too much for your sweet tooth or food capacity, then finish with the Polish coffee: a cup of strong coffee laced with honey vodka and topped with whipped cream.

TELEPHONE
020 7589 6117

OPEN
Daily

CLOSED
Christmas Day, New Year's Eve, some holidays (call to check)

HOURS
Daily 11:30 A.M.–11 P.M., continuous service; set-price lunch Mon–Fri noon–3 P.M.

RESERVATIONS
Not necessary

CREDIT CARDS
MC, V

PRICES
À la carte £10–18; set-price (lunch only) £10 noon–3 P.M. 2 courses, wine, and coffee

SERVICE
Discretionary

Daquise is only a few doors away from the South Kensington tube station and convenient to the museums in Kensington.

NOTE: There is a nonsmoking section.

FRANCOFILL (8)

1 Old Brompton Road, South Kensington, SW7
Tube: South Kensington

TELEPHONE
020 7584 0087
OPEN
Daily
CLOSED
2 days at Christmas and New Year's
HOURS
11 A.M.–11 P.M., continuous service
RESERVATIONS
Accepted and preferred for 6 or more
CREDIT CARDS
AE, MC, V
PRICES
Restaurant: à la carte £9–20; bar: £5–8; set-price lunch: Mon–Fri £8.95 2 courses, £10.95 3 courses
SERVICE
12.5% service charge

Fast food à la française in London? *Mais oui* . . . at FrancoFill, a *très bon* Great Eat done up in the colors of the French flag. The bright interior features red, white, and blue in the wide plank floors and paper table dressings, black-and-white pictures of Paris, and a sizable French-speaking waitstaff nattily attired in denim shirts. The signature dish is FrancoFill, a country loaf filled with your choice of cooked-to-order char-grilled meats or vegetables, engagingly sauced with either *moutard* (mustard), *Provençale* (tomato-based), *herbes et ail* (fresh herbs and garlic butter), *champignon et estragon* (mushroom and tarragon), *poivre vert* (green peppercorns), or béarnaise. These FF sandwiches are accompanied by *les frites* (french fries) or *une salade*. Other dishes on the French-accented menu include a bold ragout, ratatouille, steak *frites, croque monsieur* (grilled ham and cheese), *canard à l'orange, moules frites* (steamed mussels served with fries and bread and butter), the *plat du jour,* and several salads. The last thing to watch for is their version of *tarte tatin* (the famous French upside-down apple pie), with the British addition of caramel sauce and cream. The bar, with street-side window viewing, is a pleasant place for a relaxing beer, a glass of traditional Breton cider, or an afternoon snack ordered from the small bar menu.

NOTE: There is a nonsmoking section.

HILAIRE ($, 11)

68 Old Brompton Road, South Kensington, SW7
Tube: South Kensington

TELEPHONE
020 7584 8993/7601
OPEN
Mon–Sat
CLOSED
Sat lunch, Sun, holidays, Aug, Dec 24–Jan 8 (approximate dates)
HOURS
Lunch Mon–Fri 12:15–2:30 P.M., dinner Mon–Sat 6:30–11 P.M.

Sprays of fresh orchids and crisp, off-white linens on tables set with shining crystal and flatware set the formal tone at Hilaire's, a well-known South Kensington landmark for fine dining. If I am going with someone special, I like to sit upstairs at a corner banquette in the back, but if I am alone, I prefer one of the tables by the two front windows, and never, ever the table next to the wait station.

The kitchen is acclaimed for its new twists on familiar favorites and consistently delivers dishes that have freshness, good flavor, and excellent presentation in common. For instance, bufala mozzarella is served with baked rather than raw tomatoes and dressed with tapenade, rather than simple olive oil. A delicious warm fennel salad comes on a bed of wild rocket with fresh Parmesan shavings, and a plain artichoke and French green-bean salad gets a new look with the addition of lightly seared pigeon and foie gras glazed with truffle oil. Main courses keep up the pace with seasonally fresh fish such as roast sea bass with a leek risotto and red wine sauce, or char-grilled swordfish with lentils and a lusty salsa verde. If you like lamb, you will love the herb-crusted rack of lamb served with fried garlic, which isn't all that new, but when you taste the rich *gratin dauphinois* that accompanies it, you will be glad nothing has changed here. Desserts display both a resourcefulness with unusual ingredients and a nod to the known and loved. I thought the grilled pineapple slice with a chili and coconut sorbet had a great kick to it, and that the tried-and-true crème brûlée surrounded by a pastiche of winter berries was richly comforting. Service by a trio of waitresses wearing oversize men's shirts and neckties is polite and precise. Wine prices can be intimidating, but there are several varieties by the glass, and the house red or white are both certainly acceptable.

RESERVATIONS
Essential
CREDIT CARDS
AE, DC, MC, V
PRICES
Set-price lunch: £16 1 course, £19.50 2 courses, £22.50 3 courses, £15.50 2 starters, £6 desserts; dinner: 6:30–7:30 P.M. and after 10 P.M. £19.50 2 courses, 7:30–10 P.M. £35 2 courses, £39.50 3 courses, £25.50 2 starters, desserts £8
SERVICE
12.5% service charge

KHOBKHUN (4)
9A Gloucester Road, Kensington, SW7
Tube: Gloucester Road

If you like unusual food and are not afraid to experiment, consider Khobkhun. I was first attracted to this narrow Thai restaurant because it looked so fresh and clean, with flowers in the window box outside and pretty blue-and-white dishes on linen-covered tables inside. The best sign of all was the lunch clientele: all Thais. They obviously were on to something that I needed to know more about. Those of us who like Thai food know that it can be hot and spicy, sometimes too much, if caution and common sense are not exercised. The food here manages to capture the tastes, aromas, and subtleties of Thai food without sacrificing Western digestion at the same time. Please remember, when ordering you can ask to have the spiciness adjusted, but you must ask or it could be turned on full force.

The menu, with more than sixty selections, makes for tantalizing reading. Those with cast-iron stomachs can order the stir-fried squid with garlic and chilies or the

TELEPHONE
020 7584 9514
OPEN
Mon–Sat; Sun dinner only
CLOSED
Sun lunch, holidays
HOURS
Lunch noon–3 P.M., dinner 6–11 P.M.
RESERVATIONS
Not necessary
CREDIT CARDS
MC, V
PRICES
À la carte £10–20; set-price £15–18 for 6–9 dishes, 2-person minimum
SERVICE
10% service charge

pomfret (whitefish) with a fiery sauce. The most popular dish, and certainly one of the best, is surprisingly mild and almost soothing—No. 72, fried noodles Siam style. It comes beautifully arranged on a tray with side dishes of prawns, eggs, bean sprouts, peanuts, and fried noodles. It is not only pleasing to look at, but pleasing to eat as well. There are two set-price menus, but the best way to go here is to order individually according to your own taste and heat tolerance.

NOTE: Takeaway is available.

OGNISKO POLSKIE (1)
55 Prince's Gate (at 55 Exhibition Road), Knightsbridge, SW7
Tube: South Kensington, Knightsbridge

TELEPHONE
020 7589 4635
OPEN
Daily
CLOSED
3 days at Christmas and Easter
HOURS
Lunch 12:30–3 P.M., dinner 6:30–11 P.M.
RESERVATIONS
Accepted and preferred for 4 or more
CREDIT CARDS
AE, DC, MC, V
PRICES
À la carte £22–25; set-price lunch £9.50 3 courses
SERVICE
Discretionary

Ognisko Polskie (Polish Heart Club) was founded more than fifty years ago by the Polish aristocracy exiled in London after World War II. Princess Alexandra of Britain is the patroness, and the many photos hung throughout the faded, once elegant rooms assure you that this was once *the* gathering place for Polish expatriates. Today you will see aging Poles who come to eat, drink, and reminisce about home and families left behind or lost during the world wars. Many of these patrons have been fixtures on this scene long before most Great Eats readers were born. The time-warped setting rambles through several high-ceilinged rooms, creating the impression that nothing much has changed in the minds of its members, who perhaps find yesterday's memories preferable to the harsh realities of today.

The club is open to visitors and is a good place for tea and cakes after a visit to the trio of nearby museums (Victoria and Albert, Natural History, and Science and Technology). If you need something a bit more bracing, stop by the bar and order the Polish national drink: *Slivovice*—a potent fruit brandy that will definitely make your head spin. Or, order a Great Eat set-price lunch for less than £10, featuring at least one native dish. Watch for the platter of Polish sausages and ham, stuffed dumplings, pork knuckle, pheasant with red cabbage and cranberry sauce, and pancakes rolled with sweet cheese and jam. In the winter you will be served in the formal dining room and seated on a little gold chair. In the summer, service is on the terrace overlooking a lovely garden. The music is classical, the waitstaff Polish, and the experience nostalgic if you have any ties to this part of Europe.

ROTISSERIE JULES (9)
6–8 Bute Street, South Kensington, SW7
Tube: South Kensington

See Rotisserie Jules in W11, page 113, for a full description. This branch is unlicensed; BYOB, £1.50 corkage fee. All other information is the same.

TELEPHONE: 020 7584 0600, 020 7221 3331 (free delivery)

OPEN: Daily

CLOSED: Christmas Day

HOURS: Noon–11:30 P.M., continuous service

TEXAS LONE STAR SALOON (6)
54 Gloucester Road, South Kensington, SW7
Tube: Gloucester Road

For a taste of home—Texas style—grab your boots and Stetson and head for the Texas Lone Star Saloon. While hardly the spot for a first date, it is a great place to go with your pals any day of the year (except Christmas). Close your eyes and imagine a Texas honky-tonk with wagon-wheel lights and pine booths in which you are served by a waitress named Sally Sue, who is wearing tight jeans and an even tighter T-shirt, and you will have this place down pat. Country music straight from KJ97 FM in San Antonio, Texas, keeps everyone happy and humming along with Loretta Lynn, Conway Twitty, and Dolly Parton.

The rib-sticking chow is as real as the atmosphere, and it naturally comes in Texas-size portions. The mound of nachos topped with refried beans, tomatoes, onions, jalapeños, and melted cheese carries this warning: "slightly messy but oh-so good!" Slabs of barbecued ribs with cole slaw, T-bone steaks with au gratin potatoes or fries, Texas chili, burritos, tacos, and assorted burgers are guaranteed to keep everyone off a diet. There are other choices, ranging from a Mexican platter to grilled fajita plates dubbed "a sizzling fiesta," and potato skins served with sour cream, chives, or blue cheese. If this isn't enough chow to fill you, try braving the Texas Sundae, an oversize hot-fudge sundae made with five scoops of ice cream. Libations include buckets of beer, Michelob and Dos Equis by the bottle, margaritas, wines, and assorted cocktails that the menu identifies as "SHOOTERS . . . for real cowboys (and girls)." There is a kids' menu, along with coloring books (BYO crayons), and from October to April, a magician performs on Sunday afternoon between 1 and 3 P.M. For everyone,

TELEPHONE
020 7370 5625

OPEN
Daily

CLOSED
Christmas Day

HOURS
Noon–11:30 P.M., continuous service

RESERVATIONS
Not accepted

CREDIT CARDS
AE, MC, V

PRICES
À la carte £10–18

SERVICE
12.5% service charge

there's live toe-tapping music on Wednesday, Thursday, and Sunday from 8 to 11 P.M.

NOTE: Takeaway is available.

TOOTSIES (14)
107 Old Brompton Road, Kensington, SW7
Tube: South Kensington

See Tootsies in W1, page 69, for a full description. All other information is the same.

TELEPHONE: 020 7581 8942

OPEN: Daily

CLOSED: Christmas Day

Pubs

SWAG AND TAILS (3)
10–11 Fairholt Street, Knightsbridge, SW7
Tube: Knightsbridge

TELEPHONE
020 7584 6926

FAX
020 7581 9935

EMAIL
swag&tails@mway.com

OPEN
Mon–Fri

CLOSED
Sat–Sun, holidays

HOURS
Pub 11 A.M.–11 P.M.; lunch noon–3 P.M., dinner 6–10 P.M.

RESERVATIONS
Advised for lunch

CREDIT CARDS
AE, MC, V

PRICES
À la carte £12–18

SERVICE
10% service charge

Annemaria Boomer-Davies has a fifteen-year-old success on her hands, and she has worked very hard to achieve it. The Swag and Tails is in one of London's prettiest and most exclusive neighborhoods, the type we would all live in if we could afford it. It is worth a visit if only to admire the mews houses, with their brightly painted doors and pretty postage-stamp front gardens, which look straight from the pages of *Town and Country.* It is only a few minutes by foot to Harrods and the bustle of Knightsbridge shopping, but this attractive pub-restaurant seems miles away. If you are a nonsmoker, you will want to sit at one of the wooden tables in the middle section. Otherwise, the glass conservatory in back, decorated with a flowering plant on each table and framed Chinese textiles, is appealing on a sunny day. If it is cold and blustery, relax in a high wingback chair in front by the tile-framed fireplace and sip your imported wine or beer. There will be no pinball machines, no rowdies, and no invasive music to disturb your reverie.

The menu roams the globe, and I honestly wondered how the kitchen could turn out the United Nations–inspired fare. With only a few exceptions, everything I tried was good and something I would order again. I thought the smoked duck and mango salad with a poppy seed and chili dressing would be either too hot or too weird. It was neither, but delicately seasoned and not overpowering. Other preludes you can count on include homemade soup, Caesar salad (either plain or with chicken), Oriental spring rolls with a sweet chili sauce, and a caramelized red onion and goat cheese tart. Main plates are not left behind, especially the permanent dishes: sirloin steak sandwich, duck pancakes with spring onion and hoi-sin sauce, quesadillas with guacamole, blini with smoked salmon, and a soul-satisfying pasta and risotto. No one should dismiss the lead item for the perennials: a homemade burger on a sesame bap (bun) served with a salad and shoestring french fries. When Annemaria tried to remove this, her regulars rebelled. Finally, there are the desserts, which are not something you see much of in pubs; here you have a satisfying dilemma—a choice between Annemaria's own mandarin sorbet or caramel ice cream, bread-and-butter pudding with crème anglaise, date-sponge pudding, or chocolate tart with sweet mascarpone.

SW10

South Kensington and West Brompton

TOURIST ATTRACTIONS
King's Road shopping,
Chelsea Embankment

South Kensington flows from SW7 into SW10 and, along with West Brompton, is mainly a residential area.

RESTAURANTS IN SW10 (see map page 194)

Calzone	**208**
Chelsea Bun Diner	**208**

PUBS

The Chelsea Ram	**210**

Restaurants

CALZONE (17)
335 Fulham Road, South Kensington, SW10
Tube: South Kensington

See Calzone in W11, page 110, for a full description. All other information is the same.

TELEPHONE: 020 7352 9797
OPEN: Daily
CLOSED: 4 days at Christmas

CHELSEA BUN DINER (16)
9A Limerston Street, South Kensington, SW10
Tube: Sloane Square, then bus 11, 19, or 22 down King's Road; from Earl's Court tube, take bus 31 to last stop

TELEPHONE
020 7352 3635
OPEN
Daily
CLOSED
2 days at Christmas
HOURS
Mon–Sat 7 A.M.–midnight, Sun 9 A.M.–7 P.M., continuous service
RESERVATIONS
Not necessary
CREDIT CARDS
MC, V

"CALORIES, CALORIES, CALORIES!! Who's counting? Enjoy yourself and indulge in gastronomic ecstasy!!"

This is the mantra for the Chelsea Bun Diner, where the chant for excess is tempered by the following posted public notice: "We do provide indigestion tablets for customers who find our portions to hard to handle."

Calling all bargain-seeking Great Eaters in London who think portion control is a culinary sin: The Chelsea Bun Diner is the place to go! It attracts hordes of munchers from eighteen to eighty with its good-humored, casual ambience, its low, low prices, and its wide-ranging menu. It has been here since the days of Jonathan Swift, who is reported to have bought a bun here for a penny. When you arrive, don't expect much in the way of decor or gracious service; do expect good food served in gargantuan helpings geared toward big-league appetites. Breakfast, with more than forty choices, is served until 6 P.M., during which time marathon eaters should consider the Ultimate Breakfast, which the restaurant bets you can't finish, and I agree. For less than £8.50 you get three eggs, hash browns, three Scotch pancakes with maple syrup and clotted cream, bacon, country sausage, mushrooms, a beef burger, and French toast, plus a large mug of tea or coffee. They don't mention needing a wheelchair to get out after this feeding frenzy. At the other end of the spectrum is the Low Cholesterol Breakfast, which has a choice of muesli or other dry cereals; two slices of brown toast with jam, honey, or marmalade; fresh orange, apple, or tomato juice; and tea or coffee. Even though the second bowl of cereal is free, this is really a dull choice by comparison. The Chelsea Bun Mega Omelette has four eggs and is filled with ham, salami, and cheddar and comes with french fries or country-style spuds and a salad. This could feed three! The burgers range from regular to "all the way," which is topped with ham, egg, cheese, lettuce, and a tomato on a one-hundred-percent beef patty and includes fries or country-style potatoes, a mixed salad, and a relish tray.

Other dishes definitely worth attention include potatoes stuffed, baked, fried, or mashed; pasta at least eight ways; homemade meat pies; super sandwiches that come "overfilled" (or, with triple the filling mix) on granary bread, ciabatta olive bread, or brown baps (buns); and mega desserts, including a banana split and homemade apple crumble with custard. These dishes keep the hard chairs filled from dawn until almost midnight. Don't have time to sit down and eat? Don't worry; they also prepare everything to go.

NOTE: Restaurant is unlicensed; BYOB (£.50 corkage fee). They'll call a cab if you do not have a designated driver. Daytime limit on tables one hour and fifteen minutes, evening limit two hours. The Chelsea Bun Diner has another location in SW11, an area not covered by *Great Eats London.* It's at 70 Battersea Bridge Road (Tel: 020 7738 9009).

PRICES
À la carte £6–10, minimum charge £4 at lunch, £6 at dinner

SERVICE
Discretionary

Pubs

THE CHELSEA RAM (18)
32 Barnaby Street, Chelsea, SW10
Tube: Sloan Square, South Kensington, very long walk

TELEPHONE
020 7351 4008
OPEN
Daily
CLOSED
Christmas, New Year's, call to check on other holidays
HOURS
Pub: Mon–Sat 11 A.M.–11 P.M., Sun noon–10:30 P.M.; lunch daily noon–3 P.M., dinner Mon–Sat 7–10 P.M., Sun until 9:30 P.M.
RESERVATIONS
Accepted for 4 or more
CREDIT CARDS
AE, MC, V
PRICES
À la carte £15–25
SERVICE
Discretionary

At first glance, the Chelsea Ram looks like countless other London pubs: worn, dark, bare floors in a meandering room with a few tables in front for serious drinking, and more in the back for serious eating. At lunch the scene is professional and businesslike, with the patrons wearing designer-label power outfits and checking their office messages on mobile phones. In the evening, the entire space is a sea of successful, black-clad trendsetters, secret lovers, and singles who come to schmooze, flirt, brag, drink, and maybe work up a business deal or snag a weekend date. Around 9 P.M. they sit down to eat. And eat well they do, from a menu that has shed its country-bumpkin-pub image and replaced it with an urban cool selection of trendy twenty-first-century dishes. Five-spice duck spring rolls and marinated vegetable crostini with bufala mozzarella and wild rocket have the edge on the starters. The wild boar loin with Parma ham, beets, green beans, garlic mash, and thyme gravy had too much going on, but not the succulent roast chicken with creamed leeks and mushrooms in puff pastry, or the pork and apple sausages with garlic mashed potatoes and onion gravy. Lest we forget this is still a pub, on Sundays, a traditional Sunday roast leg of lamb or beef, complete with potatoes and assorted vegetables, sells out quickly.

NW1

Regent's Park

The five-hundred-acre Regent's Park was once Henry VIII's hunting forest and later provided London with hay and dairy products. Today there are two boating lakes, Queen Mary's Gardens, the London Central Mosque on the west side, and the London Zoo on the north. Close by is Madame Tussaud's Wax Museum, one of the top tourist attractions in the country—even though it is overrated, snaked lines lasting two to three hours are common during peak tourist time. Next door is the London Planetarium.

The area's most famous resident was Sherlock Holmes, who, even though fictitious, still receives letters addressed to him at "221B Baker Street."

Since the fifteenth century, a church has stood on the site where the present St. Marylebone Church is now. This church was built by Thomas Hardwick and was where Robert Browning married Elizabeth Barrett. Charles Dickens lived nearby on Devonshire Terrace, and his son was baptized in the church, which he described in his novel *Dombey and Son.*

TOURIST ATTRACTIONS
London Planetarium, Madame Tussaud's, London Zoo, British Library, Sherlock Holmes Museum

RESTAURANTS IN NW1

WINE BARS

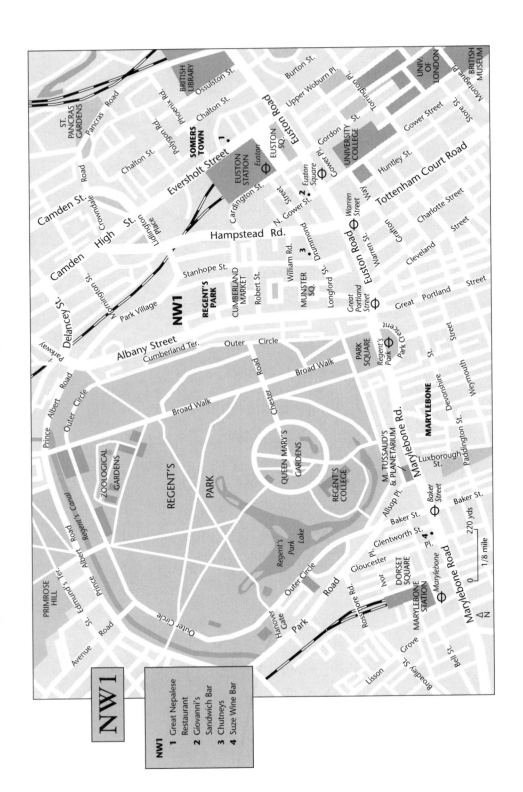

Restaurants

CHUTNEYS (3)
124 Drummond Street, Regent's Park, NW1
Tube: Euston Square, Euston

Tired of sandwiches? Had it with burgers and chips? Burned out on pub grub? Looking for a Great Eat that is well-priced, different, tastes good, and is not a heart attack on a plate? Head for London's "Little India" and try Chutneys—home of some of the best Indian vegetarian food in the area. Card-carrying Great Eaters in London will get their ticket punched at the buffet lunch, which is served Monday to Saturday from noon until 2:45 P.M. and all day Sunday for the almost giveaway price of £5.95 for as much as you can pile on your plate. The fare varies daily, but it always includes a sampling of their homemade chutneys and other dishes covering the gastronomic diversity of the subcontinent. There are hot starters from Farsan, cold appetizers from Bombay's Chowpaty, *thali* from Gujarat, and southern Indian dishes from Madras. Everything is neatly labeled and prepared fresh daily. If you are not familiar with the variety Indian food offers, Chutneys is the place to change that.

NOTE: On Sunday, only the buffet is served, no à la carte.

TELEPHONE
020 7388 0604

OPEN
Daily

CLOSED
4–7 days at Christmas

HOURS
Mon–Sat buffet lunch noon–2:45 P.M., dinner 6–11:30 P.M., Sun buffet only noon–10:30 P.M., continuous service

RESERVATIONS
Not necessary

CREDIT CARDS
MC, V

PRICES
Set-price lunch: Mon–Sat, all-you-can-eat buffet £5.95 (served all day Sun); set-price dinner: Mon–Fri £10.95 multiple dishes

SERVICE
No service charge for the buffet, 10% service charge added for dinner

GIOVANNI'S SANDWICH BAR (2)
152 North Gower Street (at Euston Road), Euston, NW1
Tube: Euston Square, Euston

Giovanni's Sandwich Bar has hundreds of clones all over London, all doing about the same thing: dispensing filling food, coffee, talk, opinions, and good cheer to the friends, neighbors, and geezers who check in daily to keep up with the local goings-on. If you are around Euston and need a quick bite, pop in here and pull up a chair at one of the four shared tables inside. In the morning, the drill includes variations on the full English breakfast of eggs, bacon, sausage, beans, tomato, toast, chips, and strong coffee or tea. Around noon, sandwiches, filled spuds, or a hot dish are on the plates. This is the time to watch for the lasagna and shepherd's pie, made by Giovanni's mother. In between, you can order peanut butter or Marmite on toast, a cappuccino, or a bottle of fruit juice. Decor, well, there isn't much of that

TELEPHONE
020 7383 0531

OPEN
Mon–Sat breakfast and lunch only

CLOSED
Sun, holidays (sometimes open if there is business), sometimes closes if the weather is bad

HOURS
Mon–Fri 7 A.M.–3:30 P.M., Sat 8 A.M.–2 P.M., continuous service

RESERVATIONS
Not accepted

CREDIT CARDS
None

PRICES
À la carte £3.50–7.50

SERVICE
No service charged or expected

here, but Giovanni does have an interesting collection of black-and-white photos of old London, and the blackboard lettering was done by a pal in Phoenix, Arizona.

GREAT NEPALESE RESTAURANT (1)
48 Eversholt Street, Euston, NW1
Tube: Euston

TELEPHONE
020 7388 6737/5935
OPEN
Daily
CLOSED
2 days at Christmas
HOURS
Lunch Mon–Sat noon–2:45 P.M., Sun noon–2:30 P.M., dinner Mon–Sat 6–11:30 P.M., Sun 6–11:15 P.M.
RESERVATIONS
Advised and preferred
CREDIT CARDS
AE, DC, MC, V
PRICES
À la carte £12–20; set-price £15.50 3 courses
SERVICE
10% service charge, minimum charge £6.50

The Great Nepalese Restaurant continues to get my vote as one of the best Indian-Nepalese dining experiences in London. The outside has had a face lift and has a new frosted front window, a new sign, and a new awning and railings. The inside is pleasant and comfortable, with hand-carved wooden screens, a teak ceiling, and a few Nepalese masks on the walls.

A first visit usually means many returns to this friendly place, run by Gopal Manandhar and his three sons. Their service is professional, courteous, and always helpful. They will suggest a menu for the uninitiated, selecting for taste, interest, and price. Nepalese cooking uses fresh herbs and more spices than most Indian-inspired food, but there are many mild dishes available, and the kitchen will always adjust seasonings to suit a customer's wishes. House specialties include Nepalese starters *masco-bara* (two black lentil pancakes with curry) and the *haku choyala* (barbecued diced mutton with hot spices, ginger, and garlic). You will need a bottle or two of the Kathmandu Nepalese beer to temper the flames of this one. Main-course standouts are the tandoori dishes and the curries made with chicken, lamb, mutton, or pork. One of the most popular is the *bhutuwa* chicken, a flavorful, mild dish with chicken cooked in ginger and garlic and flavored with green herbs. Vegetarians have more than twenty-five dishes from which to choose, including *aloo kerau ko achar* (a cold dish of potatoes, peas, green chili, and sesame seeds) and *mutter panir* (homemade cheese and peas in curry). For dessert, try the house rice pudding, flavored with bay leaves, cardamom, and cinnamon and flecked with raisins. To finish your culinary tour of Nepal, order a glass of Nepalese Coronation rum, made in 1975.

NOTE: Takeaway is available at a 10 percent discount.

Wine Bars

SUZE WINE BAR (4)
1 Glentworth Street, Marylebone, NW1
Tube: Baker Street, Marylebone

Tom and Susan Glynn's Suze Wine Bar is a quiet wine bar and restaurant celebrating the food, drink, and hospitality of their native New Zealand. In addition to the daily specials, look for seared New Zealand rack of lamb, baby Australian snapper on top of lemon roasted potatoes with a fennel and chili relish, and their specialty, shelled green mussels in a creamy wine sauce, all accompanied by an interesting vintage of New Zealand red or white wine. Equal care is invested in the desserts, especially the New Zealand and Australia favorite, pavlova, a meringue filled with cream, fruit, and calories. Seating is either upstairs on a sidewalk terrace or downstairs in a light room displaying artwork for sale. For those who might find the need, catering is available.

TELEPHONE
020 7486 8216

FAX
020 7935 3827

OPEN
Mon–Fri

CLOSED
Sat–Sun, holidays

HOURS
11 A.M.–11 P.M.; lunch noon–3 P.M., snacks 3–5:30 P.M., dinner 5:30–10:30 P.M.

RESERVATIONS
Not necessary

CREDIT CARDS
AE, DC, MC, V

PRICES
À la carte £18–22

SERVICE
Discretionary

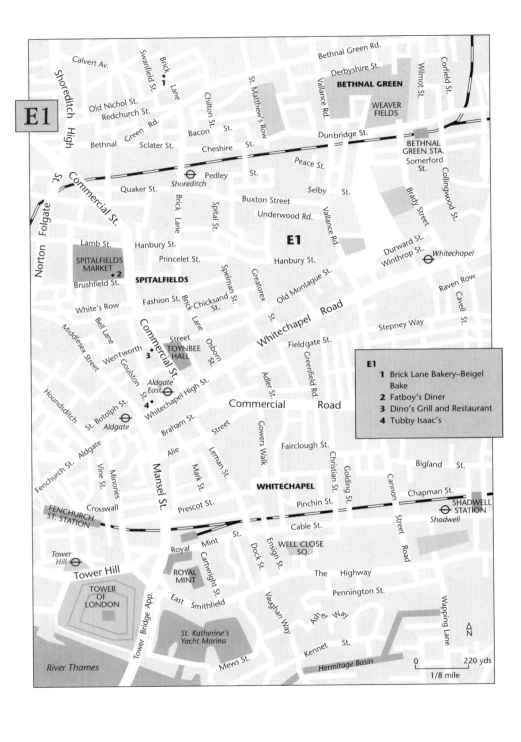

E1

Calvert Av.

Shoreditch High St.

Bethnal Green Rd.

Derbyshire St.

BETHNAL GREEN

Wilmot St.

Corfield St.

Old Nichol St.

Redchurch St.

Swanfield St.

Brick Lane

• **1**

Chilton St.

St. Matthew's Row

Vallance Rd.

WEAVER FIELDS

Green Rd.

Bacon St.

Dunbridge St.

Bethnal

Sclater St.

Cheshire St.

BETHNAL GREEN STA.

Somerford St.

Commercial St.

Peace St.

Pedley

Shoreditch

St.

Collingwood St.

Quaker St.

Selby St.

Brick Lane

Brady Street

Folgate St.

Spital St.

Buxton Street

Vallance Rd.

Underwood Rd.

E1

Norton

Lamb St.

Hanbury St.

Princelet St.

Hanbury St.

Durward St.

Winthrop St.

Whitechapel

SPITALFIELDS MARKET

• **2**

Brushfield St.

SPITALFIELDS

Greatorex St.

Raven Row

Cavell St.

White's Row

Fashion St.

Chicksand St.

Spelman St.

Old Montague St.

Brick Lane

Bell Lane

Middlesex Street

Wentworth

Coulston St.

Street

TOYNBEE HALL

• **3**

Osborn St.

Whitechapel Road

Fieldgate St.

Stepney Way

Aldgate East

Adler St.

Greenfield Rd.

Houndsditch

St. Botolph St.

• **4** Whitechapel High St.

Aldgate

Braham St.

Commercial **Road**

Fenchurch St.

Aldgate

Alie Street

Mark St.

Leman St.

Gowers Walk

Fairclough St.

Bigland St.

Vine St.

Minories

Mansel St.

Prescot St.

WHITECHAPEL

Christian St.

Golding St.

Cannon Street Road

Chapman St.

SHADWELL STATION

Crosswall

Pinchin St.

Shadwell

FENCHURCH ST. STATION

Cable St.

Tower Hill

Royal Mint St.

Dock St.

Ensign St.

WELL CLOSE SQ.

Tower Hill

ROYAL MINT

Cartwright St.

The Highway

Pennington St.

Wapping Lane

TOWER OF LONDON

East Smithfield

Vaughan Way

Asher Way

Tower Bridge App.

St. Katherine's Yacht Marina

Kennet St.

River Thames

Mews St.

Hermitage Basin

N

0   220 yds

1/8 mile

E1
1 Brick Lane Bakery–Beigel Bake
2 Fatboy's Diner
3 Dino's Grill and Restaurant
4 Tubby Isaac's

E1

Spitalfields and Whitechapel

In the Spitalfields and Whitechapel areas of London's East End, you can buy a bagel, eat at a cheap Asian or Indian restaurant, worship at a synagogue or Indian temple, visit the Spitalfields Heritage Center, which displays the history of the area's immigrants, buy organic fruit and produce at the Spitalfields Market on Sunday mornings, and see the latest in London's avant-garde art movement at the Whitechapel Art Gallery. This is an area far removed in mind and spirit from the West End, but is a vital and vibrant part of London's far-reaching makeup.

TOURIST ATTRACTIONS
Spitalfields Market

Restaurants

DINO'S GRILL AND RESTAURANT (3)
76 Commercial Street, Spitalfields Market, E1
Tube: Aldgate East

Dino Bragoli and his right-hand helper and mom, Peggy, have been running this Great Eats outpost since the early sixties. It is a good, clean bet in an eyebrow-raising area around the Spitalfields fruit and vegetable market and the sleazy garment district surrounding Petticoat Lane. The emphasis is on back-to-basics food for breakfast and lunch, the stuff we all loved before sun-dried tomatoes, chèvre, and arugula took over the menus of more stylish eateries.

Truckers and market workers arrive at Dino's Grill around 6 A.M. for fry-ups of eggs, beans, bacon, sausage, chips, and slabs of fried bread. If you want just a cup of

TELEPHONE
020 7247 6097

OPEN
Mon–Fri; Sun breakfast and lunch only

CLOSED
Dinner, Sat, holidays

HOURS
Grill: Mon–Fri 6 A.M.–4:30 P.M., Sun 6 A.M.–2 P.M.; restaurant: Mon–Fri noon–3 P.M.

RESERVATIONS
Not necessary

CREDIT CARDS
AE, DC, MC, V

PRICES
À la carte £5–11 for the grill or restaurant
SERVICE
Discretionary

java and a pastry, order one of their famous homemade and well-named Rock Cakes, which are similar to heavy-duty scones, studded with raisins. By 11:30 A.M., regulars stream in for steak and mushroom pie, overflowing plates of pasta and grilled meats, bangers and mash (sausage and mashed potatoes), roast meat served with two vegetables, and fried fish. The specialty of the house is *pasta al Dino,* spaghetti with a choice of sauces, topped with ham and/or a fried egg and Parmesan cheese and then run under the broiler. Let's just say it is different. Desserts? This is a meat-and-potatoes place, so desserts are not part of the main attraction, unless you have room for the tiramisu.

In an effort to attract a wider clientele, the downstairs red-brick basement was turned into a separate restaurant with its own entrance. The good Italian grub on the menu is almost the same as the food served upstairs, but if you eat down here, you will miss all the fun and local color that comes with your meal upstairs.

FATBOY'S DINER (2)
Inside Spitalfields Market (off Commercial Street), Spitalfields, E1
Tube: Liverpool Street, Aldgate East

TELEPHONE
020 7375 2763
OPEN
Daily
CLOSED
5 days at Christmas
HOURS
Mon–Fri 10 A.M.–4 P.M., Sat until 9 P.M., Sun 9 A.M.–7 P.M., continuous service
RESERVATIONS
Not accepted
CREDIT CARDS
None
PRICES
À la carte £8–12
SERVICE
Discretionary: "Don't be a nickel squeezer: if you enjoyed your meal, leave a tip."

Fatboy's Diner was built in Worcester, Massachusetts, by the Worcester Lunch Car Company and shipped in 1955 to Georgetown, Massachusetts, where truckers, high-school students, businessmen, local cops, and tourists always kept it filled. Relocated to London about twenty years ago and restored to its 1950s splendor, it is now inside the Spitafields Market and still going strong in the same rock 'n' roll atmosphere.

It has lots of chrome, stools, fry cooks behind the counter, and loud American music from the fifties and sixties booming nonstop. No one stands on dining ceremony here. Your food order is shouted to the cooks and served by the fast-working waitstaff. You can eat breakfast anytime, or stuff yourself with the Hillbilly Fatburger, a double burger with cheese, bacon, barbecue sauce, and topped with chili. Or there is the A.B.C. burger, a giant Fatburger covered with avocado, bacon, and cheese, and for you health hippies, a veggie cheeseburger. Hot dogs get fair exposure, and you will, too, if you indulge in the Hotbreath, with chili, Swiss or American cheese, and raw onions. To complete the meal, add a thick chocolate malt, the Flamingo F (a cream soda float with strawberry ice cream). or the "burn it and let it swim"—that is, a Coca-Cola float with chocolate ice cream. Slabs of apple or blueberry pie and double-chocolate brownies (all à la mode, of course) will take you further down memory lane. No, it isn't the stuff gastronomic thrills are made of, but for a Great Eat that will take you back—way back—it is fun. Long live Fatboy's Diner!

TUBBY ISAAC'S (4)
Goulston Street (near Aldgate East tube station), Spitalfields, E1
Tube: Aldgate East

Since 1919, the Isaac family has been selling jellied eels, rollmops (rolled-up pickled herring), mussels, oysters, fresh boiled crabs, prawns, cockles, and sea snails from a red-and-white cart near the Aldgate East tube station. The founder, Isaac Brenner, was fat and little, so everyone called him Tubby Isaac, and the name has stayed with this well-loved East End institution. The man standing in front of me waiting for his eels told me, "I'm 82, and I remember this stand as a boy. I have always loved it." Their fast-food stand-up specialty is jellied eels, which is an acquired taste that takes a great deal of determination and practice. It is included here as a Great London Eat appealing only to those eager to collect cuisine experiences they can talk about once they return home. How do you eat a jellied eel, which is boiled, then cut up and served in its own gelatinous consommé in a Styrofoam cup? Very carefully. As anyone at Tubby Isaac's will tell you, the proper way to eat a jellied eel is to put a whole piece into your mouth, taking care to chew around the bone in the center. The lemon-colored jellied consommé in which the eels are served is helped by heavy doses of chili vinegar and chunks of bread from the bread bin. The best days to hit Tubby's are Thursday through Sunday, when the biggest selection is offered—just in case you didn't come for the eels.

Can't decide what to serve at your next party? Impress your friends with a spread from Tubby's—they cater!

TELEPHONE
None

OPEN
Daily

CLOSED
2 days at Christmas

HOURS
10 A.M.–10:30 P.M., continuous service

RESERVATIONS
Not accepted

CREDIT CARDS
None

PRICES
À la carte £1.80–5

SERVICE
No service charged or expected

Tearooms, Pâtisseries, and Bakeries

BRICK LANE BAKERY–BEIGEL BAKE (1)
159 Brick Lane, East End, E2
Tube: Aldgate East, Liverpool Street

TELEPHONE
020 7729 0616

OPEN
Daily

CLOSED
Never

HOURS
24 hours a day, 7 days a week

RESERVATIONS
None

CREDIT CARDS
None

PRICES
Bagels 12 pence each, 20 pence–£2.50 filled, £23 for 14 dozen

SERVICE
No service charged or expected

Twelve pence buys you one plain bagel, 75 pence a half dozen, and £23 will bag you fourteen dozen of the best, most authentic bagels in London. No matter how you spell it (bagels, beigels, or baigels), these are the real thing: a round roll with a hole in the middle, first boiled, then baked so they will be just crispy enough on the outside and slightly chewy inside. This East End institution is open twenty-four hours a day, 7 days a week, 365 days a year, and dispenses more than 8 million bagels (four thousand on Sundays), which are consumed plain, buttered, piled high with smoked salmon and cream cheese, or stacked with slices of the Brick Lane's own salt beef (twenty-five of these are cooked per day). Don't look for blueberry, poppy seed, or the "everything" bagel. There are only two choices: "ordinary," which are sold daily, and "salty," which are added on the weekends. Also available are a variety of rye, wholegrain, white, and black breads, pastries, and cheesecake. And, as the owner reminded me, "Everything you see is made here. We only bring in the ingredients."

The trip from the tube stop to 159 Brick Lane is a fifteen- to twenty-minute hike through an Indian, Pakistani, Bangladeshi neighborhood lined with more than forty cheap-food dives and trashy-clothing outlets. It is probably most interesting on Sunday mornings around 11 A.M., when families are shopping along here and at the Petticoat Lane Market. It looks a whole lot worse than it really is. You are okay in the daytime, but at night don't make the trek alone; go as a group for added safety.

DIRECTIONS: From the tube stop, walk east on White Chapel High Street and turn left on Osborn Street, which becomes Brick Lane. You will know you are close when you see the line outside at the counter.

EC1

Farringdon and Clerkenwell

In the late nineteenth century, Clerkenwell was a seedy, rundown slum. Now the slums are gone, and the area is enjoying a renaissance of sorts, thanks to its proximity to the West End. However, other than some exceptionally good restaurants, Clerkenwell and Farringdon hold little interest for most tourists. Smithfield Market, off Farringdon Road, has been in operation since the twelfth century. It is London's main wholesale meat market, and its annual turnover of more than two hundred thousand tons of goods makes it one of the largest meat and poultry markets in the world.

Leather Lane is a busy street market selling goods ranging from fruits and vegetables to sweaters and Levi's. Hatton Garden, the center of London's diamond trade, is here, and so are the London Silver Vaults, several ancient pubs, and the oldest Catholic church in London—St. Etheldreda's.

TOURIST ATTRACTIONS
Barbican Centre, Museum of London

RESTAURANTS IN EC1

Chez Gérard	**224**
City Lazeez	**224**
Clark and Sons	**224**
G. Gazzano and Sons	**225**
Moro ($)	**225**
Quality Chop House ($)	**226**
YO! Sushi and YO! Below	**226**

PUBS

Fox and Anchor	**227**
Viaduct Tavern	**228**
Ye Old Mitre Tavern	**228**

($) indicates a Big Splurge

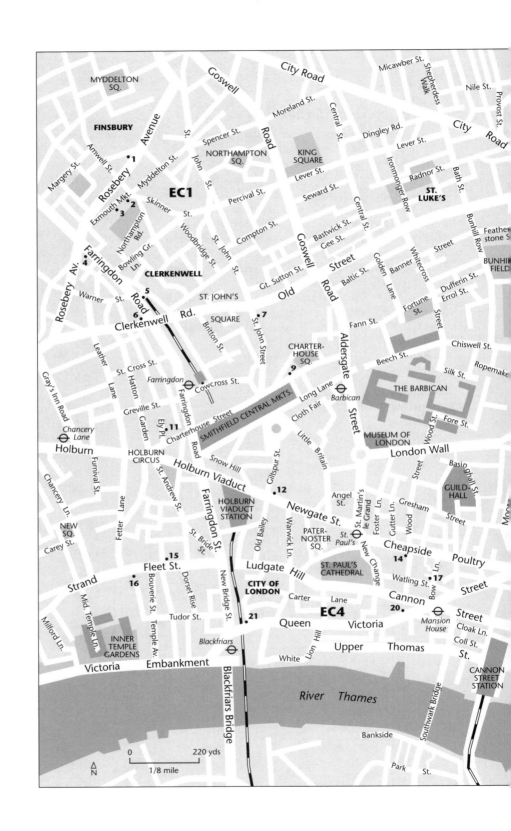

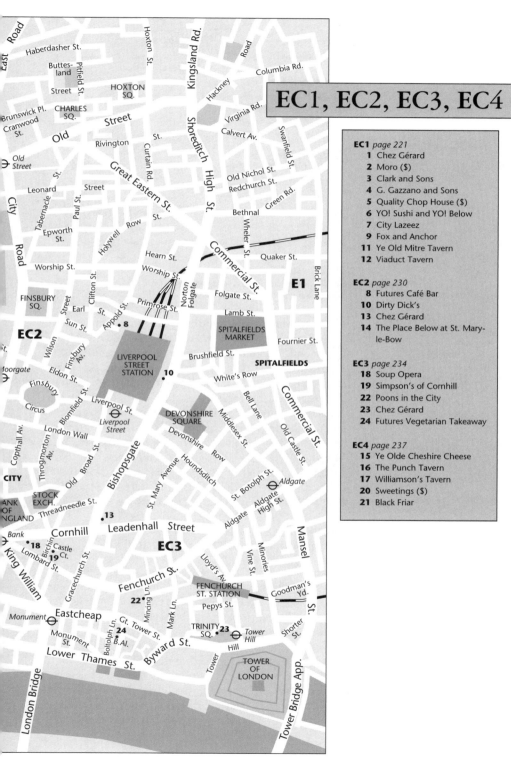

Restaurants

CHEZ GÉRARD (1)
84–86 Rosebery Avenue, Clerkenwell, EC1
Tube: Farringdon, Angel

See Chez Gérard in W1, page 45, for a complete description. All other information is the same.

TELEPHONE: 020 7833 1515
FAX: 020 7833 9118
OPEN: Mon–Sat
CLOSED: Sun, holidays
HOURS: Mon–Sat noon–11 P.M., continuous service
PRICES: Set-price lunch and dinner, £14 2 courses, £17 and £27 3 courses, £5 supplement for 4 courses

CITY LAZEEZ (7)
88 St. John Street, Clerkenwell, EC1
Tube: Farringdon

TELEPHONE
020 7253 2224
FAX
020 7253 2112
OPEN
Mon–Sat
CLOSED
Sun, holidays
HOURS
11 A.M.–10:30 P.M.
PRICES
À la carte £20–30
SERVICE
12.5% service charge

City Lazeez is a unique bar and restaurant in an architecturally listed building with an open, modern style. The restaurant, which has kept its industrial overtones and character, has been transformed into a minimalist space with exposed air ducts and pipes and an open kitchen providing diners with a direct view of the chefs creating their meals. Seating is either at the casual bar in front or in the conservatory, which is bright and well lit during the day and has a warm and intimate feel in the evening through the use of candles and soft lighting. The exposed brick wall along the side dates from the fifteenth century. The cuisine here is as light, delicious, and appealing as it is at Café Lazeez, Soho, W1, page 43, and in South Kensington, SW7, page 201.

CLARK AND SONS (3)
46 Exmouth Market, Clerkenwell, EC1
Tube: Farringdon

TELEPHONE
020 7837 1974
OPEN
Mon–Sat
CLOSED
Sun, holidays
HOURS
Mon–Thur, 10:30A.M.–4 P.M.,
Fri until 5:30 P.M., Sat until
5 P.M.
RESERVATIONS
Not accepted
CREDIT CARDS
Not accepted

You will see them all lined up here: cabbies, pensioners, pin-striped businessmen, scholars in tweeds, blue hairs in pearls, and the odd Mercedes and Rolls-Royce owners, all eager to down another meal of London's well-known comfort and soul food: pie and mash. Go early to nab one of the front booths or a table in the back, or be prepared to spend time waiting in the line that extends beyond the front door. The place opened sixty years ago and has remained largely unchanged: white-tiled walls, wooden benches, stationery tables, and gentle ladies dishing up minced beef pies, stewed or jellied eels in a green parsley-based sauce, and a scoop or two of mash, finished off with cherry pie with custard for dessert. No liquor is served or allowed BYOB, but everything you see can be packed for takeaway.

PRICES
À la carte £3–5
SERVICE
No service charged or expected

G. GAZZANO AND SONS (4)
167–169 Farringdon Road, Clerkenwell, EC1
Tube: Farringdon

G. Gazzano and Sons, across the street from the Quality Chop House (see page 226), is considered the oldest Italian deli in London. It has been in the same family since 1901, providing Italians and would-be Italians with the best deli supplies this side of Milan. If you are nearby, it is worth a stop if only to buy a little bucket of their home-cured olives, which are sold every way, from plain, with the pit, to fancy-pitted green olives stuffed with sun-dried tomatoes. Salami, Parma ham, roast beef, prosciutto, smoked cheese, tomatoes, and artichokes can be mixed, matched, and piled high on your choice of ciabatta or focaccia bread, crusty rolls, or buns. Assorted Italian wines, packaged sweets, and other cooking staples will add to any Italian meal or picnic you plan. However, everything is for takeaway; there is no seating.

TELEPHONE
020 7837 1586
OPEN
Daily
CLOSED
Holidays
HOURS
Mon, Sat 8 A.M.–5 P.M., Tues–Fri 8 A.M.–6 P.M., Sun 10:30 A.M.–2 P.M.
RESERVATIONS
Not accepted
CREDIT CARDS
MC, V
PRICES
£2.50 and up
SERVICE
No service charged or expected

MORO ($, 2)
34–36 Exmouth Market, Clerkenwell, EC1
Tube: Farringdon

The stripped-down surroundings are sleek, the service functional, and the food first-rate at Moro, one of the best restaurants in this gourmet eating corridor in Clerkenwell. It is destination dining at its best if you enjoy modern Spanish and Mediterranean cooking with Moorish overtones. The imaginative food packs in the crowds, ranging from well-dressed executives to babes with body piercing, all of whom enjoy themselves in a big way. The menu, all à la carte, changes often, and the addictive sourdough bread is baked daily in a wood-burning oven. The first-course grazing might start with a simple leek and yogurt soup, braised spinach with pine nuts and raisins, or an unusual salad with warm chorizo sausage tossed with chestnuts. The rich Moroccan-spiced pigeon pie is tempered with a tangy orange and chicory salad, but there was nothing to lighten the heavy roasted duck under a cloying pomegranate molasses sauce, or the underseasoned tabbouleh that came with it. A lighter, more appealing choice was the vegetable paella, bursting

TELEPHONE
020 7833 8336
FAX
020 7833 9338
OPEN
Mon–Sat
CLOSED
Sat lunch, Sun, holidays
HOURS
Bar: Mon–Fri, 12:30–10:30 P.M., Sat 6:30–11:30 P.M. for tapas; lunch: Mon–Fri, 12:30–2:30 P.M.; dinner: Mon–Sat 7–10:30 P.M.
RESERVATIONS
Essential for dinner
CREDIT CARDS
AE, MC, V
PRICES
À la carte £24–28
SERVICE
Discretionary, 12.5% service charged for 7 or more

with artichokes and peppers. Desserts to complement the main courses are light and refreshing, especially the Seville orange tart, Malaga raisin ice cream served with Pedro Ximenez dessert wine, or the rosewater and cardamom ice cream. A wide range of sherry is served, and often special ones are recommended to go with specific dishes.

QUALITY CHOP HOUSE ($, 5)
94 Farringdon Road, Clerkenwell, EC1
Tube: Farringdon

TELEPHONE
020 7837 5093
OPEN
Daily
CLOSED
2 weeks at Christmas and New Year's
HOURS
Lunch: Mon–Fri, noon–3 P.M., Sat–Sun till 4 P.M.; dinner: Mon–Sat 6:30 –11:30 P.M., Sun from 7 P.M.
RESERVATIONS
Essential
CREDIT CARDS
MC, V
PRICES
À la carte £26–30
SERVICE
Discretionary, 10% service charge for 5 or more

The Quality Chop House is a destination restaurant far afield from the basic tourist path. When you go, be sure to book a table and arrive by taxi. Otherwise, especially after dark, you will find yourself with a long hike to and from the tube through a sketchy part of London. The clock stopped ticking on the premises in 1869, when it first opened as a laborers' café. The old motto "Progressive Working Class Caterer" is still etched on the front window. The inside is also unchanged, from the original tilted bench seats you will undoubtedly have to share to the yellowing walls and black-and-white-tiled floor. The blue-collar interior, however, has no bearing on the simple elegance of the food prepared by Charles Fontaine, a former chef at La Caprice. Since opening in 1989, he has won praise for his competent preparations of old standards, proving that the Quality Chop House is aptly named.

It is important that you arrive starved and prepared to indulge in grilled lamb chops, steak and kidney pie, Toulouse sausages with mash and onion gravy, or grilled Dutch calf's liver with bacon. For other appetites, there is always beautiful fresh fish, salmon fish cakes, and raw oysters. The line is long for the Sunday brunch, which includes a jug of bucks fizzes or Bloody Marys, eggs Benedict, or egg and bacon waffles. Not planning ahead for dessert would be a serious mistake, since everything is made here. Although they sound potentially heavy after a big meal, you won't be sorry with the creamed rice pudding or the caramel cheesecake.

YO! SUSHI and YO! BELOW (6)
95 Farringdon Road, Clerkenwell, EC1
Tube: Farringdon

Here we YO! again with conveyor-belt sushi, vegetarian bento boxes, and a bar with singing waiters, tarot-card readings, massages, and cocktails. For complete details on this unabashed McDonald's of Japanese-style food gimmickry, please see YO! Sushi, Soho, W1, page 75. All other details are the same.

TELEPHONE: 020 7841 0777

Pubs

FOX AND ANCHOR (9)
115 Charterhouse Street, Smithfield Market, EC1
Tube: Farringdon, Barbican

The food served at the Fox and Anchor is a carnivore's dream and a heart specialist's nightmare. The record for London's most gigantic breakfast stands unbroken at this pub, less than a block from the Smithfield Market (the world's largest wholesale meat market). While the price tag on breakfast may seem high, you will actually save money, because you won't need to eat for the rest of the day, and possibly the next.

As you can imagine, the butchers and pitchers (men who unload the trucks) demand the best quality meat, and the Fox and Anchor serves it to them in abundance every weekday. The pub opens at 7 A.M. for workers to have an eye-opening pint or two before tackling the morning meal, which is served until 3 P.M. Insiders generally ignore the menu and order the house favorite, which is not listed: the Mixed Grill. (If you want this, you must call ahead to order it.) Only hard-core meat lovers need apply for this feast, which includes sausage, kidneys, steak, liver, black pudding, eggs, mushrooms, tomatoes, french fries, and endless cups of coffee. Another blowout is the full English breakfast: bacon, two sausages, black pudding, fried egg, tomato, baked beans, fried bread, and a pint of Guinness recommended as the chaser. If you feel you are not up to the Mixed Grill or the full English breakfast, consider a 5- to 8-ounce steak with two of the following side dishes: baked beans, bacon, black pudding, sausages, tomatoes, mushrooms, fried egg or fries. For the prissy, they do have a vegetarian breakfast . . . but here? Please. This is a place where the protein-rich, animal-fat-loaded food is the only thing to order. If you can't bring yourself to down one of the heavy-hitting breakfasts, go elsewhere.

TELEPHONE
020 7253 5975

OPEN
Mon–Fri

CLOSED
Sat–Sun, holidays

HOURS
Pub: 7 A.M.–8 P.M., breakfast until 3 P.M., (no food at all after 3 P.M.)

RESERVATIONS
Advised for breakfast before 9 A.M., required to order the Mixed Grill

CREDIT CARDS
AE, MC, V

PRICES
À la carte £8–14

SERVICE
Discretionary

VIADUCT TAVERN (12)
126 Newgate Street (across from Old Bailey), EC1
Tube: St. Paul's

TELEPHONE
020 7606 8476
OPEN
Daily
CLOSED
Sun, Christmas Day
HOURS
Pub Mon–Sat, 11 A.M.–11 P.M.,
food service noon–9 P.M.
RESERVATIONS
Not accepted
CREDIT CARDS
AE, MC, V
PRICES
£5–7
SERVICE
No service charged or expected

The first public building in London to have electricity now functions as the Viaduct Tavern. Originally standing just outside the city walls, it was a debtors' prison linked to Newgate Prison, which is now Old Bailey. Some of the original twelve-by-six cells still exist beneath the bar and make up the Viaduct's cellars. They are said to be inhabited by Fred, the ghost of a prisoner, who is blamed for all the noises and mishaps that have inexplicably happened here over the years. The small, dark cells make it easy to imagine the horrible conditions in which prisoners existed, being stacked twenty deep in these airless cubicles with holes in the ceiling as the only ventilation. On request, the staff will conduct tours. Behind the Viaduct is St. Bartholomew's Hospital, which was founded in 1123 and is the oldest hospital in England standing on its original site. Inside are paintings by Hogarth. To learn more about this fascinating part of London, I recommend joining one of the London walking tours that give in-depth insight into the history and lore of the area. The best walks are given by Original London Walks. Look for their monthly brochures at your hotel, or call them at 020 7624 3978

As a pub, the Viaduct was a fashionable drinking spot for the upper classes of London society. The stone reliefs around the walls represent the heads of the sixteen hanging judges of Old Bailey. In the back you can see an original etched-glass booth from which the landlady issued tokens that were exchanged at the bar for drinks because the bartenders could not be trusted with money.

History and ghosts aside, the Viaduct Tavern serves predictable pub food, concentrating on sandwiches, Cumberland sausage with mash and onion gravy, and jacket potatoes with gooey fillings.

YE OLD MITRE TAVERN (11)
1 Ely Place, Holborn, EC1
Tube: Chancery Lane

TELEPHONE
020 7405 4751
OPEN
Mon–Fri
CLOSED
Sat–Sun, holidays
HOURS
11 A.M.–11 P.M., food service
until 9:30 P.M.

Look for the old street lamp that marks the entrance to Ely Court, a narrow passageway linking Ely Place and Hatton Garden, which is a street lined with London's jewelry traders. In 1546, when the bishops of Ely lorded over this part of London, the Mitre Tavern was built for their palace servants. Rebuilt in the late eighteenth century, its oak-paneled rooms are filled with antiques and relics dating back to the origins of the pub. In the corner of the bar is the preserved trunk of a cherry tree that grew on the boundary between the bishop of Ely's land and that of Sir Christopher Hatton, who was a great favorite of Queen Elizabeth I. In fact, she once danced the "maypole" around this tree. During the English Civil War, the tavern was used as a prison and a hospital, but judging from its size, it could have held only a handful of prisoners and patients.

Today, the pub is popular with local office workers, who treat it as their private club and enjoy sitting and relaxing in a quiet atmosphere free from loud music or pinball machines. There is no hot food served, but it is a worthwhile stop for a freshly made sandwich and a pint of ale, and to savor one of London's most charming and authentic pubs. The sandwiches, which cost a whopping £1 to £2, are served Monday to Friday from 11 A.M. to 9:30 P.M. The choice is not large: four made with cheese and two with sausage.

RESERVATIONS
Not accepted

CREDIT CARDS
None

PRICES
À la carte £1–2

SERVICE
No service charged or expected

EC2

The Barbican

The Barbican opened in 1984 and covers sixty acres. It is still one of the most impressive and controversial buildings in London. It was built around the remaining portion of the old Roman wall as an ambitious scheme to promote the area as a residential quarter rather than only as a place to work. The plan has met with mixed results. While definitely improving the neighborhood and attracting business, it has not become the residential hot spot developers had hoped for. It contains high-rise flats, shops, offices, pubs, the City of London School for Girls, the sixteenth-century church of St. Giles Cripplegate, the Museum of London, the performance hall of the London Symphony Orchestra, and the Guildhall School of Music. The Bank of England and the Stock Exchange make this the financial hub of the country.

RESTAURANTS IN EC2 (see map page 222)

PUBS

Restaurants

CHEZ GÉRARD (13)
64 Bishopsgate, the City, EC2
Tube: Liverpool Street

You will need reservations almost a week in advance at this Chez Gérard, which serves breakfast and is open during the week from Monday through Friday. See Chez Gérard in W1, page 45, for a complete description. All other information is the same.

TELEPHONE: 020 7588 1200
FAX: 020 7588 1122
OPEN: Mon–Fri
CLOSED: Sat–Sun, holidays

HOURS: Breakfast 8–10:30 A.M., lunch noon–3 P.M., dinner 6–10:30 P.M.

RESERVATIONS: Essential

PRICES: À la carte: breakfast £3–11, lunch and dinner £20–26; set-price lunch and dinner: £14 2 courses, £17 and £27 3 courses, £5 supplemental course

FUTURES CAFÉ BAR (8)
2 Exchange Square, Broadgate Complex, Spitalfields, EC2
Tube: Liverpool Street

The Futures Café Bar on Exchange Square is a bold, bright, classy vegetarian grazing ground for the buttoned-down office workers, junior executives, fashionable cute young things, and a few tarnished older models who populate this stunning, renovated section of London above Liverpool Street Station. The decor and atmosphere of the contemporary, glass-enclosed dining room make it more reminiscent of California than of London, and so does the beautifully executed and presented food, which is geared toward a lunchtime feeding blitz, followed by a more subdued afternoon and evening, when it is filled with the BPs (beautiful people) back for wine and evening snacks.

It is always a good sign when you feel you could eat anything on the menu, and at Futures you can expect to do that. Breakfast stays the same day in and day out with omelettes, poached eggs on English muffins, homemade cereals, seasonal fruits, and freshly squeezed juices, plus the usual retinue of coffees and teas. The lunch choices change every two weeks and feature a short list of appetizers, beautifully sculpted salads, pastas, stir-frys, and desserts destined to wreak havoc on one's dieting willpower. My lunch starter of grilled vegetables with a cucumber relish and peanut saté sauce was the perfect support for the sweet potato mille-feuille served with woodsy oyster mushrooms and leeks. For dessert, the apple custard tart was the perfect finale.

DIRECTIONS: Finding Futures Café Bar requires the latest detailed street map of London available, as the area has undergone a massive renovation. The best approach is to enter Exchange Square opposite Earl Street, walk up the stairs, and look for the huge bronze statue of Venus of Broadgate. Futures will be on one corner of the square. Another approach is to exit the Liverpool Street tube station on Bishopsgate and turn left. Walk to Primrose Street and turn left. Exchange Square with Venus of

TELEPHONE
020 7638 6341

FAX
020 7621 9508

EMAIL
Futures.Restaurants@ BTInternet.com

INTERNET
www.1e.btwebworld.com/ futures1/

OPEN
Mon–Fri

CLOSED
Sat, Sun, holidays

HOURS
Breakfast: 7:30–11:30 A.M., lunch noon–2:30 P.M.; wine bar: Mon–Wed 2:30–10 P.M., Thur–Fri until 11 P.M.

RESERVATIONS
Advised for lunch

CREDIT CARDS
AE, MC, V

PRICES
À la carte £14–19; set-price lunch £9.50 2 courses, £12 3 courses

SERVICE
Discretionary, 12.5% service charge for 5 or more

Broadgate will be in front of you. Still lost? Probably. Ask any of the security guards wearing white navy officers' hats, and they will direct you.

NOTE: No smoking at lunchtime before 2 P.M. Futures has a vegetarian takeaway at 8 Botolph Alley, EC3. Please see page 235 for details.

THE PLACE BELOW AT ST. MARY-LE-BOW (14)
St. Mary-le-Bow Crypt, Cheapside, the City, EC2
Tube: Mansion House, St. Paul's Bank

TELEPHONE
020 7329 0789
FAX
020 7248 2626
INTERNET
www.theplacebelow.co.uk
OPEN
Mon–Fri, breakfast and lunch
CLOSED
Sat–Sun, Holidays
HOURS
7:30 A.M.–4 P.M.; breakfast pastries 7:30–11:30 A.M.
RESERVATIONS
Not accepted
CREDIT CARDS
MC, V
PRICES
À la carte £6–12; 11:30 A.M.–noon, all main courses £2 less
SERVICE
Discretionary

The St. Mary-le-Bow church serves as a religious and cultural landmark in the City. It has long been known that those born within earshot of its famous bells are considered to be the true Cockneys of London. The church, one of Sir Christopher Wren's masterpieces, houses another masterpiece in its eleventh-century crypt: Bill Sewell's the Place Below, a brilliant example of just how delicious vegetarian cooking can be in the hands of an imaginative and creative chef. Sewell has received awards and rave reviews for his meatless cuisine and has now gone on to develop other culinary interests, but he still keeps his fingers in the pies here, and he is ably assisted by another young and promising chef, Jo Hopwood.

Naturally, everything is made here, from the moist olive and garlic bread to the smoothies and freshly squeezed orange juice. Breakfast and lunch are self-service and emphasize quiches, breads, soups, salads, wonderful hot dishes, and tempting desserts. When I was there, highlights included a mushroom bisque soup and tabbouleh with lemon-spiced carrots, eggplant puree, and marinated green beans. The treacle tart was good, and the rich tiramisu just sweet enough, but I wished my favorite chocolate zucchini cake had been available.

The two-room space, with a garden courtyard area for summer tables, is positively packed for lunch. You absolutely must arrive early for the best table selection—no reservations are taken. If you arrive between 11:30 A.M. and noon, all prices are £2 less, but you might have to contend with the cleanup crew finishing its work.

NOTE: Restaurant is unlicensed; BYOB (no corkage fee). Takeaway is available, and if you want to bring some of Bill's magic cooking home with you, purchase a copy of his cookbook, *Food from the Place Below,* available here for around £10.

Pubs

DIRTY DICK'S (10)
202 Bishopsgate, the City, EC2
Tube: Liverpool Street

The story of Dirty Dick's is written on the walls around the upstairs rooms of the pub: "In a dirty old house lived a dirty old man. Soap, towels or brushes were not in his plan; for forty long years as his neighbors declared, his house never once had been cleaned or repaired. 'Twas a scandal and shame to the business-like street, and a terrible blot on a lodger so neat; the old shop with its glasses, black bottles and vats, and the rest of the mansion a run for the rats."

As historic London pubs go, Dirty Dick's is hard to beat. It is named after one of the most famous characters in the City of London, who inherited the property, a bonded warehouse for port and sherry, in the early eighteenth century from his father. Dick was a messy person, with a scruffy reputation he did not care about changing. At one point he was engaged to be married, but the bride to be died the day before the wedding. Dirty Dick was so emotionally bereft that he locked up the wedding table he had prepared for his wedding night, and it was not seen again until someone found it after his death.

Today the pub consists of three distinct eating and drinking areas with a limited bar menu served for lunch only in the ground floor pub and downstairs in the vaulted wine cellar. Frankly, the food is the last reason to go to this pub. Instead, go for a peek into the lives of some of London's colorful persons, and have a pint of beer while you are at it.

TELEPHONE
020 7283 5888

OPEN
Mon–Fri

CLOSED
Sat–Sun, holidays

HOURS
Mon–Fri 11 A.M.–10:30 P.M., lunch noon–2:30 P.M.

RESERVATIONS
Not necessary

CREDIT CARDS
AE, MC, V

PRICES
À la carte £5–8

SERVICE
No service charged or expected

EC3

Lloyd's of London, Leadenhall Market, and Tower of London

The world's most famous insurance company, Lloyd's of London, occupies a futuristic building with an observation deck that's open to the public, but only by written request. Close to Lloyd's is Leadenhall Market, the beautiful Victorian glass and iron market where smart cafés and pubs coexist with the few remaining meat and fish mongers and colorful produce stalls.

Perhaps the most famous castle in the world, the Tower of London was the largest fortress in medieval Europe and the palace and prison of English monarchs for five hundred years. It was first built by William the Conqueror to both protect and control the City. Over time it has also served as the nation's storehouse for weapons and public records, kept the Crown Jewels, and housed the Royal Mint and the Royal Menagerie.

RESTAURANTS IN EC3 (see map page 222)

Restaurants

CHEZ GÉRARD (23)
14 Trinity Square, Tower of London, EC3
Tube: Tower Hill

Please see Chez Gérard on page 45 for details. All other information is the same

TELEPHONE: 020 7480 5500

FAX: 020 7480 5588

CLOSED: Sun

FUTURES VEGETARIAN TAKEAWAY (24)
8 Botolph Alley, the City, EC3
Tube: Monument

If you are considering your breakfast or lunch options, there are two Futures markets for you. Both are tough to locate without a compass and steely determination (see Futures Café Bar, EC2, page 231). At this Futures, the vegan and vegetarian fare is strictly cash-and-carry takeaway or delivery. The food choices are brief yet imaginative, prepared in a huge underground kitchen almost the size of a London city block. In addition to a brisk takeaway, Futures faxes its menus to surrounding offices and delivers daily to a devoted lunch crowd of eight hundred people.

Kick off your day on a healthy note with the breakfast special, a bowl of toasted oats covered in natural yogurt and fresh fruit. Add one of their own muffins and a glass of fresh orange or apple juice, and you will be set for the day. Real porridge cooked with milk and honey is another healthy bet. The lunch menu is never the same two days in a row, but it always lists unusual soups, a pasta or two, stir-frys, salads, and desserts.

DIRECTIONS: Exit the Monument tube stop on the Eastcheap side, walk east to Lovat Lane, turn right, and the first little street will be Botolph Alley.

TELEPHONE
020 7623 4529

FAX
020 7621 9508

EMAIL
Futures.Restaurants@
BTInternet.com

INTERNET
www.1ebtwebworld.com/
futures1/

OPEN
Mon–Fri breakfast and lunch only

CLOSED
Sat–Sun, holidays

HOURS
Breakfast 7:30 A.M.–10 A.M., lunch 11:30 A.M.–3 P.M.

RESERVATIONS
Not accepted

CREDIT CARDS
None

PRICES
À la carte £3–9

SERVICE
No service charged or expected

POONS IN THE CITY (22)
Minster Pavement (lower ground level), Minster Court, Mincing Lane, the City, EC3
Tube: Tower Hill, Monument

At this location of Poons, it is important that budget-watching Great Eaters dine in the fast-food café; otherwise, the bill will fast approach the Big Splurge category. Takeaway is available. In all dishes, MSG can be omitted on request. See Poons in W2, page 93, for a full description.

TELEPHONE: 020 7626 0126
FAX: 020 7626 0526
OPEN: Mon–Fri
CLOSED: Sat–Sun, holidays
HOURS: Fast-food café: Mon–Fri 11:30 A.M.–2 P.M.; restaurant: 11:30 A.M.–10:30 P.M., continuous service
RESERVATIONS: Advised for lunch in the restaurant
CREDIT CARDS: AE, DC, MC, V
PRICES: Fast-food café £8–20; restaurant £20–25
SERVICE: £1.75 cover charge in restaurant, 10% service charge in fast-food café and restaurant

SIMPSON'S OF CORNHILL (19)
38½ Castle Court (at Ball Court, off Cornhill), the City, EC3
Tube: Bank

TELEPHONE
020 7626 9985
OPEN
Mon–Fri lunch only
CLOSED
Sat–Sun, holidays
HOURS
11:30 A.M.–3 P.M.
RESERVATIONS
Not accepted
CREDIT CARDS
AE, DC, MC, V
PRICES
À la carte £10–14
SERVICE
Discretionary

Finding Simpson's of Cornhill (not to be confused with the touristy and overpriced Simpson's-in-the-Strand) is not easy: walk along Cornhill, turn right on St. Michael's Alley, then right on Castle Court, walk until you come to Ball Court, and turn right again. To say it is a hidden find is quite an understatement! But the search for the old-fashioned English food with old-fashioned prices to match is definitely worthwhile. For my lunching pound, this is the best food value in the City, as this square mile of London is known.

The restaurant was founded in 1757, and for generations the traditions and customs of male-dominated London eating houses were strictly maintained: not until 1916 were women admitted to this conservative male bastion. Today, women are welcomed in both the upstairs restaurant and in the downstairs grill room. The food is heavy and hearty, so skip the starters and concentrate on a main course of grilled meat or the daily hot joint (roast meat). Liver and bacon, steak and kidney pie, poached or cold Scottish salmon, and a stew of some sort are always on board. The popular Simpson's fish cakes, served once a week, are equally recommended. For an after-meal savory treat, everyone orders the stewed cheese. This is a crock of melted cheddar cheese mixed with Worcestershire sauce and seasonings to spread on toast. You must try one. It is the house specialty, and the kitchen cannot turn them out fast enough.

NOTE: You can't call for reservations because they don't take them. By 12:15 P.M., it is completely full, so for assured seating, plan to arrive at noon at the latest.

SOUP OPERA (18)
56-57 Cornhill, the City, EC3
Tube: Bank

Please see Soup Opera, page 66, for details. All other information is the same.
TELEPHONE: 020 7621 0065
CLOSED: Sun

EC4

The City

Dating back to the Romans, the City is an almost perfect square mile in the heart of London. During the week, it teems with executives, office workers, and a constant rush of people on the go. On the weekends and at night it becomes silent, populated only by pigeons and the stray sightseer. It owes its appearance to Sir Christopher Wren, who was the chief architect after the Great Fire of 1666. He designed fifty-one churches to replace the eighty-nine that were destroyed. St. Paul's Cathedral, in fact, was built by Wren between 1675 and 1710 on the site of the medieval cathedral destroyed in the fire. It serves as the bishopric of London and the parish church of the British Commonwealth. Today, it retains its great dignity and grandeur in spite of the huge tower blocks surrounding it.

Fleet Street used to be the newspaper and journalist headquarters of London. All major British daily papers had their offices here, and the pubs were full of journalists. No more. The offices have moved to the suburbs, but many still refer to Fleet Street as the home of the British press.

Old Bailey, the Central Criminal Court, is open to the public, and it is a show worth seeing. You can visit an actual case in progress by participating in one of the daily walking tours in London. Consult your hotel for brochures.

TOURIST ATTRACTIONS
St. Paul's Cathedral, Thames River, Fleet Street, Dr. Johnson's House

RESTAURANTS IN EC4 (see map page 222)

Sweetings ($)	**238**
Ye Olde Cheshire Cheese	**238**

PUBS

Black Friar	**239**
The Punch Tavern	**240**
Williamson's Tavern	**240**

($) indicates a Big Splurge

Restaurants

SWEETINGS ($, 20)
39 Queen Victoria Street, the City, EC4
Tube: Mansion House

TELEPHONE
020 7248 3062
OPEN
Mon–Fri lunch only
CLOSED
Sat–Sun, holidays
HOURS
11:30 A.M.–3 P.M.
RESERVATIONS
Not accepted
CREDIT CARDS
None
PRICES
À la carte £25–35
SERVICE
Discretionary

"We don't take reservations, accept credit cards, or serve coffee—we do serve the best fish you will eat in London," states owner Pat Needham. Generations of loyalists and I agree with her, and now patrons arrive with their children and grandchildren on a regular basis. Sweetings has been serving lunch on the same corner in London's financial district for more than a hundred years (the only change in this time seems to have been the prices), and it is required eating. The yellowed walls, a front window loaded with tubs of wine, and longtime customers milling around one of the long mahogany bars waiting for their favorite table set the tone. The fish is fresh daily from the Billingsgate fish market, and the oysters are supplied directly from West Mersea in Essex.

Every regular has his or her own favorite dish—whether it's the Dover sole, salmon, smoked haddock, halibut, or crab salad—and would never consider experimenting with something else. Familiar desserts such as bread-and-butter pudding, baked jam roll, and steamed syrup pudding, along with excellent wines sold by the glass or bottle, complement the meal.

NOTE: If you are in a hurry, you can sit at the front counter.

YE OLDE CHESHIRE CHEESE (15)
145 Fleet Street (off Wine Office Court), the City, EC4
Tube: Blackfriars

TELEPHONE
020 7353 6170
FAX
020 7353 0845
OPEN
Mon–Sat; Sun lunch only
CLOSED
Sun dinner, several days at Christmas, holidays
HOURS
The Chop Room: Mon–Fri noon–9:30 P.M., continuous service; Sat noon–3:30 P.M. and 5:30–9:30 P.M., Sun noon–3 P.M.; Johnson Restaurant: Mon–Fri noon–2:30 P.M. and 6–9:30 P.M.; bar: Mon–Fri lunch noon–2:30 P.M.

Seventeenth-century chop houses were the forerunners of today's wine bars, and this centuries-old bar and restaurant is one of the most famous. It is almost impossible to pick up a guide to London restaurants without reading something about Ye Olde Cheshire Cheese. Even though this fame brings flocks of international tourists to the door, the restaurant has managed to remain true to its heritage. In the thirteenth century, the site formed part of a Carmelite monastery, but since 1538, a pub has been in business here. Rebuilt in 1667, the year after the Great Fire, the Cheshire Cheese has preserved the atmosphere of the intervening centuries, spanning the reigns of sixteen kings and queens. Pictures and artifacts adorn the multiroomed pub, giving an account of the people and events that have left their mark. Today, little has changed: the original wooden floors are sprinkled with sawdust each day, the hard benches are worn smooth, and the same rickety staircase leads to the upstairs rooms. In the Chop Room you can still see the long table at which Dr. Samuel Johnson, Oliver Goldsmith, and Charles Dickens dined.

Prices lean on the high side in the Johnson Restaurant, so thrifty Great Eaters will want to dine in the bar (lunch only) or the Chop Room. The food is predictably English, but for the historical value it is worth a visit, if only to step up to the bar and order a drink.

NOTE: Available for private parties.

RESERVATIONS
Accepted for the Chop Room and Johnson Restaurant
CREDIT CARDS
AE, DC, MC, V
PRICES
Chop Room: à la carte £15–20; Johnson Restaurant: à la carte £20–30; bar: £6–11;
SERVICE
Discretionary

Pubs

BLACK FRIAR (21)
174 Queen Victoria Street, the City, EC4
Tube: Blackfriars

The best reason to visit the Black Friar is to see one of the richest and strangest pub interiors in London. In the 1960's, the pub was scheduled to be torn down, but thank goodness the great public outcry saved it. This Art Nouveau fantasy, built in 1903 from designs by H. Fuller Clarke and sculptor Henry Poole, pays homage to the Dominicans, or black friars, who had a monastery on this site many years ago. The friars were known for being more interested in drinking than divinity, and their devotion to the bottle sets the theme for this amazing building. Outside over the door stands a figure of a good-natured friar, hands folded across his impressive beer belly. Mosaics on either side show other friars eating, drinking, laughing, and having fun. The remarkable interior features polished stone, colored marble columns, and bronze bas-reliefs. The room in back, known as the Side Chapel, has a vaulted black, white, and gold ceiling and reflecting mirrors encircled by friezes of inebriated friars. They are accompanied by crouching demons, fairies, and carved alabaster animals. All around the room are mottoes of the friars: "Tell a gossip," "Finery is foolery," and "Haste is slow."

The main bar area has an enormous bronze-canopied fireplace and a small horseshoe bar. The tiny wedge-shaped front part of the pub is where hot and cold

TELEPHONE
020 7236 5474
OPEN
Mon–Fri; Sat lunch only
CLOSED
Sat dinner, Sun, holidays
HOURS
Mon–Fri 11:30 A.M.–11 P.M., Sat noon–5 P.M.; lunch Mon–Sat noon–2:30 P.M.
RESERVATIONS
Not accepted
CREDIT CARDS
AE, MC, V
PRICES
À la carte £3–6
SERVICE
No service charged or expected

lunches are served. The food is not as spectacular as the surroundings, but it is basic pub fare at decent prices. Please note that *only* crisps and peanuts are served after 2:30 P.M.

THE PUNCH TAVERN (16)
99 Fleet Street, the City, EC4
Tube: Blackfriars, Temple

TELEPHONE
020 7353 6658

OPEN
Mon–Fri

CLOSED
Sat–Sun, week between Christmas and New Year's, holidays

HOURS
Mon–Fri 11 A.M.–11 P.M., lunch daily noon–2:30 P.M., bar snacks until 5 P.M.

RESERVATIONS
Not accepted

CREDIT CARDS
AE, MC, V

PRICES
À la carte £4–7

SERVICE
No service charged or expected

In its early days, prisoners were brought here for their "last one for the road" as they were taken to Newgate Prison (now Old Bailey) to be hanged. Later it served as the watering hole for employees of *Punch* magazine. Now, the magnificently restored Punch Tavern is a living museum and memorial to that famous London periodical, and it is the quarterly meeting place for the Punch Appreciation Society. The original plans for the pub were used in detail when it was recently restored to its former glory, keeping the original prints, etched-glass mirrors, and fireplaces in place. A glass display case houses an interesting collection of *Punch* memorabilia. The pub is a mob scene at lunch, with office workers ordering freshly cut sandwiches to have with their pints of beer.

While you are here, don't miss a visit to St. Bride's Church next door, which has the highest spire designed by Sir Christopher Wren and was the inspiration for the first tiered wedding cakes. The first printing press with movable type was brought to the church in 1500, and that is the reason St. Bride's is referred to as the Printer's Cathedral and the Journalist's Church. John Milton lived in the churchyard at one time, Samuel Pepys was baptized here, Samuel Johnson lived across the street, Dickens up the road, and in 1587, Virginia Dare's parents were married here. Virginia Dare was the first child of European descent born in colonial America.

WILLIAMSON'S TAVERN (17)
1–3 Groveland Court, Bow Lane, the City, EC4
Tube: Mansion House

TELEPHONE
020 7248 6280

OPEN
Mon–Fri

CLOSED
Sat–Sun, holidays

Williamson's Tavern is appealing for its historic background, warm atmosphere, and better-than-usual food. Like many pubs in the City, it claims to be the oldest, a fact that is obviously determined in several creative ways. It does, however, mark the exact center of the City of London. Built after the Great Fire of 1666, it was a former mansion house and the residence of London's lord mayors until 1753. The wrought-iron gates guarding the entrance of the alley that leads to the pub were presented by William III and Queen Mary to the lord mayor of London. Before its transition into a pub in the eighteenth century, it was Sir John Falstaff's home, and long before that the site of a Roman villa. The tiles used around the fireplace on the first floor were found ten feet below ground level during the most recent renovation a hundred years ago.

There are three parts to the pub: the Tavern Bar, a typical pub complete with loud music and pinball machines; the Williamson's Bar, a quiet sanctuary on the ground level; and Martha's Bar downstairs, where a large variety of interesting wines are served. What's to eat? The hands-down favorite is the house special: a four-ounce sirloin steak sandwich, char-grilled and served with parsley or garlic butter and a small salad, all for less than £7.

HOURS
Pub: 11:30 A.M.–11 P.M.; Tavern Bar food service: noon–9 P.M.; Martha's Bar food service: noon–2:30 P.M. and 5–9 P.M.

RESERVATIONS
Not accepted

CREDIT CARDS
AE, DC, MC, V

PRICES
À la carte £7–10

SERVICE
No service charged or expected in pub, service discretionary in restaurant

SE1

South Bank

TOURIST ATTRACTIONS
Shakespeare's Globe Theatre, Southwark Cathedral, Imperial War Museum, Tate Modern, Tower Bridge, Waterloo Bridge

The South Bank of the Thames was bombed flat during World War II, but rose from the ashes and has become a hub for the arts in London. Stretching from Lambeth Bridge to Blackfriars Bridge, the area includes the Royal Festival Hall, the National Film Theatre, Old Vic Theatre, Young Vic Theatre, the London Eye, and the Royal National Theatre, just to mention a few of the attractions in this rapidly redeveloping area of London. The importance of the area is reflected in the number of visitors, which is expected to nearly double from 7 to 12 million, aided by the opening of a new Southwark tube station, the Millennium Bridge (the first crossing of the River Thames in a century), and the impressive Tate-Modern, dedicated to modern art. The magnificent views of the City from Waterloo Bridge have inspired generations of painters, including J. M. W. Turner, whose works are at the Tate-Britain, across the river.

The Southwark Cathedral, a fine example of Gothic architecture, contains the Harvard Chapel, dedicated to the founder of Harvard University, who was baptized in the church in 1607. (Southwark is pronounced SUTH-uk).

The Tate Modern, housed in an old power station along the Thames, exhibits international modern art from 1900 to the present.

RESTAURANTS IN SE1

PUBS

Restaurants

THE APPRENTICE–THE BUTLERS WHARF CHEF SCHOOL (6)
The Cardamom Building, 31 Shad Thames, SE1
Tube: London Bridge, Tower Hill

At this training institute for chefs and other restaurant personnel, you can taste gourmet cooking for much less than what a regular restaurant would charge to have it prepared by a fancy, name-brand chef undoubtedly represented by an agent and a public relations firm.

At the Apprentice, students practice what they have been taught on willing guinea pigs, i.e., us. Putting theory into practice doesn't always turn out the way it was planned, so you must allow for certain gaffes occasionally in both cooking and service. Still, the constantly changing menu, devised by the students, rotates through a roll call of currently fashionable modern British dishes, and most of them pass muster. Around Christmastime, I was happy to start with an unusual curried parsnip brûlée that came with a peppy tomato and red-onion chutney. The prawn and artichoke risotto was nothing new, but it was creamy and rich, just the way a risotto should be. The roast cod on marinated tomatoes with a lemon and parsley couscous elevated this overworked fish to a higher level, but the venison casserole with chestnut fritters needs to be reworked—the taste was too gamey and strong. Other main courses of salmon with truffle-scented mash, and stuffed turkey escalope with cranberries, were tops in their class. Flunking the vegetarian test were the rubbery spinach and potato dumplings, overpowered by ratatouille and a blob of Gorgonzola cream sauce. Top honors in the dessert class went to the zippy iced ginger and white chocolate cake with prune and Armagnac ice cream, the port-soaked Stilton cheese with crisp biscuits and tart plum chutney, and the cloudlike orange pudding soufflé with fresh peach sorbet.

The interior of the restaurant is devoid of charm and character, and it needs some acoustic engineering, but you are not here to admire the surroundings. You are here to eat, and you will do that quite well.

TELEPHONE
020 7234 0254

OPEN
Mon–Fri

CLOSED
Sat–Sun, holidays

HOURS
Lunch noon–1:30 P.M., dinner 6:30–8:30 P.M.

RESERVATIONS
Essential, sometimes one week in advance

CREDIT CARDS
AE, DC, MC, V

PRICES
Set-price: lunch £11.50 2 courses, £15 3 courses; dinner £17 2 courses, £20 3 courses

SERVICE
The Apprentice has a policy of not charging for service, but gratuities are welcome and will be used to support student training

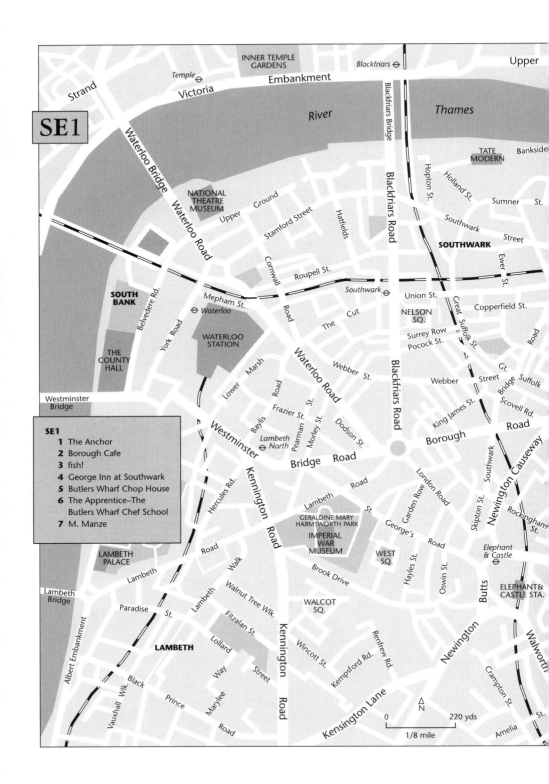

SE1

Strand

Victoria

Temple ⊖

Embankment

INNER TEMPLE
GARDENS

Blackfriars ⊖

Upper

River

Thames

Waterloo Bridge

Blackfriars Bridge

Blackfriars Road

TATE
MODERN

Bankside

Hopton St.

Holland St.

Sumner   St.

Southwark   Street

SOUTHWARK

Ewer   St.

NATIONAL
THEATRE
MUSEUM

Upper   Ground

Stamford Street

Hatfields

Waterloo Road

Cornwall

Roupell St.

Southwark ⊖

Union St.

Copperfield St.

SOUTH
BANK

Belvedere Rd.

Mepham St.

⊖ Waterloo

WATERLOO
STATION

Road

The   Cut

NELSON
SQ.

Surrey Row

Pocock St.

Great   Suffolk   St.

Road

York Road

Marsh

Webber   St.

Webber   Street

Gt.   Suffolk

THE
COUNTY
HALL

Westminster
Bridge

Lower

Road

Frazier St.

St.

Waterloo Road

Dodson St.

Blackfriars Road

King James St.

Bridge

Scovell Rd.

Road

SE1

1 The Anchor
2 Borough Cafe
3 fish!
4 George Inn at Southwark
5 Butlers Wharf Chop House
6 The Apprentice–The
   Butlers Wharf Chef School
7 M. Manze

Baylis

Pearman

Morley St.

Westminster

Lambeth
North ⊖

Bridge   Road

Borough

Kennington   Road

Hercules Rd.

Lambeth   St.

George's

London Road

Southwark

Garden Row   Road

Skipton St.

Newington Causeway

Rockingham St.

LAMBETH
PALACE

GERALDINE MARY
HARMSWORTH PARK

IMPERIAL
WAR
MUSEUM

WEST
SQ.

Hayles St.

Oswin St.

Elephant
& Castle
⊖

Road

Walk

Brook Drive

Lambeth
Bridge

Lambeth

Road

Paradise   St.

Fitzalan St.

Walnut Tree Wlk.

WALCOT
SQ.

Butts

ELEPHANT&
CASTLE STA.

Albert Embankment

LAMBETH

Lollard

Way

Street

Wincott St.

Kempsford Rd.

Renfrew Rd.

Newington

Walworth

Crampton St.

St.

Vauxhall Wlk.

Black

Prince

Marylee

Road

Kennington   Road

Kennington Lane

N

0   220 yds

1/8 mile

Amelia   St.

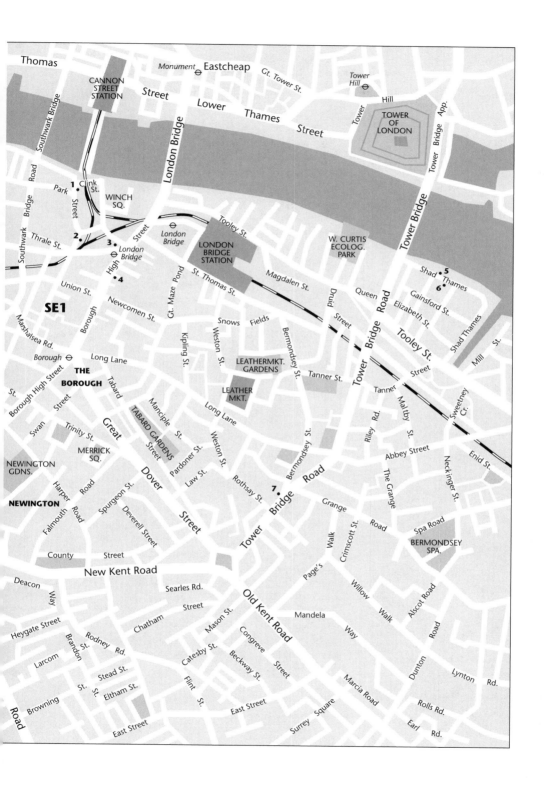

BOROUGH CAFE (2)
11 Park Street, Southwark, SE1
Tube: London Bridge

TELEPHONE
020 7407 5048
OPEN
Mon–Sat
CLOSED
Sun, 1 week between Christmas
and New Year's, holidays
HOURS
Mon–Fri 4:30 A.M.–3 P.M., Sat
4:30 A.M.–1 P.M.
RESERVATIONS
Not accepted
CREDIT CARDS
None
PRICES
À la carte £2.50–5
SERVICE
Discretionary

For a taste of something pure and simple in the rapidly vanishing village life of Southeast Londoners, a meal at the Borough Cafe is required eating. Even though it is a small place on a backstreet, a meal here is never boring. For forty-plus years, Mamma Amalia Moruzzi and her daughter Mariarenza have been feeding everyone from the police and market people to lawyers and film stars, all of whom happily share the twenty seats squeezed into the tiled room with café curtains hanging at the steamy windows. The open kitchen allows Mariarenza and Amalia to banter back and forth with everyone who eats here, taking a personal interest in them all by keeping close tabs on the ups and downs of their business and love lives. Their homemade turkey, ham, and steak pies and proper vegetable soups are always popular, and for less than three U.S. dollars, they should be! However, the big sellers are the bubble and squeak, and their signature dish, which they call Bacon and Stuffing. This is homemade stuffing made with vegetables, plenty of garlic, herbs, and cheese, wrapped in lean bacon and fried until the bacon is crispy on the outside. "It is a work of art you can either climb or eat," claim both mother and daughter. They don't do much in the dessert department, other than a homemade bread pudding served in a portion I defy you to finish.

NOTE: BYOB (no corkage fee); unlicensed. If you are here on a Saturday, be sure to visit the exceptional produce market that operates near Southwark Cathedral. Just ask for directions. Also, please ask Mariarenza about her little dog, Zoey, a stray she adopted and adores.

BUTLERS WHARF CHOP HOUSE (5)
Butlers Wharf Building, 36E, Shad Thames (off Tower Bridge Road), Southbank, SE1
Tube: Tower Hill, London Bridge

TELEPHONE
020 7403 3403
OPEN
Daily
CLOSED
2 days at Christmas
HOURS
Bar: Mon–Sat lunch noon–
3 P.M., dinner 6–11 P.M., Sat–
Sun brunch noon–3 P.M.;
restaurant: Mon–Fri, Sun lunch
noon–3 P.M., Mon–Sat dinner
6–11 P.M.

Eat in the bar at this Conran-run standby along the Thames and you will have an affordable Great Eat. Slip into the restaurant and be prepared for a Big Splurge for food that comes out of the same kitchen as the bar meals do. No corners are cut on the quality of the bar menu, which has a lineup of smoked Scottish salmon, fresh lobster, raw Irish rock oysters, grilled steaks, roast beef, and Yorkshire pudding; set-price menus for both lunch and dinner; and a super weekend brunch that includes a Bloody Mary, John Smith's or Kronenbourg beer, or fruit juice. On top of this, you share the same magnificent view of London and the River Thames as the high-rollers in the restaurant. Is there any question here?

RESERVATIONS
Advised

CREDIT CARDS
AE, DC, MC, V

PRICES
Bar: à la carte £20–25; set-price Mon–Fri lunch and dinner, Sat dinner £9 2 courses, £11 3 courses, Sat–Sun brunch £15 2 courses, £18 3 courses, includes one drink; restaurant: à la carte £28–38, set-price lunch £21 2 courses, £25 3 courses

SERVICE
12.5% service added

fish! (3)
Cathedral Street, Borough Market, Southwark, SE1
Tube: London Bridge

At fish! they care about the fish they serve and might even be able to tell you the name of the boat that caught the fish on your plate. Of course, we all know that fish is lean and easily digested protein, low in calories, and high in minerals and vitamins. To make matters even healthier, nothing served here is breaded or deep fried, and of course everything is absolutely fresh. The menu tells you what fish is available, and you tell the kitchen how you want it cooked and add your choice of sauce: salsa, hollandaise, herb and garlic butter, olive oil, or red-wine fish gravy. Otherwise, opt for one of their recommended dishes of spaghetti with tuna Bolognaise, a swordfish club sandwich, or a tuna burger with all the trimmings. Children have their own menu and a few fishy games to play at the table. fish! is toward the back of the Borough Street Market in a wrap-around glass pavilion that looks like an aquarium. The Borough Street Market is a great addition to this part of London and has developed into a foodie mecca, especially on the third Saturday of the month, when there are more vendors. The market is open every Saturday from 9 a.m. to 4 p.m.

NOTE: fish! can deliver fresh fish anywhere in London on the same day or overnight to anywhere on the mainland U.K.

TELEPHONE
020 7234 3333 (reservations), 020 7407 3801 (deliveries)

FAX
020 7234 3343

EMAIL
fish@bgr.plc.uk

INTERNET
www.fishdiner.co.uk

OPEN
Daily

CLOSED
Sun dinner, 2–3 days at Christmas and New Year's

HOURS
Lunch: Mon–Sat 11:30 A.M.– 3 P.M., Sun noon– 4 P.M.; dinner: Mon–Sat 5:30–11 P.M.

RESERVATIONS
Essential

CREDIT CARDS
AE, DC, MC, V

PRICES
À la carte £18–28

SERVICE
12.5% service charge

M. MANZE (7)
87 Tower Bridge Road (near Bermondsey and Caledonia Markets), SE1
Tube: London Bridge, then bus 1, 42, or 188

TELEPHONE
020 7407 2985
OPEN
Mon–Sat lunch only
CLOSED
Sun, holidays
HOURS
Mon 11 A.M.–2 P.M., Tues–Thur 10:30 A.M.–2 P.M., Fri 10 A.M.–2:15 P.M., Sat 10 A.M.–2:45 P.M.
RESERVATIONS
Not accepted
CREDIT CARDS
None
PRICES
À la carte £2.50–5
SERVICE
No service charged or expected

"My grandfather, father, and now I have been eating at Manze's for over a hundred years total, and we are all well and healthy," said the man standing ahead of me in the ten-deep queue to get to the counter for an order of pie and mash. Judging from the constant stream of customers of all ages, there are many more people who can also make this claim. Pie and mash remains the comfort food of the London blue-collar worker, and Manze's on Tower Bridge Road has been feeding them since the 1890s and is recognized as the oldest pie and mash shop still standing in London. It was founded by Robert Cooke in 1892, bought by his son-in-law, M. Manze, in 1902, and is now owned and run by M. Manze's grandsons Graham, Geoffrey, and Richard Poole. What is pie and mash? It consists of individual ground-beef pies, mashed potatoes, liquor (a parsley-based sauce) with a squirt or two of chili vinegar added at the table, and eels—stewed or jellied. It's an experience, all right.

You order and collect your food from the counter to take away or to eat here (it's open for lunch only). If you take your pie and mash with you, you can BYO thermos or have it poured into a plastic carton with a lid. But half the fun of Manze's is the people and the surroundings. When you eat here, you sit at marble-slab tables in the original green, white, and brown tile interior; see the boiling pots in the window; and watch the matronly, rosy-cheeked women ladling up the orders as fast as they can. Statistic junkies take note: twenty-five hundred pounds of potatoes, fifty to sixty pounds of eel, and between four and five thousand pies are sold here per week. Now that adds up to success.

NOTE: Restaurant is unlicensed; no alcohol allowed.

Pubs

THE ANCHOR (1)
34 Park Street (at Clink Street), Southwark, SE1
Tube: London Bridge

The Anchor is a well-worn eighteenth-century pub with a maze of rambling corridors joining dark, low-ceilinged rooms with open fires and wooden benches. The pub used to play host to William Shakespeare, whose Globe Theatre is close by, and later on, Dr. Samuel Johnson had a special room in which he wrote his famous dictionary. In all, there are five small bars, three restaurants, and an outdoor terrace with a spectacular view across the Thames to St. Paul's Cathedral. For these reasons, I think it is an interesting pub. There are restaurants here as well, but please don't come for the forgettable food. Rather, on a nice day, when you can sit outside and enjoy the magnificent view along the Thames, it is worthwhile to stop by for a beer and a look around.

TELEPHONE
020 7407 1577

OPEN
Daily

CLOSED
Christmas Day

HOURS
Pub: 11 A.M.–11 P.M., hot food served Mon–Fri noon–3 P.M., Sat–Sun until 5 P.M.; restaurant: Mon–Sat noon–2:30 P.M. and 6–9 P.M., Sun noon–9 P.M.

RESERVATIONS
Advised for the restaurant

CREDIT CARDS
AE, DC, MC, V

PRICES
À la carte pub £5–9, restaurant £22–28

SERVICE
No service charged or expected in pub, 10% service charged in restaurant

GEORGE INN AT SOUTHWARK (4)
77 Borough High Street, Southwark, SE1
Tube: London Bridge, Borough

The George Inn is a taste of London as it was fifty years after Columbus arrived in America, when Henry VIII reigned and Sir Francis Drake was sailing around the world. The inn has stood on this spot since Elizabethan times and is the last galleried coaching inn from that period still standing in London. The current inn is only a quarter of its original size and dates from 1542. It was rebuilt in 1676, following the Great Fire of Southwark. Its purpose then was to provide food, drink, and lodging for travelers en route to Kent and the port of Dover. Inside the walled yard, tradesmen had offices, plays were performed, and musicians entertained, while lords and ladies relaxed in front of roaring fires after their strenuous journeys. Later on, Charles Dickens ate and drank here, but he became a patron only after he had become rich and famous. As a child, visiting his father in the Marshalsea prison just down the road, he would have been too poor to enter. Today, the inn is part of the

TELEPHONE
020 –7407 2056

FAX
020 7403 6956

EMAIL
george.southwark@ whitbread.com

OPEN
Daily

CLOSED
Never

HOURS
Pub: Mon–Sat, 11 A.M.–11 P.M., Sun until 10:30 P.M., hot food served Mon–Fri noon–3 P.M., Sat–Sun until 4 P.M.; restaurant: lunch Mon–Fri noon–2:30 P.M., dinner Mon–Sat 6–9:30 P.M.

RESERVATIONS
Advised for the restaurant

CREDIT CARDS
MC, V

PRICES

À la carte: pub £5–9, restaurant
£16–25; set-price: Sunday-roast
lunch £8

SERVICE

No service charged or expected
in pub, service discretionary in
restaurant

National Trust for the Preservation of Historic Sites and still provides food and drink to its many customers every day.

The ground-floor bars are small, with bare wooden floors and benches. In the back bar is a parliamentary clock, from the time when Parliament imposed a tax on all timepieces. The bar front in the half-timbered wine bar is from a French church. Some of the old coaching bedrooms that overlook the cobblestone courtyard are now part of the Coaching Rooms Restaurant. More bedrooms make up the George Room function area, where you can spot a photo of Franklin Roosevelt to the right of the brick fireplace. The Talbot Room is reported to be haunted by a ghost who appears when the pub installs any new equipment to make sure that new installations never work on the first try. The large courtyard has picnic tables and benches, and in summer it's full of people eating and drinking. The menus in the various eating areas of the inn highlight all the English favorites: roast meats, grills, hot and cold pub food, meaty sandwiches, and fattening desserts.

Glossary of English Food Terms

The English have really everything in common with the Americans, except of course language.
—*Oscar Wilde*

The English speak English, we speak American. It doesn't matter that we share the same language; London is still a foreign capital, and you are a foreigner in it. Sure, you won't have the serious communication problems you would have in Moscow or Tokyo, but you will have to deal with some different meanings and terms. To *queue* is to line up (and you will find yourself doing this often). A *subway* is an underground walkway, but the actual underground transportation system is referred to as *the Underground* or *the tube*. If you are going to see a stage play, you are going to *the theatre,* and for a film, you head for *the cinema*. You *ring* the restaurant to make a reservation, but you *call* your dog. The following list of food terms and related words should help you sort out any dining dilemmas.

A

aubergine	eggplant

B

banger	sausage
bangers and mash	sausage and mashed potatoes
bank holiday	legal holiday, many restaurants and pubs closed
bap	soft bun, like a hamburger bun
bill	check (restaurant)
biscuit	cookie or cracker
black or white?	black or milk/cream in your coffee?
broad bean	lima bean
bubble and squeak	mashed potatoes mixed with cabbage and fried (sometimes leftover meat is added)
bucks fizz	drink similar to a mimosa

C

caff	inexpensive café; rhymes with "half"
chicory	endive
chips	french-fried potatoes
cooker	stove
Cornish pasties	meat, onion, and vegetables wrapped in pastries
cottage pie	similar to shepherd's pie, but the meat is ground
courgettes	zucchini
crisps	potato chips

crumpet	like an English muffin, but with bigger holes and more of them
cuppa	cup of tea or coffee (slang)

D

doorstops	type of pub sandwich, and as heavy as the name suggests

F

fish-and-chips	cod, plaice, skate, or other whitefish dipped in batter and deep fried
fool	fresh whipped cream mixed with seasonal fruit
French beans	green beans
fry-up	fried breakfast of eggs, sausage and/or bacon, baked beans, toast or fried bread, with additions of mushrooms and tomatoes, depending on the poshness of where you are eating

G

grease-out	see *fry-up*

J

jacketed potato	baked potato, usually served with a variety of toppings
jam	jelly
jelly	Jell-O
joint (meat)	roasted meat on the bone (leg of lamb would be a joint of lamb)

L

Lancashire hot pot	mutton and vegetables in a rich sauce, cooked in a pastry crust

M

mains	main courses (slang)
mange tout	snow peas
Marmite	savory yeast spread that can be found in hot drinks, soups, and stews
marrow	squash
martini	straight vermouth (to get a real martini, ask for a double gin or vodka with ice)
mince	ground meat, usually beef

O

off-license	retail liquor store
other half	either another half-pint of beer or your spouse, depending on your location

P

peckish	a little bit hungry
pickled wally	pickled dill cucumber
ploughman's lunch	pub lunch consisting of cheese or pâté with crusty bread, a pickle, and sometimes chutney or an onion
plum pudding	served at Christmas, made from suet and dried fruit, steamed and then soaked in brandy or other similar liquor
pub grub	pub food
publican	manager of a pub
pudding	dessert
puds	desserts (slang)

R

rasher (bacon)	slice of bacon
ring	to call on the telephone for a reservation, as in "to ring for a booking"
rocket, roquette	arugula

S

salt beef	corned beef
sausage and mash	sausage and mashed potatoes
Scotch egg	hard-cooked egg encased in ground sausage and bread crumbs, which is then fried
shepherd's pie	diced meat and vegetables covered with gravy, topped with mashed potatoes, and baked in a casserole
spirits (drink)	liquor
spotted dick	steamed sponge cake with diced fruit and raisins, served warm with soft custard sauce
steak and kidney pie	mixture of pieces of steak, kidneys, and mushrooms in gravy, cooked in its own deep-dish pastry crust
sticky, toffee pudding	similar to spotted dick, but without the fruit, served with a warm butterscotch sauce
sultana	raisin
sweet	dessert
sweets	candy
Swiss roll	jelly roll

T

tatties	potatoes
toad-in-the-hole	sausage baked in batter, served plain or with ale gravy
toasties	type of pub sandwich
top-up	refill

treacle	molasses
trifle or tipsy cake	sherry-soaked sponge cake, layered with raspberry preserves and topped with cold custard sauce and whipped cream

W

Welsh rarebit	melted cheddar cheese and mustard or Worcestershire sauce served on toast
whitebait	tiny whole fish, deep-fried

Index of Restaurants

Readers' Comments

The listings in *Great Eats London* are described as they were when the book went to press, and as I hope they will stay, but as seasoned travelers know, there are no guarantees. This is especially true when it comes to prices; in fact, there is usually a 10 to 20 percent price increase between editions of this guide. Inflation, fluctuating exchange rates, wage increases, new ownership or staff, revised holiday periods, and the whims of managers can all result in changes, and often higher prices—sometimes overnight. Although every effort has been made to ensure the accuracy of the information presented, the author and publisher cannot accept responsibility for any changes that may result in loss or inconvenience to anyone. The publisher and author also cannot be held responsible for unpleasant experiences of readers while dining in any of the restaurants listed.

Great Eats London is revised on a regular basis, but there are some places I have no doubt missed, and maybe you have some new Great Eat discoveries you would like to pass along to me for the next edition. Your comments are extremely important to me, and I read, answer, and follow through on every letter I receive. Because of this, I do not provide an email address, since the volume of mail it would generate would make it impossible to personally reply to each message. I hope you will understand and will take a few minutes to send me an old-fashioned letter with your comments, tips, new finds, or suggestions for *Great Eats London.* In your letter, be sure to state the name and address of the restaurant, the date of your visit, a description of your findings, and any other information you think is necessary.

Please send your letters to Sandra A. Gustafson, *Great Eats London,* c/o Chronicle Books, 85 Second Street, Sixth Floor, San Francisco, CA 94105.

For more information about all of the books in the Great Eats and Great Sleeps series, and for updates as I travel, please visit my Website at www.greateatsandsleeps.com.